# California
# Desperadoes

## Stories of Early California Outlaws in Their Own Words

By
**William B. Secrest**

Word Dancer Press

Clovis, California

*Printed in the United States of America.*

Published by
Quill Driver Books/Word Dancer Press, Inc.,
8386 N. Madsen, Clovis, CA 93611
559-322-5917 / 800-497-4909

---

Word Dancer Press books may be purchased for educational, fund-raising,
business or promotional use. Please contact Special Markets, Quill Driver Books/
Word Dancer Press, Inc. at the above address or phone numbers.

---

**ISBN 1-884995-19-5**
To order a copy of this book, please call
1-800-497-4909.
*First Printing June 2000*

Also by William B. Secrest
*I Buried Hickok* (College Station, Texas, 1980)
*Lawmen & Desperadoes* (Spokane, Washington, 1994)
*Dangerous Trails* (Stillwater, Oklahoma, 1995)

Front cover photo: A turn of the century posed photograph of a stagecoach
robbery. John Boessenecker collection.

Quill Driver Books/Word Dancer Press Project Cadre:
Doris Hall, John David Marion, Stephen Blake Mettee
Cover and interior design by William B. Secrest

Library of Congress Cataloging-in-Publication Data

Secrest, William B, 1930-
      California desperadoes : stories of early California outlaws in their own words /
   [compiled and written] by William B. Secrest.
         p. cm
      Includes bibliographical references (p. ) and index.
      ISBN 1-884995-19-5
         1. Outlaws--California--Biography--Anecdotes. 2. Frontier and pioneer
   life--California--Anecdotes. 3. California--Biography--Anecdotes. 4.
   California--History--1846-1850--Anecdotes. 5.
   California--History--1850-1950--Anecdotes. I. Title.

   F864 .S378 2000
   979.4'04*0922--dc21

                                                                    99-088615

For my parents,
Carl and Amanda Secrest

...and Shirley,
the love of my life

*"I wish they would make lynch law
the law of the mines. It is as necessary
to wear a pistol as a shirt."*

Miner Hubert Burgess
writing home from
California in the 1850s.

# Contents

# Preface and Acknowledgments

Over the years as I have researched old newspapers, libraries, courthouses and archives for material on California's frontier days, there have been many serendipitous discoveries of autobiographical material concerning early California's outlaws and badmen. Some of these items were rare, such as the autobiography of Charles Mortimer. Others were often even more rare, such as newspaper interviews or writings by .45 calibre outlaws like Jim Smith and Dick Fellows. Since I was working on other projects at the time, these items were filed away in my own archives to await an opportune time for their use. Now, some of this fascinating and little-known material can be made available.

The excellent staff of the reference desk and the California History and Genealogy Room of the Fresno County Library deserve much credit for their skillful help, interlibrary loans and encouragement over the years. Sibylle Zemitis and others of the California Room of the California State Library have always been most helpful. At the California State Archives, W. N. Davis, Jr., David Snyder, Joseph P. Samora, Laren Metzer, Anthony R. Hoffmann and others have provided much of the raw material of this work over the years. William Roberts and the rest of the staff at the Bancroft Library helped in this and other projects. The Yosemite Natural History Association and Norman Bishop of the Yosemite Museum provided valuable information and photographs. Dale E. Floyd, Military Archives Division, and M. Thomas, Textual Reference Division of the National Archives, contributed needed aid in a timely manner. Many thanks also to the San Luis Obispo County Historical Society and to Fr. Viagilio Biasiol, O.F.M., Director, the Santa Barbara Mission Archive-Library. Wally Ohles, secretary for the "Friends of the Adobes," San Miguel, California, was most helpful and cooperative.

Individuals who have given me important data or helped in various ways: Kevin Mullen, Robert Chandler, Shirley Sargent, Troy Tuggle, Harold Edwards, Greg Martin, Bill Secrest, Jr., Richard Dillon, Kip Davis, Christian de Guigné, Linda Sitterding and Richard Nelson. Steve Mettee and Dave Marion, of *Word Dancer Press,* have been most encouraging and helpful although I am sure they wanted to "throw up their hands" at times.

John Boessenecker, who has been researching this area of California history for many years, has been a particular partner and friend. A lawyer, writer and historian of great ability, John has shared his own research and brought several first-hand outlaw items to my attention. His generosity and companionship as we prowled California state and local archives is much appreciated.

Perhaps most of all, I owe a debt to my wonderful wife whose patience and understanding contribute so much to my work. I love you, Shirl, and you are appreciated more than you will ever know.

To you all and anyone I might have overlooked, thank you again.

W. B. S.

# Introduction

For many years I have researched and written about early California stage robbers, killers, rustlers and badmen with a view towards generating an interest in California's rightful place in our "Wild West" history. The result has been a great many articles and several books. Hopefully, some of this has made the public more aware that outlaws, shootouts and brave and colorful lawmen were as plentiful in early California as they were in Deadwood, Tombstone and old Dodge City. If we haven't reached the point where Western novels and films are set in California as often as in Texas, Arizona and Wyoming, perhaps we are at least making some progress.

In researching the stories of early California lawmen or desperados, a great many sources have to be utilized. The old newspapers are a primary source of information, along with court documents, reminiscences, prison registers, old county histories and census records. Over the years I have collected enough material to fill a group of filing cabinets with these stories of California's early peace officers and badmen.

Scattered among all these thousands of documents are a few rare, first-person accounts of these criminals. Some are personal accounts, booklets published in obscure paperback editions of which few have survived. Others are newspaper articles and interviews written by convicts or dictated to reporters. Some are confessions taken down in the shadow of the gallows or made to prison officials. All are the raw stuff of California's "Wild West" history.

These first person accounts are inevitably edited to some minor degree when they are transcribed by a newspaper reporter, printer or prison stenographer. Even so, the aura of violence can be strong indeed when a murder or robbery is described succinctly by someone who actually committed the crime.

In order to retain the flavor and character of the actual spoken language of the California desperadoes, I have done very limited editing of the first-person narratives in this book. I have allowed the characters to speak in their own voices—voices rich with colloquialisms, slang, and argot of the outlaws and their cohorts.

In many cases, the, misspellings and word discrepancies are the result of transcriptions by semi-literate individuals—prison stenographers, citizen witnesses, court reporters, and even self-educated lawyers and newspapermen. These transcriptions often reveal the linguistic idiosyncrasies of the scribes as much as they divulge the personality and story of the speaker.

As is customary in extracted material, I have allowed the language to stand—as is—and have made infrequent changes in the sometimes eccentric or incorrect spelling, grammar, punctuation and usage. The few changes I have made were to prevent total incomprehensibility.

In March of 1864 two thieves and rustlers named George Strong and Tom Heffernan made arrangements to buy a large herd of sheep from a rancher named Taylor near San Luis Obispo. Telling Taylor they would pay him off at Hill's Ferry if he would help them drive the sheep there, the two outlaws waited for an opportunity to murder the unsuspecting sheepman along the way. One morning Strong shot a duck for breakfast. While Taylor was watching the bird's retrieval, Heffernan suddenly shot him in the neck. As the rancher went down, Strong walked over to the body. He later wrote:

> Seeing that Heffernan had shot him too low, I cocked my revolver and shot him just above the right eye, which immediately finished him.

The two killers then sat down for breakfast, Heffernan remarking, "see how the damned rascal bleeds." Tying the body to a fifty-pound sack of sand, the murderers threw him into a slough and then continued driving the sheep to Hill's Ferry. The whole murderous transaction is described in a few lines of type and the brutality of the two killers would send shivers down the spine of a statue.

Despite the coarseness and brevity of some of these narratives, the human side of these criminals sometimes struggles to the surface. Strong has no problem writing of visits to his parents after detailing a long series of thefts and murders. Longtime stage robber Jim Smith, on the other hand, saw the humorous side of a highwayman's life and enjoyed telling whimsical stories of botched holdup attempts.

The humor that often lurked just beneath the surface of a criminal psyche was sometimes manifest in curious ways. When a mass escape was made from the Martinez jail, located across the bay from San Francisco, Sheriff

Hunsaker found a note the next morning in place of his recent prisoners. It was published in the *Stockton Argus* of January 8, 1857:

Contra Costa Co., Jail, 12 M

Sir:—Excuse the liberty I have taken of absconding premises at this unexcusable hour of the night; nothing but business of the utmost importance prompts me to pursue this course. I am sincerely grateful for the kind treatment I have received from you during my brief sojournment at your hospitable mansion. As a token of friendship, I will leave you a lock of my hair. If, when you wake up in the morning, you should find any one missing in my sleeping apartment, please give the alarm immediately, so that the officers may be on the alert to apprehend the kidnappers....

Educated stage robber Dick Fellows drank his way into a life of crime, but he wrote of his exploits with a keen sense of humor and an eye for history. He realized he had lost all sense of honor and decency and accepted prison as his fate, grateful that the institution had at least forced him to give up drinking.

Chris Evans, a dangerous killer and train robber, actually wrote a thoughtful, futuristic novel while in Folsom State Prison.

Some of these memoirs are sketchy at best and generally pay scant attention to the common decencies of life that most of us take for granted. Although sometimes boastful in tone, for the most part these confessions are of a cleansing nature. The criminals seem to be honestly baring their souls in the hope they will perhaps be spared their fate in either this world or the next, if they just confess their sins.

And yet these confessions, of whatever nature, are quite rare. It took a certain type of person to confess his crimes to the world and few were willing to do so. Whatever cleansing of the soul might be accomplished, there is something very final about a confession. Once committed to this course of action, for whatever reason, it was all over.

You couldn't change your mind. A confession would haunt you forever. Still, it must be borne in mind that the bad guys only told what they wanted told. "I wouldn't tell my own brother about some of (my crimes)," mused outlaw Pierre Ridge.

Strangely enough, some criminals listening to their gallows being built, did reveal their misspent lives and disclose terrible crimes. Perhaps it was the ultimate act of a despairing hopelessness—a sense of knowing you had reached the end and were about to enter some new sphere of spiritual existence. A few actually wrote of these feelings and declared they were ready to meet their God. There was little else they could do.

As for the social value of these tales, I can only say they are important in revealing character insights, clues to obscure crimes and, most importantly, sometimes show where that fatal misstep was made from which there was no return.

On the other hand, perhaps we can only assess these personal outlaw stories as a window on a time and place long gone. Looking back over the centuries it seems obvious that criminals will always be with us despite the great advances in social consciousness and technology that have taken place. In the past, society has been incapable of dealing with these problems and even today understanding the criminal mind is an evolving frontier. Conceivably, the only lesson here is that despite the circumstances of cultural heritage and healthy environment, criminals will continue to evolve, haunting and demeaning our society. Perhaps there are no answers to these questions.

In many ways, these personal tales of stage robbers and desperadoes are the ultimate history, told at the time by those who experienced it. Hopefully, the author's notes and additional research and text will aid in bringing these stories to life. Read now, in the outlaw's own words, of a time when there were few fences in a wild and often lawless land of mountains, swamps, plains and rivers. And of a time when even the badmen were pioneers.


William B. Secrest
Fresno, California

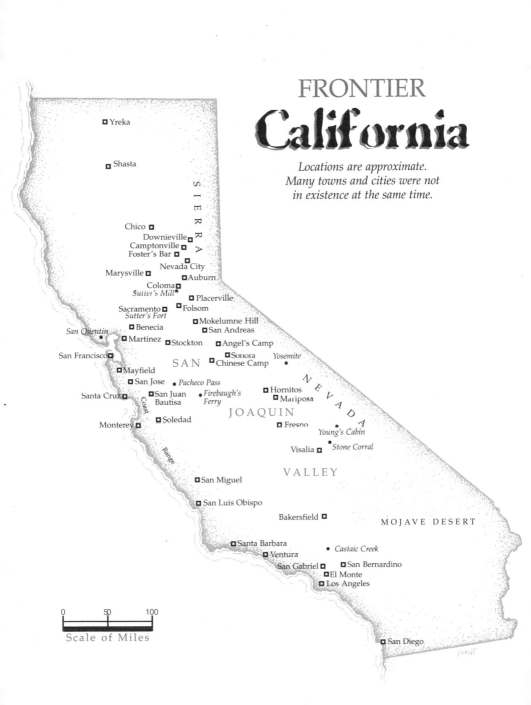

FRONTIER
# California

*Locations are approximate.*
*Many towns and cities were not*
*in existence at the same time.*

Yreka

Shasta

SIERRA

Chico

Downieville
Camptonville
Foster's Bar
Nevada City
Marysville
Auburn
Coloma
*Sutter's Mill*
Placerville
Sacramento
Folsom
*Sutter's Fort*
San Quentin
Benecia
Mokelumne Hill
San Andreas
Martinez
Stockton
Angel's Camp
San Francisco
SAN
Sonora
*Yosemite*
Chinese Camp
Mayfield
NEVADA
San Jose
*Pacheco Pass*
Santa Cruz
San Juan
Bautisa
*Firebaugh's*
*Ferry*
Hornitos
Mariposa
JOAQUIN
Monterey
Soledad
Fresno
*Young's Cabin*
Visalia
*Stone Corral*

VALLEY

San Miguel

San Luis Obispo

Bakersfield

MOJAVE DESERT

Santa Barbara
Ventura
*Castaic Creek*
San Gabriel
San Bernardino
El Monte
Los Angeles

Coast

Range

0      50      100

Scale of Miles

San Diego

Described by contemporary travelers as a desolate and treeless location, the Mission Nuestra Senora de la Soledad (top) was a dark gathering ground for a group of murderous misfits in December of 1848. Soldiers and sailors deserted in droves in the early days of the gold rush as illustrated by the old engraving above. Author's collection and William T. Sherman: Memoirs.

# 1 "I heard a blow of an ax"

## The Slaughter at Mission San Miguel

Reported by descendants to be a portrait of Petronilo Rios, partner of William Reed. Friends of the Adobes, Inc.

**"G**old! Gold! Gold from the American River."

Waving his hat and holding aloft a glistening bottle of gold flakes, a man ran into the middle of the plaza of old San Francisco. It was May, 1848, and Sam Brannan was announcing to the world that there was gold in California.

A wily Mormon printer and merchant, Brannan had learned of the gold discovery in the foothills east of the bay city. John Marshall, a partner of John Sutter in the building of a sawmill at Coloma, had picked up some flakes of gold on the morning of January 24, 1848. Sutter was apprehensive that his extensive land holdings in the new territory would be overrun by gold seekers and he and his sawmill employees agreed to keep the discovery a secret, at least for awhile. Such secrets cannot be kept for long, however.

Brannan was one of the first to hear the news in his store at Sutter's Fort on the site of the future city of Sacramento. When he was sure of the validity of the discovery, the shrewd merchant began stocking his shop with mining tools and supplies.

On March 15, 1848, Brannan printed a small notice of the discovery in his San Francisco newspaper, *The California Star*. The article, however, caused barely a ripple of excitement. A more extended account was printed in the issue of April 1, addressed to the *New York Herald* and placed aboard an eastbound ship. The following month Brannan shouted his news in the San Francisco Plaza and the greatest gold rush in history was soon underway.

While American legends and frontier traditions dictated that women and children were held to be inviolate during our frontier days, this was never completely true. In the early years of the Gold Rush, Joaquin Valenzuela, one of notorious Joaquin Murrieta's lieutenants, reportedly kidnapped a young girl after murdering her parents. The Mexican woman Josefa was lynched at Downieville in 1852 and there were others. Before the great Gold Rush had fairly commenced, however...before there was even a formal system of government in the new territory, the most monstrous crime against women and children in the history of the state took place.

Like any frontier region, California had its share of crime and criminals as it struggled toward becoming an organized society. The first great crime in the state's history, however, is little-known today primarily because of the lack of population at the time and the primitive state of the new territory's society .

It happened just after the Mexican War

Sutter's Mill at Coloma, California, where the Von Pfister murder took place. From a daguerreotype ca. 1851. California State Library.

and the Treaty of Guadalupe Hidalgo. When gold was discovered in January of 1848, the first arrivals in the gold fields were those closest to the West Coast. Crews aboard ships anchored along the California coast, or other points between Oregon and South America, quickly responded to the news. American army posts and naval vessels accepted desertion as an increasingly serious problem. The commander of the U.S. Pacific fleet was offering $500 each for the first four naval deserters who had jumped ship in July. The easygoing life of pastoral Mexican California was changing forever.

As early as late 1848, Australian convicts began arriving—"Sydney Ducks" who mingled in the mines and towns with Mexicans, Chilenos, Californios and a scattering of others from around the world who happened to be in the area.

Although excited foreigners were arriving in a steady and growing stream, few knew anything about mining. Many newcomers hardly knew where to look for a good claim and didn't know what to do next if they found one. When they finally figured out or were shown what to do, they also discovered that placer mining was very hard work. Soon many disappointed adventurers were roaming about the mining country. With their money

Sutter's Fort as it appeared at the time of Raymond's escape. J. W. Revere, A Tour of Duty in California, 1849.

running low, some quickly became envious of those who were more successful and a peaceful and busy utopia slowly began to unravel.

Strangely enough, the dreadful story begins at Sutter's mill, where the original gold discovery had been made. The sawmill itself was not in operation that fall of 1848 and was utilized as quarters for some of the local residents. About the first of October, those sleeping in the mill were awakened one night by a man named Peter Raymond who was drunk and calling for whiskey. It is not known just when Raymond came to California, but he was a member of Fremont's California Battalion in 1846 and was apparently mining in the area at this time.

John R. Von Pfister got out of his blankets to talk to Raymond. A practical man, he shoved a knife in his belt for protection. He had apparently pacified the drunken man when Raymond suddenly seized Von Pfister's knife and plunged it into his heart. Others were awake by now and heard what transpired. They seized the killer and the following day took him downriver to Sutter's Fort where he was confined until a trial could be held. Heralded as the first murder in the gold mines, the killer escaped later in the month and a reward notice was printed in the *San Francisco Californian*, October 28, 1848:

$5,000 REWARD—Will be paid for the apprehension of Peter Raymond, the murderer of John R. Von Pfister, or for his head, in case he cannot be taken prisoner. The following is the description of said

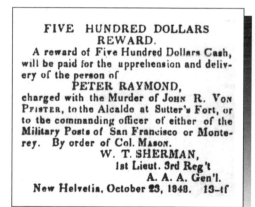

FIVE HUNDRED DOLLARS REWARD.
A reward of Five Hundred Dollars Cash, will be paid for the apprehension and delivery of the person of
PETER RAYMOND,
charged with the Murder of JOHN R. VON PFISTER, to the Alcalde at Sutter's Fort, or to the commanding officer of either of the Military Posts of San Francisco or Monterey. By order of Col. MASON.
W. T. SHERMAN,
1st Lieut. 3rd Reg't
A. A. A. Gen'l.
New Helvetia, October 23, 1848.  13–tf

Ad appearing in the Monterey Californian, October 28, 1848, with the reward offer for Raymond. Author's collection.

Raymond: height, about 5 feet 7 inches; hair, brown; complexion, dark, and is very robust and stout in nature, has a downcast look and places great emphasis on his word when conversing. He is well known to the old residents of the country. The above reward of $5,000 will be paid on his delivery (or that of his head) at the office of the Alcalde.

San Francisco, Oct. 21, 1848

The amount was apparently a misprint since notices in the *Monterey Californian* noted a $500 reward for the murderer.

When an Indian reported Raymond was at Swartz's, a tule house opposite Sutterville on the Sacramento River, a posse was promptly dispatched. Riding downriver several miles, the posse commandeered a canoe to cross over. When the overloaded canoe capsized, the yelling and splashing possemen made so much noise, Raymond quickly guessed what was happening and disappeared.

Making his way out of the area, Raymond joined three other men who were traveling to the coast. One was a German named Joseph Lynch, alias Fisher, while the other two were prospectors leaving the mines for the winter. Lynch was a former corporal in the First Regiment of New York Volunteers who had landed at Monterey on April 4, 1847. His company had been stationed at Los Angeles where he was discharged in September of the following year. Like most of his comrades, he immediately headed north for the mining country.

Lynch and Raymond quickly found they were kindred souls. After discovering their companions were carrying an amount of gold, the two ex-soldiers murdered and robbed them, then quickened their pace across the valley. They made their way to San Francisco, then headed south, traveling through San Jose and San Juan (Bautista).

The old Spanish missions in California had been secularized in 1833, with only the chapels and priests' quarters being retained by the church. The other buildings and lands had been sold or leased as ranch property or the nucleus of a pueblo. From San Diego to San Francisco, all along El Camino Real, or the King's Highway, these old, deteriorating missions stood along the coast as silent reminders of a bygone age.

Continuing their journey south, Raymond and Lynch stopped at the old Mission Nuestra Senora de la Soledad in the Salinas Valley. Situated between Santa Barbara and Monterey, in the Coast Range, the locale was as lonely as its name. Traveler J. Ross Browne wrote that "a more desolate place cannot be well imagined." Perhaps that is why a group of deserting seamen congregated there early in December of 1848. There were plenty of rooms in the wings flanking the main chapel and adjoining Indian quarters. For food, all they had to do was kill one of the many wild cattle roaming the hills.

Raymond, now using the alias "Mike," and Lynch quickly threw in with Peter Quin and Peter Remer, two deserters from the U.S. sloop-of-war *Warren*. Another sailor named Bernard, or Barnberry, joined them. These three were down to their last few coins and were glad to accept when Raymond and Lynch offered to share their stolen gold.

The next morning the five men, accompanied by an Indian guide named Juan, resumed their journey south. The three sailors were afoot, while Raymond and Lynch were horseback. When two broken-down horses were found along the road, two of the sailors mounted and rode with the others.

It was midafternoon on December 4 when the group rode into the Mission San Miguel. Owned by ex-English sailor William Reed and a former Mexican artillery officer named Petronilo Rios, the property was being used as a ranch headquarters. Reed was glad to have some English-speaking visitors and invited them to eat and spend the night. He had recently returned after selling a herd of sheep in the mines. Reed foolishly mentioned that he had been paid in gold—"more gold than his young son could lift." Perhaps as a ploy to ascertain whether there was any money at the mission, Raymond sold Reed some thirty ounces of his stolen gold for seven dollars an ounce.

The travelers were up early the next morning and resumed their journey. The weather was bitter cold with heavy winds buffeting them as they made their way south. About two hundred yards down the road the group stopped for a discussion. Several of the men brought up the subject of Reed's gold and insisted they should go back for it. The gold was there for the taking and who knew just how much other loot might be available. The dark decision was made and they started back to San Miguel.

Mission San Miguel as it appeared in the early 1900s. The Reed family quarters were in the long building attached to the large chapel at the right. Friends of the Adobes, Inc.

*An early lithographic view of Mission San Miguel shows the road by which Raymond and his gang arrived on that deadly, December day.* History of San Luis Obispo County, 1883.

At the mission Reed was probably glad to see them again. He would be glad to feed and house them for another night if they would chop down two trees for him. They agreed and spent the rest of the day on their chore.

The early evening was spent smoking and talking around the communal fireplace. Reed's wife, Maria Antonia Vallejo, was pregnant and had left the men and retired to her room with her three-year-old son. Also with her was a younger brother, Jose Vallejo, and Josefa Olivera, a midwife looking after Mrs. Reed. Others at the mission this night were Mrs. Olivera's fifteen-year-old daughter and four-year-old grandson. Reed's old Indian shepherd and his five-year-old grandson were also on the premises, as was a young black man who worked as a cook.

As the men lounged about the fire, Reed came into the room about eight o'clock in the evening. He sat down on a bench and joined in the conversation as Barnberry was chopping some wood behind him. Throwing some kindling on the fire, Barnberry walked back behind Reed and again picked up his axe. Joe Lynch was just lighting his pipe with a coal when he saw Barnberry rise up behind Reed. "I heard a blow of an axe," he said later, "struck by this man Barnberry on Mr. Reed." As Reed tumbled to the floor, his hat and head cleaved in two, Barnberry struck him several more times. The Indian, Juan, then leaped upon the prostrate rancher, plunging a knife into the quivering body.

Standing there with blood splashed all over him and the dripping axe in his hand, Barnberry cried out: "I have struck the first blow and there is no backing out!"

Stalking through the mission buildings, the killers burst into Mrs. Reed's room. "Buenas noches, Senoritas!" Mike said, as he began the slaughter. He ran one of the women through with a cutlass as children were pulled from under the bed where they tried to hide. All were butchered mercilessly. The killers then rushed to another room and killed the old Indian shepherd and his grandson. The black cook was also found and murdered in his bed.

As the murderers stood around wondering if they had killed everyone, a horse galloped across the yard and was tied in a nearby orchard. When someone called out, the murderers quickly hid in a darkened room. The rider approached the occupied wing of the mission, then entered the interior corridor. Again he called out. As he walked down the corridor, he saw a body on the floor and froze. Something was terribly wrong.

The rider was Jim Beckwourth, a noted trapper who had recently arrived in California. At this time he was carrying mail and government dispatches between Monterey and Dana's Ranch. On this bitter cold evening he could look forward to a steaming cup of coffee and a bite to eat at Reed's place. Later he would recall that terrible night:

Jim Beckwourth, the mail rider who stumbled upon the horror at Mission San Miguel. Nevada Historical Society

"I entered the house as usual, but was surprised to see no one stirring.... I stepped into the kitchen to look for some of the inmates. On the floor I saw some one lying down, asleep, as I supposed. I attempted to rouse him with my foot, but he did not stir. This seemed strange, and my apprehensions became excited; for the Indians were very numerous about, and I was afraid some mischief had been done. I returned to my horse for my pistols, then, lighting a candle, I commenced a search. In going along a passage I stumbled over the body of a woman; I entered a room, and found another, a murdered Indian woman, who had been a domestic...."

Beckwourth promptly retraced his steps and ran to his horse. Riding to the nearby ranch of Petronilo Rios, Reed's partner, he described what he had seen to those present. A party of vaqueros and Indians was quickly gathered and returned with Beckwourth to San Miguel. Now they found all the bodies piled in one room where they had been set on fire. The fire had died out while the killers had looted the rooms and then disappeared into the night.

While Beckwourth rode on to Monterey to report the news to the military authorities, two riders rode up to the mission the day after the killings. John M. Price and Francis Z. Branch, two prominent San Luis Obispo ranchers, were returning home after a visit to the mining country. Walking into the deathly quiet Reed quarters, the men were horrified when they discovered the bodies. A message was quickly sent to Santa Barbara and by December 10, a fifteen-man posse under Cesario Lataillade was on the track of the desperadoes.

In Monterey, Beckwourth reported to Lieutenant William T. Sherman, adjutant for Military Governor Richard B. Mason. Sherman's account of the meeting is concise and dramatic.

"Leftenant," Beckwourth blurted out, "they killed them all, not even sparing the baby....I tell you that Reed at San Miguel is killed, all his family and servants, not excepting the baby!"

When Governor Mason heard the news, he directed Sherman to send Lieutenant Edward O. C. Ord and a party of soldiers to pursue the killers "to the death." The troops were quickly on the trail and picked up news along the way. When they heard that the killers were headed south, they kept on El Camino Real, the old mission road, heading towards Santa Barbara. By the time the troopers arrived, they found they were not needed.

Raymond and his murderous gang had headed south, riding past the Atascadero Ranch and the village of San Luis Obispo. On December 9, they bought four horses at Rancho Los Alamos, then proceeded on to Santa Barbara, passing through that seaside village the following night.

Cesario Lataillade and his well-armed posse of three Americans and a dozen Californios failed in an effort to set up an ambush for the killers. Scouts were sent out to the hills surrounding Sycamore Canyon and the outlaws were spotted riding along the foothills paralleling the beach. The posse quickly spurred in pursuit.

Riding along the beach, the killers had just left the Rancho Ortega, some five miles below Santa Barbara, when they noticed a group of riders rapidly approaching from the north. Raymond, alias Mike, and his men must have quickly realized that judgment day was upon them. As the posse closed in on the beach, the fight was swift and deadly. After a brief exchange of gunfire, Peter Quin was wounded and posseman Ramon Rodriguez galloped up

*Santa Barbara was a sprawling collection of tile-roofed adobes when Raymond and his thugs rode through that dark December night. Author's collection.*

to Barnberry. At point-blank range the two men killed each other with well-directed pistol shots. Leaping from his horse, Raymond plunged into the surf, desperately attempting to swim out to sea. All the possemen, not otherwise engaged, opened fire on the swimmer. After taking several hits, Raymond attempted to return, but soon disappeared under the choppy water.

It was over as swiftly as it had begun. Quin, Remer and Lynch stood with their hands up in wide-eyed horror at what had happened. They probably expected to be shot on the spot, but instead were tied and led back to Santa Barbara. Raymond's body was later found on a nearby beach where it was reportedly allowed to rot. There is apparently no record of the disposition of Barnberry's body, but perhaps it too was allowed to slowly decompose on that lonely stretch of beach now called Summerland.

In Santa Barbara, a committee was appointed with Thomas Robbins as president, Lewis T. Burton as associate, and Henry S. Carnes as secretary. In this interim period between the old Mexican government and the new American system, a legal structure had not yet been established, but a quasi-legal alternative was soon in place. On December 13, the statements of the prisoners were taken in the presence of the appointed committee and three witnesses:

*Santa Barbara, California*

*December 13th 1848*

*The committee chosen by the citizens of the town of Santa Barbara to examine the prisoners under the charge of murder met pursuant to appointment at 9 o'clock this morning.*

*The members being all present proceeded in their examination—*

*Joseph Lynch examined—belongs to the Dukedom of Hesse Darnstadt—native town is Mayence—age is 28 years—The prisoner was then informed by the President that he stood indicted by the town of Santa Barbara for a murder committed in the Mission of St. Miguel. The prisoner then confessed the following; started from the gold mines in company with three men, two Americans and one Irishman. About three weeks ago, in the night, one of these three men, the Irishman named Mike (or Bill) murdered the two Americans to get the gold that they had brought with them from the mines. Mike then said to me that if I ran he would shoot me. Passing near Weaver's ranche I wished to stop there in order to work, but he told me that if I stopped he would murder me. Then divided the gold we had taken from the murdered men—I taking half and Mike the other half. Arriving at "St. Juan" Mission we bought two horses. Arriving at the Mission of "La Soledad," we met five men; three sailors (of which two are now prisoners, and one was shot in the fight) and two marines. The three sailors left the marines at the mission, not wishing to travel further with them, and joined us. We all came on together to the mission of St. Miguel. An Indian named John came on with us from the Mission of La Soledad.*

*The three sailors were afoot. About two or three miles this side of the Mission of La Soledad, we found two old horses. Two of the men who joined us mounted the horses, but one of them giving out on the road we only brought one into St. Miguel. Arrived at the Mission of St. Miguel about 3 or 4 o'clock in the afternoon. We got something to eat and stopped there all night. The next morning, about seven o'clock, we left and went on about two hundred yards. It was very cold, the wind blowing very hard. The evening we arrived at the Mission we sold the gold, about thirty ounces, that was stolen from the two murdered men, to Mr. Reed for seven dollars an ounce. Mr. Reed, the man who was living in the Mission of St. Miguel, had been talking to the boys about his trip to the mines, saying that he had more gold than his boy could lift. Some of our party began disputing, saying that Reed had a great deal of gold and that it would be best to take it. We then decided to turn back, which we did, and stopped at the Mission all day. During the evening I was talking with the prisoner Quin about the idea of robbing the gold and he decided that it was not right, which was my opinion, also. I wanted him to persuade them not to commit the robbery, but he answered that if he did they would be mad at him. During the evening the rest had come in and the man who was shot, Barnberry, said that if we had been men we would have been looking (illegible).*

*About seven or eight o'clock Mr. Reed came in the room and sat down on a bench. Barnberry was standing behind Reed cutting some sticks with an axe that he had in his hand, to throw on the fire. He stepped towards the fire and threw the sticks on, and then walked back again behind Reed. I was at this time filling my pipe. I told Quin to give me a coal of fire. Just as he was giving me the fire, I heard a blow of an axe struck by this man Barnberry on Mr. Reed—he struck him on the head. Reed fell* and after he had fallen Barnberry struck him several blows more with the axe—after this the Indian stabbed Reed with a knife.

Quin and myself ran out after this in the corridore, and Mike and Barnberry brought us back again and shut the door. Barnberry then opened the door again and told us to come on; he then said I have struck the first blow and there is no backing out. One man named Remer, one of the prisoners, went into the kitchen and killed the negro in there. He had an axe. He then came back and said "now come on." We all then went towards Reed's room. Mike opened the door. He had an old sword and his double barrel fowling piece. Upon opening the door he said, "Buenas Noches Senoritas" and all went in but myself. I ran outside of the corridore and this man after me who asked me where I was going. I heard one of the women scream whilst running and he said to me "I have stabbed one with the sword." After this they all came outside of the house—as everything was quiet they (meaning all those in Reed's room) must have all been killed.

Barnberry then said to me, "God dam you, why don't you shoot that Indian" (there was an old Indian in another room lying near the fire). I did not say anything. He had a double barrel gun that belonged to Mr. Reed in his hand and also a candle. I told him the door where the Indian was lying was shut. Remer then said, "I will dam soon open it." He gave the door a kick and it flew open. Barnberry then said to me, "Shoot him." I answered, I cannot take sight—he then raised up his gun and shot him. He then said, "He ain't dead" and told me to shoot him. My gun was lying in my arm, and I pulled the trigger and it went off, but I don't think the ball struck anywheres near him. Remer then went into the room and struck him on the head with an axe.

Barnberry then said, "Now, God dam your souls, come in here. What are you standing there for?" I then went in and saw the men in the act of taking the dead bodies into the carpenter's shop. I immediately left the room and after I came out Barnberry came out of the room with a young child in his arms and carried him into the carpenter's shop. When he came out again I heard him say, "that he could not have the heart to kill the child." The man Remer who came out afterwards then said, "I soon settled it."

Some time after this occurred, I cannot say whether it was before or after we left the mission, I heard the men say that they pulled an Indian boy from under the bed. One said that "he had a hard life," meaning that he died hard. Mike then asked Quin (a prisoner) how he hit him, and he answered that "he did not know how he hit him." Mike then said that "he had split his head open."

After this we went and drank some wine in Reed's room. The man Remer then took an axe and struck on a chest. They then commenced opening all the chests and taking out everything. The money was in the chest that was first struck by the axe.

The chests were rifled of all their contents. Barnberry got a silver watch. About half an hour after the murder was committed we left the mission and after going about a half or mile, Barnberry threw his bag of silver on the ground saying, "God dam the stuff, it is too heavy. You fellows take your share to pack and you can divide it by and by." Each man then took a share.

After we left the mission we slept some distance this side of the first ranche (Paso de Robles) and the next night we slept near a creek about two leagues this side of the Mission of St. Louis. It was here the Indian boy ran away, leaving with us two silk shawls, a woman's dress, some ribbons, etc. These things were wrapped up in a sheet worn by the Indian.

Don't recollect anything further until we got to a ranche where we met a dragoon (which proves to be the Alamos). Our party left the above place with four horses. Near a ranche amongst the mountains (The Cruces) met a Spaniard with two horses ahead of him. Barnberry wanted Remer to shoot him in order to get the horses, but he said "Do you think I am a God dam fool to kill a fellow right in the settlements?" But as the Spaniard went around the hills, the opportunity was lost.

Slept that night in a ranche amongst the mountains. The next night slept at a ranche where we bought four horses (Los Pueblos)—a palomino or cream colored horse for twenty-five dollars, with a saddle for six dollars; a black horse for twenty dollars and a mare; a white horse for twenty-five dollars and a horse. The bay mare belongs to the prisoner who is wounded (Quin). I don't remember what it cost. We passed Santa Barbara during the evening, late, and slept about a mile from the town, on or near the road. The next day about 11 o'clock A.M. stopped at a ranche about five or six miles below Santa Barbara (ranche Ortega) and bought something to eat. Saw a Spaniard arrive there and change a horse. About one o'clock left and had not proceeded more than a mile when we were attacked—

*13 December 1848—Second declaration of Lynch—*

After we left the Mission of St. Miguel, the next morning either a little before or a little after daylight, Barnberry and Mike being behind, Mike called me to him and said, "Give me your hand." I did not at first give it, being suspicious of their wishing me harm. He then said "Me," meaning himself, "and Barnberry have made you captain, and you will have to make laws which we have to obey." I gave him no answer, but never told them to do anything, nor made any laws.

This side of a ranche where there is a dry creek (Atascadero) we encamped for an hour to eat. After we had gone on again, Remer and Barnberry proposed to kill the Indian boy. I said "No!" After we had encamped beyond St. Louis, I was lying down asleep. It being Barnberry's watch, he, Barnberry, sang out to me to get up and go up on the bank and call the Indian. I went, but did not find him. I told Barnberry that *the boy had run away because he was afraid of him. Whilst we were saddling the horses that morning, Remer said "that if we had killed the damned Indian we would not have had to come there, for a dead man tells no tales."*

*The declaration of the prisoner now finished.*

*The different articles taken from the prisoners, as well as some money in gold and silver, and some gold from the mines, were then shown to the prisoner, Lynch, and he declared that he recognized them as belonging to his party.*

*The above declaration has been carefully read to me, and I do hereby solemnly swear it to be true and correct, and hereby ratify the same by my free will.*

*Joseph Lynch*

The document was then signed by three witnesses and the three-man committee. Peter Remer's confession was as damning as the Lynch document, but it was becoming abundantly clear that the prisoners were invoking that time-honored criminal privilege of assigning the principal blame on someone other than themselves, or on their dead comrades:

*Santa Barbara, California*

*13th December, 1848*

*Declaration of Peter Remer*

*Was born in Dublin—age 21 years. I was one of a party of five who stopped at the Mission of La Soledad. Two men arriving there during our stay urged three of us to join them, saying that they had a little money and as far as it went they would share it with us. We arrived at the Mission of St. Miguel at three o'clock in the afternoon. We stopped 'till next morning and then left and went on about a mile and a half from the mission. As our horses were tired out, it was concluded that it would be best for us to turn back and stay there another day. We went back and stopped that day and started at three o'clock the following day. The owner of the mission desired us to cut down a tree for him, which we did, and about 10 o'clock that night we were all of us sitting in the room. I was sitting by the fire and Mr. Reed was sitting on a bench. Behind him was Barnberry standing up against the wall with an axe in his hand. I saw Barnberry strike Reed with the axe on the back of the head. He struck him several blows afterwards and after he had fallen the Indian stabbed him with a knife.*

*I, together with Quin, endeavored to leave the room, but Barnberry said that if we did he would blow our brains out, with a gun that was near him in the corner.*

Santa Barbara, California
13$^{d}$ December 1848-

Declaration of Peter Remers-

Was born in Dublin - age 21 years-
I was one of a party of five who stopped
at the mission of La Soledad - two
men arriving there during our stay
urged three of us to join them, saying
that they had a little money and as
far as it went they would share it
with us - we arrived at the mission
of S$^{a}$ Miguel at three O'clock in the
afternoon - we stopped 'till next morning
and then left and went on about a
mile and a half from the mission -
as our horses were tired out, it was
concluded that it would be best for
us to turn back and stay there another
day - we went back and stopped
that day, and started at three O'clock
the following day - the owner of
the mission desired us to cut down
a tree for him, which we did - and

A portion of the first page of Peter Remer's confession. Santa Barbara Mission Archives.

*Lynch then got up and took his gun. Barnberry then swore that I must kill the negro with the axe or he would blow my brains out. I told him that I could not, that I could not kill a man for nothing, but he swore that if I did not he would kill me. Then Barnberry took the axe out of my hands and went in and knocked the negro on the head. After that Mike went into the room where the women were with an axe, a gun, and an old cutlass. He then hallowed for the Indian boy and me to come in. The Indian boy went in and Mike swore that if I did not come in he would come out and shoot me. When I went in he had killed the whole of them, the women were lying all over the floor. There were two little boys, one an Indian, under the bed. Mike pulled them out and killed them, too. They, Mike and Barnberry, then went out into another room where there was an old Indian. They shot two loads into him — Lynch shot one and Barnberry the other. They then went in with the axe and knocked him on the head.*

*Barnberry then wanted to set fire to the house. They then took all the bodies and put them into one room, which was the carpenter's shop. Barnberry then took his gun and worked it and swore that if I did not go into the house and search all the things, he would blow my brains out. They then made me get some tea and sugar from under the table and tie them up in two papers. I then told Barnberry that I wanted to leave the crowd, that I did not want to go any further with them, but he swore that I should not leave them. He then took my cap off my head and put a black hat (sombrero) on and threw my cap into the fire and then said that we must go. I then saw Barnberry bring an infant out of the room and take it in the carpenter's shop where the dead bodies were, and the Indian knocked the child on the head with an axe.*

*We then left and about a mile from the mission Barnberry shared the money that he had amongst us, to carry, as it was too heavy for one man. This money was taken from a chest or bureau and the next day when it was again passed out, each man had one hundred and thirty-six dollars. There were four doubloons and one five dollar piece.*

*We encamped about twenty-three or four miles from the Mission of St. Miguel. The next night stopped about four miles this side of St. Louis. Here the Indian boy ran away. Encamped the next night about two leagues this side of Capt. Dana's ranche. About a league before arriving at the next ranche (the Alamos), Lynch shot a calf. We stopped at the ranch that night and met the mail rider there. When we shot the calf we saw four or five men, besides another mail rider going to Monterey. We thought these men were coming after us for killing the calf.*

*We started early the next morning and come through the mountains and stopped at a ranche all night, but could get nothing to eat for ourselves or horses. The next afternoon arrived at a ranche where an Indian was living (Don Ortega's* ranche). I wanted to leave them there as I was tired and afoot, but they swore they would shoot me if I did not come on.

Next day stopped at a ranche about six leagues from here (Dos Pueblos) and bought four horses and two saddles. Passed the Indian rancheria late in the evening and passed through Santa Barbara and encamped about two or three miles below the town. The next day stopped at a ranche and fed the horses. Bought two bottles of aguardiente there—left immediately, and about a mile of two from the ranch we were taken prisoners.

*Question by the court*—

Have you ever heard Lynch or Mike say anything respecting a murder that had been committed at or near the Placers?

*Answer*—

I heard Lynch say that he shot a man's face off, and then they, that is Lynch and Mike, jumped on to his horses and made off with them. There was a wagon about three quarters of a mile behind.

*Question*—

Did Lynch take any active part in the murder committed at the Mission St. Miguel?

*Answer*—

I was standing near Lynch, perhaps fifteen feet off, when he fired at the Indian— "God dam him, I have hit him in the head," was the expression he made use of after he had fired.

*Question*—

Did any of your party have any gold when you arrived at the Mission? And if so, what did you do with it?

*Answer*—

Lynch and Mike had gold, which they said they dug from the placer—and they sold it to Reed for seven dollars per ounce.

The examination of the prisoner here closed.

The different articles taken from the prisoners, as well as some money in gold and silver, and some gold from the mines were then shown to the prisoner, Remer, and he declared that he recognized them as belonging to his party.

*The above declaration has been carefully read to me, and I do hereby solemnly swear it to be true and correct, and hereby ratify the same by my free will—*

*his*

*Peter X Remer*

*mark*

Peter Quin, the final prisoner brought before the committee, was not as cooperative as his pals. Surly and in pain from his wound, he at first refused to admit having anything to do with the murders:

*Santa Barbara, California*

*December 13th 1848*

*Declaration of Peter Quin*

*Born in Dublin—age 20 years—*

*This is all that could be got from the prisoner. He refuses to disclose anything and asserts positively that he knows nothing whatever in relation to the murders committed at St. Miguel Mission.*

*The prisoner was then told by the President that he could gain nothing by his silence, but on the contrary it would go far to prove his guilt—that if no evidence was brought forth to prove his being implicated in the murder, he would be set at liberty, but that if he was found guilty he must be punished according to his crimes.*

*The prisoner still insisted that not only he was not of those who committed the murder, but also that he knew nothing of it, and that the first intimation he had of it was after he was brought back to Santa Barbara.*

*The President then informed the prisoner that his obstinacy would avail him nothing—that allowing sufficient evidence could not be produced to prove his guilt, a price had been set upon his head of one thousand dollars, by Commodore Jones, for desertion from the Warren.*

*The prisoner was then remanded back to prison. The committee then resolved to adjourn 'till tomorrow morning at 9 o'clock.*

*Santa Barbara, Calif.*

*14th December, 1848*

*The committee met pursuant to adjournment at 9 o'clock this morning.*

*The prisoner Quin was called up for reexamination—The prisoner was then* asked by the President if he was ready to declare anything, or if he still insisted to keep the same silence that he did yesterday. The prisoner then said that he would declare all he knew.

I deserted from the Warren in company with two marines and three sailors— arrived at the Mission of La Soledad in company with Peter Remer—there joined a party consisting of three men, Lynch, Barnberry and Mike. We went on together so far as St. Miguel. About three o'clock in the afternoon arrived there—stopped there all night, had plenty to eat and drink. The next morning about 10 o'clock we left and went on about a mile. I was behind the rest of the party and afoot. The party agreed to go back again and stop there a week, they had such good accommodations that they would as soon stop there a week or so as not. We then went back.

The man of the house desired us to cut down a tree. We cut down an apple tree. He said it was too green, that it would not do, and he then went out with me and we cut down another one. We then carried it up to the house, and the old man (Reed) went and made some bread. I went out to ease myself and when I came back I went into a room where were Barnberry and Mike sitting by the fire. I said to Barnberry, "What in the name of God are you about?" He answered me, "Silence, you Irish son of a bitch, or I'll blow your brains out." Barnberry had an axe in his hand, holding it over the head of the negro, and Mike had a double barrel fowling piece. Just as I went in he struck him (the negro) with the axe. As soon as I saw that I ran out and hid in the bushes, and the two (meaning Barnberry and Mike) come out and found me in the bushes. They swore they would shoot me. The negro was not wounded before he was struck with the axe, but was alive.

After I ran out I heard a shot fired in the same room. I heard two shots fired, one in a room below. The first one was fired by Mike. After I was brought back Mike said to me, "You God dam son of a bitch, I have a good mind to put an end to you so that you will not sell us." I answered, "I don't care if you do, I think it is a hard thing to kill poor innocent people for nothing. It is a thing I am not accustomed to, I have never done such a thing in my life."

Then two men made a break for the women's room. They had axes, a cutlass, and a double barrel fowling piece with them. I then left the mission alone and about a half a mile from there fell in with P. Remer. (here the declaration of the prisoner was so confused and disjointed that it was almost

Lewis T. Burton, prominent Santa Barbara rancher and storekeeper, served on the committee that tried the San Miguel murderers. Author's collection.

impossible to get at his meaning. In the first place he said that he went on with Remer about four miles and then Barnberry and Mike came up to them at full speed on horseback. Then next he says that Remer staid behind and came up with the two men mentioned above, Barnberry and Mike.)

When the two came up to us, one of them said "You Irish son of a bitch, I have a mind to blow your brains out." They then said they had a good mind to shoot me any how for backing out. "For backing out from what" I said? "For backing out from the murder of those people." I said "It was most time for a person to back out from such a murder as that—I never yet murdered any one and I would not have the stain of it on my hands."

We then fell in with the man Fisher (Lynch), the two, Barnberry and Mike, then said "We have a mind to blow the brains out of all three of you." I said, "No you won't." We two poor buggers, meaning Remer and myself, had no arms, but Fisher (Lynch) had a rifle and a knife.

We traveled all night, and the next morning about 4 o'clock we put up a few miles beyond the first ranche. Stopped there two hours and then went on and put up after sun down at another ranche. Gave the horses some feed and then went on. The Indian did not join us until a couple of nights after this. Slept about four miles from the mission—the Indian left that night. He stole a pair of cloth trousers and some tobacco. He did not leave anything behind. The Indian had on a white, calico shirt and a pair of blue trousers—a colored handkerchief (red, blue, white and green) around his head. He had a calico serape (supposed to be a sheet) and a lot of white calico serapes around him. He was mounted on a dapple grey horse, had no saddle, or bridle, but had a halter. There were two white blankets under him on the horse—one had yellow and white stripes. Had pretty long hair, no beard nor mustache—about twenty or twenty-five years old, about five feet ten inches in height—had no shoes on.

We started the next morning (here the narrative of the prisoner became so confused that it was utterly impossible to make out anything of it, until they arrived at the Alamos). About a league the other side of the ranche where we slept (the Alamos) we shot a calf and whilst we were eating we saw five men on horseback—one man who was the mail rider, a dragoon, came over to us and spoke to Barnberry and Mike. I was walking along with the other two. The Spaniards went on ahead and the dragoon followed after them. We then went to the ranche. The dragoon was there eating his supper. Stopped all night at the ranche.

(illegible) on the road met a Spaniard on horseback—he was afraid to come near us and went over the mountain. (Here the narrative became confused again.) Came to another ranche (the dos Pueblos) where we bought four horses—two white, one black and one red. I bought the red horse and paid twenty-five dollars for the horse and saddle. I had a horse when I arrived there. Barnberry bought the black

horse and gave his own horse and twenty or twenty-five dollars in money. Peter Remer bought a white for twenty-five dollars and a saddle for six dollars. Lynch bought the remaining white horse and gave his own horse and about twenty or twenty-five dollars in cash. The man who sold us the horses was a tall, thin, spare man, rather old. There were three or four young men in the house. When the old man went out after the horses, a young man about twenty-five years old went out with him. The young man was of a dark complexion—had on a white hat and a red shirt—had on calconeros [calzoneras, the traditional Mexican, split-bottom breeches]. The old man appeared to be willing to sell the horses—he said he would get them the next morning, but we told him we wanted them that night and he replied that if we wanted them he would get them for us. He got them that night. Two men went into the corral and got out two horses and brought them to the house.

We rode all night—passed through Sta. Barbara about thirty yards from the mission, near enough to distinguish the towers of the church. It was now about eleven o'clock. The moon was not up so we passed through the town—heard a man sing out from the window of a house. Slept about a mile or two from the town. We could see the town very plain from where we were encamped. Got up about six o'clock the next morning—the sun was pretty high. Stopped at a ranche during the morning where we bought two bottles of aguardiente. Barnberry fired off his fowling piece here and we left the ranche about 1 o'clock.

The examination of the prisoner here closed. The different articles of the prisoners, as well as some money and gold and silver and some gold from the mines, were then shown to the prisoner, Quin, and he declared that he recognized them as belonging to his party.

The above declaration has been carefully read to me and I do hereby solemnly swear it to be true and correct and hereby ratify the same by my free will.

Peter Quin


The document was signed by three prominent Californian witnesses, besides the members of the committee. Quin must have been quite agitated to judge by the rambling nature of his statement. He was incoherent at times and his signature indicated he could either barely write his name or was terrified at the prospects of his immediate future.

A jury was selected on December 24, then adjourned since the next day was Christmas. At 9 o'clock on Tuesday, the 26th, the jury heard the case and quickly brought in a verdict of guilty. The three prisoners were sentenced to be shot. At the bottom of the court document giving the verdict is the notation:

*The foregoing findings and sentences in the cases of Peter Remer, Peter Quin and Joseph Lynch are approved by authority of Col. R. B. Mason, Gov. of Cal.*

*E.O.C. Ord, 1st Lt. U.S. Artillery*

Considering the unsettled state of California affairs, the lack of a U.S. judicial system or even any American peace officers other than the local alcaldes, the case was settled remarkably quickly...and well. Within twenty-three days the murderers had been pursued, captured, tried and shot. The Americans and the native Californians, even though they had just concluded a bitter war, functioned extremely well together in this first crisis of law and order in the new territory. It would not always be so.

The prisoners, all of the Catholic faith, were given the last rites of the church. On December 28, they were taken to a ravine near town where a nine-man firing squad ended their earthly cares. All died at the first fire and were

buried in the mission cemetery, as was Ramon Rodriguez , the posseman who had died helping effect their capture.

In a curious epilog to the tragedy, Cesario Lataillade prepared for a cattle drive early in 1849. Finding his shotgun needed repair, he took one of the captured bandit weapons to the forge behind the de la Guerra House, in Santa Barbara. He planned to replace a damaged part in his shotgun with the same part taken from the

*Lt. Edward O. C. Ord led an army patrol in pursuit of the killers. Author's collection.*

captured weapon. As Don Cesario held the bandit's shotgun in the forge, the weapon accidentally discharged, mortally wounding him. He died some thirty-nine hours later, adding yet another to the tragic list of bandit victims.

Today, tourists strolling the sandy stretches of beach at Summerland have no idea of the terrible history that was concluded in the crashing surf just south of Santa Barbara. The cruel death of Lataillade signalled the end of what was undoubtedly one of the most brutal and tragic episodes in California history.

# Chapter One / NOTES

Information on Sam Brannan and the Gold Rush can be found in Watson, Douglas S. "The Great Express Extra of the *California Star* of April 1, 1848." *California Historical Society Quarterly*: Vol. 11, No. 2, June, 1932. See also Stellman, Louis J. *Sam Brannan, Builder of San Francisco*. New York: The Exposition Press, 1953 and Lewis, Oscar. *Sutter's Fort: Gateway to the Gold Fields*. Englewood Cliffs, N.J.: Prentice-Hall, Inc., 1966.

For the early days of the California Gold Rush, see Bancroft, Hubert H. *California Pastoral. 1769–1848*. San Francisco: The History Company, Publishers, 1888; Harlow, Neal. *California Conquered, War and Peace in the Pacific, 1846–1850*. Berkeley, Los Angeles: University of California Press, 1982; Colton, U.S.N., Rev. Walter. *Three Years in California*. New York: A. S. Barnes & Company, 1850; Garner, William Robert. *Letters from California, 1846–1847*. Berkeley: University of California Press, 1970; Hawgood, John A. *First and Last Consul*. Palo Alto, CA: Pacific Books, 1970; Holliday, J. S. *The World Rushed In*. New York: Simon & Schuster, 1981.

U.S. Naval Commander Thomas A. P. C. Jones' reward offer for deserters appeared in the *Monterey Californian*, November 11, 1848. Army posts in the new territory were also hard hit by desertions. Writing to Lieutenant William T. Sherman at Monterey in October of 1848, Dragoon Captain A. Johnston complained that he had lost "some of the best men" in his company who had also taken horses and other material. U.S. Army, Records of the 10th Military Department, Letters Received, 1846–1851, National Archives. Information on the Australian penal colonies is in Hughes, Robert. *The Fatal Shore*. New York: Alfred A. Knopf, 1987.

An account of the Von Pfister murder can be found in Gay, Theressa. *James Marshall*. Georgetown: The Talisman Press, 1967. See also the *Monterey Californian*, October 14, 1848, and the *San Francisco Californian*, October 29, 1848. Peter Raymond is listed as a member of Fremont's California Battalion, Company E; see "Roster of Fremont's California Battalion, Mexican War, 1846," *The Madera County Historian*, Madera County Historical Society's quarterly, September, 1961.

Raymond's escape is recorded by William R. Grimshaw, a resident of Sutter's Fort at the time. A man named M. J. House was blamed for the escape since he had been detailed as the guard for the night. Grimshaw's recollections were written for Bancroft in 1872 and later edited by J. R. K. Kantor and published as *Grimshaw's Narrative* by the Sacramento Book Collector's Club, 1964.

For information on Joseph Lynch, see Clark, Francis D. *The First Regiment of New York Volunteers*. New York: George S. Evans & Company, Printers, 1882.

Information on Raymond and Lynch's murder of the two prospectors is in Bancroft, Hubert H. *History of California, Vol. VI, 1848–1859*. San Francisco: The History Company, Publishers, 1888, and the *San Francisco Star and Californian*, December 2, 1848.

For data on the California missions, see the series by Engelhardt, Father Zephyrin, particularly *Mission Nuestra Señora de la Soledad* and *Mission San Miguel Archangel*. Santa Barbara: Mission Santa Barbara, 1929. A well-researched and more recent study is Ohles, Wallace V. *The Lands of Mission San Miguel*. Fresno, CA: Word Dancer Press, 1997.

The history of the U.S. ship *Warren* can be found in Mooney, James L., ed. *Dictionary of American Fighting Ships*, Vol. III. Washington: Naval Historical Center, Department of the Navy, 1981. Little is known of Quin, Remer and the other naval deserters. The Department of the Navy did not begin maintaining personnel files for enlisted men until 1885, but some information can be obtained from enlistment returns and ship's muster rolls. Quin, for example, was 23 years old when he enlisted in the navy at Philadelphia on June 13, 1846. He was a native of Ireland and probably one of the huge influx of immigrants fleeing the disastrous potato famine in that tortured land. M. Thomas, Archives 1, Reference Branch, Textual Reference Division, National Archives, Washington DC, to the author, February 7, 1998.

The movements of Raymond and his gang of cutthroats is described in each of the three confessions cited later.

Information on William Reed and his family is from Bancroft, Hubert H. *History of California, Vol. V, 1846–1848*. San Francisco: The History Company, Publishers, 1886. Other data on the Reeds and the San Miguel tragedy are recounted in "Memoirs of Doña Catarina Avila de Rios, the Widow of Sergt. Petronilo Rios" (Reed's partner). Manuscript No. D-35, in the Bancroft Library, University of California, Berkeley.

Data on the actual murders at the mission is from the three confessions.

The mail rider's story is from Beckwourth, James P. *The Life and Adventures of James P. Beckwourth, written from his own dictation by T. D. Bonner*. New York, Harper, 1856 and Wilson, Elinor. *Jim Beckwourth*, Norman, Oklahoma, University of Oklahoma Press, 1972. The first serious, documented study of the San Miguel murders was by Leonard, Ralph J. "The San Miguel Mission Murders." *La Vista*, Vol. 4, No. 1, June, 1980, San Luis Obispo County Historical Society.

General William T. Sherman's comments and recollections are from "Old Times in California," *North American Review*, March, 1889. The arrival of Price and Branch is mentioned in the Rios manuscript, the Leonard article and various other early sources. The route of the killers as they fled south is detailed in the three confessions and all generally agree. An account of the fight on the beach is in Leonard and in the *San Francisco Daily Alta California*, January 25, 1849.

The three confessions and various documents relating to the trial and execution of the prisoners are in the De la Guerra Collection, Santa Barbara Mission Archives, Folder 821, 1848–50. The confessions, as presented here, were minimally edited by the author for readability. There was little paragraphing or punctuation in the originals—dashes usually taking the place of periods, for example. No words were changed by the author, although coordinating conjunctions were occasionally omitted to make two sentences from one awkward or overlong sentence.

The shooting of the three prisoners is noted in various documents, in Leonard and in the *Alta* of January 25, 1849. Other details are in the Rios manuscript. According to his widow's story, Petronilo Rios himself insisted the loot recovered from the murderers be given to the widow of Ramon Rodriguez, who was killed in the fight on the beach. See also Streeter, William A. "Recollections of William A. Streeter, 1843–1878." William H. Ellison, ed. *California Historical Society Quarterly*, Vol. XVIII, 1939.

The Reed murders and the death of Cesario Lataillade is described in Ellison, William H. and Francis Price, eds. *The Life and Adventures in California of Don Agustín Janssens, 1834–1856*. San Marino, CA: The Huntington Library, 1953 and O'Neill, Owen H., Ed. *History of Santa Barbara County*. Santa Barbara, CA: H. M. Meier, 1939. Laitillade's widow, Maria Antonia de la Guerra, gave birth to a son shortly after her husband's untimely death.

San Francisco in the early 1850s was plagued by fires, crime and sleazy politicians trying to get in on the ground floor of the new frontier. When all three elements seemed out of control, there were those brave enough to take matters into their own hands. Reviled by some, but heralded by thousands of others, the Vigilantes took over and never looked back. Author's collection.

A convict of the Australian penal colonies as he appeared ca. 1874. Thousands of these men, as they escaped or were paroled, made their way to California during the gold rush days. Many were reformed. Too many others were not. National Library of Tasmania, Hobart.

# 2 "We had hard fighting"

## English Jim and the Sydney Ducks

William T. Coleman proved to be just the right man to try to take control of a city overrun with venal politicians and thugs. Author's collection.

"**M**y true name is James Stuart...."

So begins the extraordinary confession of an Australian ex-convict in 1851. Detailing many crimes and giving names and descriptions of his confederates, Stuart's tale did much to justify the existence of the San Francisco Vigilance Committee of that year. He and a cluster of Sydney ex-convicts were responsible for much crime in frontier California, from horse stealing and arson, to bank burglaries and highway robbery. A witness described Stuart's demeanor as he recounted his many crimes:

> He went through the whole range of his many rascalities, gave vivid descriptions of his adventures, entering with great zest into the details, and it was curious to see his eye brighten and twinkle...when describing his best successes....

In other words, he was boasting to a bunch of grim-faced vigilantes in the hope that if he made a confession of his crimes, it would go easier on him. It was a fatal mistake.

During the eighteenth century many condemned English criminals were given the option of being transported to the colonies in America. After 1775 and the American War of Independence, however, England could no longer transport convicts to that distant land. Soon the British prisons were becoming overcrowded and criminals were housed aboard various ancient merchant or warships, referred to as hulks, moored in the Thames and at various coastal ports. Inevitably, this overcrowding again forced consideration of new, remote prison sites. Although Bermuda and Gibralter were later also utilized as convict dumping grounds, transportation to New South Wales (Australia) was instituted on May 13, 1787, when an eleven-ship fleet set out from England. Five hundred and eighty-six male convicts were aboard, with some 192 female prisoners, together with a group of free settlers and various government and military units. By 1868, when the practice was discontinued, about 162,000 convicts had been landed at Sydney Cove and other ports.

This initial convict transportation to New South Wales was the first step toward colonizing this far-flung British territory. A settlement was quickly established at Port Jackson, later Sydney. A previously unseen land, the area consisted of dangerous inland deserts contrasted with sandstone cliffs and bluffs covered with eucalyptus, palms and ferns. Flocks of cockatoos and other exotic birds filled the forests. It was a paradise that was to become a convict's hell.

*Ticket-of-Leave men as depicted in an engraving from a photograph ca. 1862. Author's collection.*

Prior to 1815, transportation to New South Wales was hideously cruel. Many of the contracted ships were former slavers whose captains crowded the convicts unmercifully to make room for goods to be sold at inflated prices in Sydney. In the early years, death rates were high, food was bad and exercise among the shackled convicts was mostly nonexistent. Later, as conditions improved, there were a few shipboard mutinies, but they were ruthlessly suppressed and rarely repeated. The first fleet had taken 252 days to reach Botany Bay, but by the 1830s the trip was being made in just over three months.

Many of these "transports" were repeat offenders—poor farm workers or urban laborers forced to steal from necessity. The balance were prostitutes, professional criminals or Irish political exiles. Sentences ranged from seven years to life.

At Sydney, the colonists began constructing the homes and outbuildings for their farms, while the convicts began building their own prison, roads, various public works and government buildings. Other convict colonies were established, also, and the names of Van Diemen's Land (Tasmania), Norfolk Island, Port Arthur and Macquarie Harbor became synonymous with desperation. Fortunate convicts would be doled out to work for private settlers in the Crown's behalf. Escape was sometimes possible, but there was nowhere to go. The option was to die at sea or in the outback. The floggings, bad food, brutal officers and long work days in chains forced many to make the choice, however. If you were tough enough, you became a "bushranger," and lived by banditry. Conditional pardons were possible, while four years of good conduct made prisoners eligible for a "ticket-of-leave" from a seven-year sentence. This meant that a convict was "free" to work in the colony for the balance of his sentence, although many left the country. Most served out their time, returning to England or taking a job in the Australian towns or villages.

One of these convicts was a man named James Stuart, but he had many aliases. Acquaintances called him "English Jim." According to his own account, Stuart—if that was his real name—was born to a family of eleven children in Brighton, Sussex County, England, on March 3, 1819. His parents were good people and he was raised in the church, but in 1835, when only sixteen years of age, he committed a forgery and was transported to New South Wales for life. After serving six years, friends secured his release and he spent several years in Adelaid, on Australia's southern coast. He couldn't return to England since he hadn't served out his term and punishment could be death. He was just a boy when he had been thrown into the company of hardened criminals and prisons have always been exeplary schools for crime.

Stuart soon shipped out for South America where he spent several years living by his criminal wits. Early in 1849, he made his way to Panama.

Australian convict work gang ca. 1830. *National Library of Australia, Canberra.*

Signing up as a crewman on the steamer *Tennessee*, he arrived at San Francisco in November of that year.

In California, Stuart mined and worked at various jobs throughout the gold country. He was always on the lookout for a fast buck, however, whether it be highway robbery, horse theft, or burglary. He was described as being about five feet, nine inches tall, with sharp features and dark hair and whiskers. "Exceedingly handsome," one acquaintance described Stuart, while another

*San Francisco Bay as it looked in 1851. The bay was choked with abandoned ships from all over the world, many of them being used as habitations. It was here that the ship* James Caskie *was attacked by Stuart and his men. California State Library.*

noted his features suggested the traditional pictures of Christ. A man who worked with him stated he did little but always had money with which to gamble. At Foster's Bar, on the North Fork of the Yuba River above Marysville, he was accused of selling some stolen property. When he offered some gold as security, it was recognized as having been stolen from the gambling house of Dodge & Company. He was nearly lynched by a mob, but during the course of his trial before Judge Oliver P. Stidger in early October 1850, he managed to escape jail.

Fleeing to San Francisco with Jim Burns, alias "Jimmy from Town," Stuart quickly associated with a gang of Australian thugs. When he was tipped off that the brig *James Caskie* was carrying a large amount of coin, Stuart put together a gang. On the night of October 25, 1850, Stuart, John Edwards, Jim Brown and George Smith boarded the ship. The captain put up a desperate resistance and was shot at a number of times. Finally, one of the pirates knocked him down with a slung shot. The *Daily Alta California* reported:

> Outrage—On Friday night five men went on board the brig *James Caskie* off Clark's Point and demanded of the captain his money. The captain refusing, they beat him senseless, and until his wife, who feared they would kill her husband, delivered to the robbers the money, about $900....They were all masked and otherwise disguised.

The captain's wife was later reported as "insane at times" as a result of her ordeal. Stuart meanwhile fled the city. In early December he was again in the Yuba River area, above Marysville, traveling with several horse thief companions. They had apparently lost all their money gambling, and while riding near Dobbin's Ranch, they lamented the poor state of their pocketbooks. All agreed that they might as well be dead, as dead broke. When the trio met one Charles E. Moore on the road, they had their first victim. Stuart killed him with a shotgun blast and his possessions were divided among them. The murder was reported in the *Sacramento Transcript* in mid-December 1850:

> Murder—Last Saturday Mr. Charles Moore and his two partners left their camp to come down to Dobbins' Ranche on the Yuba River. When about four miles from their destination they separated....Mr. Moore...had twenty-three hundred dollars belonging to himself and partners....After a short time a Spaniard came to the Ranche and said there was a man who had been shot, lying dead above. The next day...they found Mr. Moore lying in a small ravine, dead, with three slug wounds upon him.

The body was discovered on December 7. Some articles of merchandise were found close by which were recognized by W. W. Dobbins who kept a store at his ranch. Dobbins remembered selling the items to Jim Stuart and two companions a few days previously. This was enough to put Moore's partner, Thomas Broadwater, on the trail of the suspected murderers.

Tracking the killers through Marysville to Sacramento, Broadwater found Stuart jailed on a housebreaking charge on the Sacramento prison brig. The *Sacramento Transcript,* December 14, reported:

> Yesterday two gentlemen arrived in the city from Yuba County having a warrant for the arrest of James Stewart (sic), or "English Jim," an individual charged with the murder of Charles Moore, on the Yuba River and robbing him of $2,500. These gentlemen visited the prison ship and recognized the murderer in the man arrested on Thursday night.

While Broadwater was discussing the matter with local authorities, Stuart again managed to escape. Working with three other prisoners, he managed to cut a hole through the floor of their cell with a pen knife. Dropping down into the hold of the bark, the men crawled out a porthole and fled in a rowboat. Stuart again headed for San Francisco where he could lose himself among the Australians living in the notorious Sydney Town, a collection of saloons, boarding houses and shanties at the base and running up the ravines, of Telegraph Hill. The *San Francisco Daily Alta California* noted:

> In the valley on the North side of Telegraph Hill, is a community which has well selected a locality hidden from the city's eye. They have picked out a spot separated from their fellows by the lofty hill. This place has been christened "Sydney Valley." Here are gathered the immigrants from that unpopular portion of the globe, and bad rum at a rial a glass, dirty and bloated faces marked with crime are the features of this locality.

San Francisco's first city jail was the brigantine Euphemia, *the first expenditure of the city's* ayuntamiento, *or city council. Sacramento soon followed suit, the city prison from which Stuart escaped being the 259-ton bark* La Grange, *shown above. The 314-ton bark* Strafford *was the Sacramento's first jail. California State Library.*

By May 1851 some 11,000 Australians had migrated to California. Although there were many honest immigrants among the so-called "Sydney Ducks" or ex-convicts, many were of the Stuart ilk who lived by crime. Some of these outlaws ran saloons and boarding houses, always giving them alluring and innocent appearing names such as Cottage of Content, Bird in Hand, Uncle Sam, Live and Let Live, Rose Cottage and Heart in Hand. Actually, many were dens for hiding fugitives where crimes were plotted and loot was fenced. After the fifth great San Francisco fire in May 1851, some $10,000 worth of stolen property was found hidden in Sydney Town.

Joining forces with a gang of other Sydney men, Stuart sallied forth on various robbing expeditions. Although many of these offenses were later confessed by the participants, murder and the more heinous crimes were not mentioned for obvious reasons.

When a Stuart confederate, one Samuel Whittaker, mentioned he had seen some $10,000 to $15,000 being brought into a popular dry goods establishment, Stuart began making plans. On the evening of February 19, 1851, Stuart, Whittaker and six accomplices descended on C. J. Jansen & Company on Montgomery street. There were few street lights in those days and the muddy roads were only illuminated by the lights of the saloons and businesses along the way. Waiting until they were sure Jansen was alone, John Morgan went in first, followed by Stuart. The others waited outside. In a matter of minutes Jansen had been beaten senseless and the robbers had fled with some $1,500 in gold coin.

Charles Jansen described his assailants to the police and the next day an Australian named Thomas Burdue was picked up. The police had been keeping an eye out for "English Jim" Stuart after his escape from the Sacramento prison brig and Burdue not only matched Stuart's description, but he was a reported ex-convict from Sydney. Despite frantic declarations that he was innocent of any crime, Burdue was held as not only the Jansen robber, but the killer of Moore in Yuba County, also. The following day another Australian named Robert Windred was arrested as the other Jansen robber. When the badly beaten Jansen tentatively identified the two prisoners from his bed, large crowds yelling "Lynch 'em!" followed the procession to the nearby justice court on Portsmouth Square.

As the examination of the prisoners progressed, the crowds outside became aware that the notorious Stuart was one of the robbers, although it was Burdue who was in custody. Soon, several thousand excited people were milling about. As witnesses began testifying for the defense—perjured witnesses were a frequent ploy of criminals—the mob outside began shouting and milling about. When court was adjourned until Monday morning, a rush was made for the prisoners in the courtroom, but it was beaten back by officials and portions of a nearby militia unit. Although many in the crowds had drifted away at this point, late that Saturday afternoon people again began assembling around City Hall. After a variety of speeches were made, a committee was appointed to consult with the authorities and help guard the prisoners.

It was a critical time in the city's history. Not only did crime seem to be on the increase in recent days, but the courts had seemed ineffective with packed juries, bought witnesses and lawyers paid for with stolen funds.

Criminals were quickly back on the street to continue their depredations. A speech given by Mormon merchant Sam Brannan summed up the frustration of many city residents:

> I am very much surprised to hear people talk about grand juries, or recorders, or mayors. I'm tired of such talk. These men are murderers, I say, as well as thieves. I know it, and I will die or see them hung by the neck. I'm opposed to any farce in this business. We had enough of that eighteen months ago when we allowed ourselves to be the tools of these judges, who sentenced convicts to be sent to

*Large crowds swarmed around the San Francisco City Hall, February 22, 1851, demanding justice.* Annals of San Francisco.

the United States. We are the mayor and the recorder, the hangman and the laws. The law and the courts never yet hung a man in California; and every morning we are reading fresh accounts of murders and robberies. I want no technicalities. Such things are devised to shield the guilty.

The next day nearly eight thousand people assembled around the courthouse. Mayor John Geary and other authorities addressed the crowds preaching moderation, but their suggestions were ignored. Merchant William T. Coleman recommended a committee of twelve men be appointed to retire and devise a course of action. The committee immediately recommended that a trial should be conducted by the people and that the legal authorities could participate if they so chose. Helpless when opposed by such a huge crowd, the authorities withdrew and Coleman and other prominent citizens took over.

Sam Brannan, the merchant who insisted on sending a firm message to the criminal element. Author's collection.

The trial took place immediately, with the selection of a judge, jury, Coleman as prosecutor and two prominent attorneys as the defense team. Other officers were appointed and the trial commenced. It was near midnight when the jury retired, but they were unable to reach a verdict. When they were finally dismissed and the crowd outside advised as to what had occurred, there were shouts of "Hang them anyhow!" Again there was a great tumult and it was with much difficulty that the crowds were pacified and urged to return to their homes. It was close to one o'clock Monday morning when the committee voted to adjourn and the streets were again cleared.

Burdue and Windred were turned over to the authorities and again tried. This time both were found guilty and sentenced to fourteen years imprisonment. Windred managed to carve his way out of the local jail and quickly disappeared. Burdue steadily maintained his total innocence, but he had been identified by numerous witnesses as Stuart and he now wore the subdued look of one who had no choice but to accept his fate. In March the resigned prisoner was escorted to Marysville to be tried for the Moore murder.

The Sydney Ducks and other criminals hadn't taken the events after the Jansen robbery seriously, however. Homicides and robberies still seemed to be prevalent; at least that must have been the general perception. Certainly, great crowds of citizens were stirred up about something. Prisoners continued to escape from the city jails with alarming regularity, when not being released on technicalities.

Fires, too, were a constant concern. Four disastrous conflagrations had destroyed large portions of the city. Several were thought to be the work of arsonists. As early as December 1850, a letter published in the *Alta* vented the frustrations of the populace:

Mr. Editor—The crime of arson has in all ages and countries been classed amongst the highest grades of offenses, not only for the reason that life and property are jeopardized when its owners and inmates are most defenseless, but because of the impossibility, except by the most distant chances, of the detection of the culprit. The motive for the perpetration of the crime in this country and especially in this

*The great San Francisco fire of May 4, 1851.* Annals of San Francisco.

city seems to be to afford an opportunity for plunder and house robbery while the occupants are engaged in extinguishing the conflagration. I would suggest one mode by which the incendiary may meet the reward of his crime....When any person shall be caught in the act of stealing at a fire, let him receive Lynch law, and suffer death.

Although signed merely, "Justice," the editor noted the writer was "one of our most respectable citizens and a lawyer." Later writers would suggest that the fires were set by merchants eager to destroy market-glutted goods for the insurance, but this does not make sense. That merchants would destroy large sections of the city for their own selfish reasons seems highly unlikely, not to mention extremely dangerous. Burglars and thieves had a usual routine of taking a room in a boarding house or hotel, then in the early morning hours set a fire and in the resulting smoke and confusion rob the rooms of the fleeing tenants. Often the fires were set as distractions since there was no more terrifying occurrence in a city or town in those faraway times. And, it was often the Sydney men who were picked up as suspects.

On May 4, 1851, the fifth and worst fire wiped out three-quarters of the business section of the city, destroying nearly two thousand buildings. It had started late at night in the paint shop of Baker & Meserve on the south side of the town plaza. According to the *San Francisco Evening Picayune*, the owners were known to be particularly careful, again raising the question of incendiaries. Rebuilding had scarcely commenced when arsonists struck again.

On May 21 the Stockton *San Joaquin Republican* reported: "Incendiarism— An attempt was made on Saturday last, at San Francisco, to fire the City Hospital, in which there were a large number of persons confined to their beds. Two other attempts to fire the city have been reported."

The same issue of the *Republican* reported an attempt to ignite the Verandah, a well known hotel on Kearny and Washington streets. There was no doubt just who was responsible for the rash of recent fires both in the bay city and Stockton, according to the *Republican*:

In our columns will be found no less than four reports of fresh attempts at incendiarism at the Bay City. It appears that the majority of persons are agreed to fasten the foul crimes of arson which have recently been perpetrated, upon Sydney convicts and expirees. Doubtless the surmise is a correct one.

On June 2, a notorious Sydney man named Benjamin Lewis was accused of setting a fire on San Francisco's Long Wharf. Lewis was staying at the Collier Hotel and was caught leaving the place as a fire was burning between two mattresses in his room. As witnesses were giving testimony in police court the following day, a cry of fire was raised and there was much scurrying about in court before the fire was pronounced a false alarm. Meanwhile, a large crowd was gathering around the building and it looked like a repeat of the Burdue hearing. Suddenly cries of "Lynch him, hang him!" were heard, but a rush into the courtroom was unproductive when it was discovered the prisoner was not present. The mayor addressed the crowd and managed to disperse them, but the *Alta* commented; "Lewis...may thank a combination of circumstances for his present existence, as had the crowd around the city hall waited two minutes longer he would have been brought into the courtroom where he could easily have been seized."

William D. M. Howard was elected president of the vigilantes. Author's collection.

On June 9 the *Alta* reported a series of six fires set underneath the California Street Wharf with a kind of timed fuse device called "slow matches." One of the sites was directly under a pile of lumber and hay piled on the wharf. The *Alta* had no doubt that these incidents were deliberate:

> This could not possibly have been the result of accident, and it is now rendered positive and beyond a doubt, that there is in this city an organized band of villains who are determined to destroy the city. We are standing as it were upon a mine that any moment may explode, scattering death and destruction.

The *Alta* did not yet realize that the arsonists didn't want to destroy their plundering fields, but merely create havoc that they might steal in the confusion. The stage was now set for the next act of the unfolding drama.

Disturbed at the faltering criminal justice system and the recent fires, several prominent businessmen stopped by the office of Sam Brannan on Sunday, June 8, 1851. The formation of a safety committee or patrol was discussed and notice was sent out of a general meeting at a local firehouse the following day. As members were being signed up, officers were selected, a constitution was drawn up and the name "Committee of Vigilance" was adopted. William D. M. Howard was elected president, with J. R. Snyder and Samuel Brannan as vice presidents.

On Tuesday evening some one hundred men had been enrolled and the meeting adjourned when a vigorous knock sounded on Brannan's office door. Three men were admitted with a thief in custody who had just been caught in the act. A Sydney man calling himself John Jenkins had stolen a small safe from a business office on Long Wharf. A large man, Jenkins had tried to make his escape in a boat, but had been chased and captured by other boatmen. He was held prisoner by the vigilantes, who quickly arranged for a trial. Unrepentant and constantly cursing his captors, Jenkins was easily convicted and sentenced to death.

Firehouse bells tolled throughout the city. At two o'clock in the morning the vigilantes and their prisoner moved through town towards Portsmouth Square. At Clay and Kearny streets a rescue was attempted by the Australian's friends, but they were unsuccessful. The police, too, tried to interfere but withdrew under the threat of vigilante pistols. A rope was rigged on the porch of the old adobe Custom House and the *San Francisco Evening Picayune* chronicled the terrible, closing moments:

> Another and a last attempt was now made to rescue him; a fierce contest ensued, but only for a minute; pistols were levelled, and the

*The hanging of Jenkins on the plaza of San Francisco, June 11, 1851. More were to come.* Illustrated London News, *August 9, 1851.*

Stuart was returning from a visit to the Mission Dolores, pictured above, when he was accosted by a group of men searching for a thief. Author's collection.

assailants fell back; and at a quarter past two o'clock, the rope was manned, and, with a jerk, the unhappy man lifted from the ground. As he stood a little distance from the house, he fell, when raised, against the railing, and the blood spurted from his nose and mouth. He struggled for some moments desperately, but, at last, drawing up his knees with a convulsive jerk, he expired.

The first Australian had fallen and the vigilantes had triumphed. Most of the local press justified the action. Horrified and helpless, there was little the authorities could do as they watched the vigilante ranks grow to over seven hundred in the next few weeks. Against such odds, the seventy-five man police force could do little, if anything.

English Jim Stuart had meanwhile done some traveling to Monterey and the mining country. By July 1, he was back in San Francisco. He was startled at the Jenkins lynching and quickly learned that the vigilantes were investigating crimes, warning certain Australians to leave town and shipping others back where they came from.

After scouting a robbery site out near the Mission Dolores the next day, Stuart was returning to the city when he saw some men who seemed to be searching the area. Actually, Jim Adair and some friends were seeking a housebreaker who had stolen a trunk containing some clothes. Stuart wanted to keep out of sight, for obvious reasons. He tried to avoid the searchers, but when Adair called to him, Stuart paused and joined him. The suspicious traveler was noted to be wearing a pistol and large knife.

Inconsistencies in his story as to why he was in the area resulted in the suspect being taken to vigilance committee headquarters. Stuart's blood must have run cold. He merely smiled and acted cheerfully, however, and claimed he was anxious to meet the famous vigilantes.

The prisoner gave his name as William Stevens and told a story that was readily believable, yet with curious inconsistencies. He had gone out to the Mission Dolores that morning to see a cousin who worked at a bakery there. When detained on his return, it was pointed out to him that his route would have taken much longer over the sand hills than if he used the mission plank road. This was enough to send several vigilantes to the mission to check on his story. They found no cousin working at either of the bakeries there and no one had asked to see an employee. The prisoner was in serious trouble now.

Stuart was still sweating in his cell the next morning when a new guard came on duty. It was John Sullivan, a boatman who had helped capture the lynched Jenkins. Sullivan was a shady character himself, but because he had an acquaintance with many of the Australians and had helped in the Jenkins capture, he was allowed to join the vigilantes. Later a vigilante recalled how the new sentry stuck his head in the door now to see who he was guarding:

> ...He espied in a corner of the room, one whom he had formerly known, and he sung out to him "Halloo, Jim! How did you come here!" The person accosted pretended not to know him, and Sullivan said, "You needn't pretend not to know me; I know who you are. I worked for you six months at Foster's Bar." He then closed the door, and called to me, as I happened to be near, and said, "Mr. Schenck, do you know who you have got here?...Why you have got English Jim, or Jim Stuart, the man who murdered the Sheriff of Auburn [Charles Moore], and I was present when he was about to be lynched at Marysville, when the rope broke and he escaped.

Jacob Van Bokkelen, head of the vigilante police, and other officers quickly confronted the prisoner, but he steadfastly denied his real identity. He was shaken by the unexpected appearance of Sullivan, but he had escaped from the law many times before and he now desperately looked for a way out of his situation.

The vigilantes quickly rounded up witnesses who had known Stuart in San Francisco. At the same time they sent a warning letter to Marysville alerting the officers there that the real Stuart was in their custody and Burdue was probably innocent. They also requested some of the Marysville witnesses be sent to the bay city so as to identify the captive there. Although hesitant as to admitting that they were trying an innocent man, the Marysville authorities complied with part of the request and soon a damning array of witnesses arrived to confront the prisoner, all identifying him as Stuart.

Frank M. Pixley was a noted criminal attorney who had defended Stuart many times. For a time he lived near San Quentin since he had so many criminal clients. California State Library.

Glowering in his irons and chains, Stuart still insisted that they had the wrong man. It had happened to Burdue, he protested, and now they were persecuting another innocent man.

When he heard the voice of Frank M. Pixley in an anteroom, Stuart looked up from his bench. Pixley was the local city attorney and had previously represented Stuart during his Sacramento incarceration. He knew he could depend on Pixley. Jake Von Bokkelen administered an oath to the lawyer before he entered Stuart's cell. "Pixley, will you say on your word of honor if this man is the man whom you have defended time and again in the lower courts?" The lawyer replied, "I will, gentlemen." Pixley and several vigilantes then entered Stuart's room.

The prisoner stood up with a big smile as Pixley walked in. He assumed it was his moment of freedom. There would be bail or some sort of deliverance. Even the vigilantes couldn't ignore the city attorney.

"Is that Stuart or not?" growled Von Bokkelen.

"You have no authority to ask me any questions," the attorney replied. "You are an illegal body." Vigilantes in the corridor had heard what transpired and began shouting "Hang him! Hang him!"

The vigilantes smiled. They had found out what they wanted to know when Stuart and his lawyer obviously recognized each other.

Witnesses who had known and worked with Stuart made out affidavits making a clear case as to his identity. It was one of the oddest circumstances in California history and confused everyone involved in the situation.

The *Alta* commented:

> It is placed almost beyond a doubt that this man here is the real Jim Stuart, and that Burdue is innocent of the charge of the murder of Moore, as Stuart is well known to be the murderer, and that it is a case of mistaken identity. To account for this it is said that there are three men in this country, all noted scoundrels, who in appearances very much resemble each other so as easily to be taken one for the other. These are Jim Stuart, Thomas Burdue and James Briggs, who escaped from the Station House some time since....

Briggs was a minor criminal who had once been jailed with Stuart. The *Sacramento Union* of June 2 had noted that Burdue had been convicted of the Moore murder and was now awaiting sentence. Working with the Marysville authorities, the vigilantes saw to it that Burdue was exonerated of any complicity in the two crimes of which he stood convicted. He had been identified by many witnesses as the real Stuart and the physical similarities between the two men were said to be remarkable. "It does seem," commented a chagrined *Marysville Herald*, "that after this, no one could positively identify his own brother."

Burdue returned to San Francisco where a large purse was collected to help compensate for his long months of incarceration. He sued the state also, but the legislature knew better than to open a can of worms of that sort. Burdue was last seen running a monte table on the Long Wharf.

Stuart saw that his race was run. There seemed to be only one way to save himself now and he didn't hesitate to call in members of the vigilance committee. He at last admitted to being James Stuart. Accused of the Moore murder and the Jansen

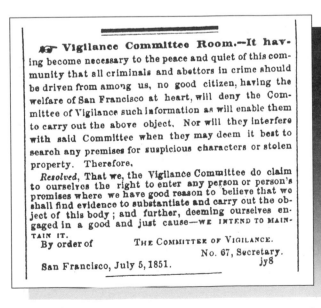

☞ **Vigilance Committee Room.**—It having become necessary to the peace and quiet of this community that all criminals and abettors in crime should be driven from among us, no good citizen, having the welfare of San Francisco at heart, will deny the Committee of Vigilance such information as will enable them to carry out the above object. Nor will they interfere with said Committee when they may deem it best to search any premises for suspicious characters or stolen property. Therefore,

*Resolved*, That we, the Vigilance Committee do claim to ourselves the right to enter any person or person's premises where we have good reason to believe that we shall find evidence to substantiate and carry out the object of this body ; and further, deeming ourselves engaged in a good and just cause—WE INTEND TO MAINTAIN IT.

By order of  THE COMMITTEE OF VIGILANCE.

No. 67, Secretary.

San Francisco, July 5, 1851.  jy8

robbery, he knew he would have no chance if left to the tender mercies of the vigilantes. He must bargain now and he didn't have to ponder long over betraying his friends to save his own skin.

The deal was simple. He would make a full confession. He would tell all his crimes and implicate by name all the members of his gang. In return he asked merely to be turned over to the civil authorities. He was told there would be no deals. If he told the whole truth, however, his suggestion would be considered by the committee . Surrounded by John F. Spence, William T. Coleman and others, Stuart began his confession in the evening:

*Vigilance Committee Room, July 8th 10 1/2 PM*

*Confession of James Stuart—alias English Jim—alias James Campbell alias William Stevens alias James Carlisle—*

*My true name is James Stu[a]rt. I was born in Brighton, Sussex Co Eng. I left Eng. about 16 years of age for New South Wales (where) I was transported for life on a charge of forgery. I served nearly 6 years of that sentence and through the intercession of friends I received my emancipation. I went from there to South Australia, Port Adelaid. I lived in Adelaid 5 years or more & then went to Calleo. I was on the Coast of South America 2 or 3 years. At last I got to Payta in the Bark J W Coffin and from there I went to Panama in a La[u]nch of 5 or 6 tons. I then ship'd as a hand on board Steamer* Tennessee *to San Francisco.*

*On my arrival in San Francisco, I went directly to the mines. I joined the Rock Mining Co. the day I arrived there—this was at Foster's Bar. I worked in the Rock Mining Co. one month. I hired one John Sullivan to work for me one month. I then went down the river about 4 miles and worked by myself at mining. I worked about 2 weeks, then went up and got John Sullivan to come down and work for me. He finished his month out here and then I got him to work two days over his time. Then we went up to Foster's Bar together.*

*I then bought a claim and paid 300$ for it. I bought a life boat for 400$—used it as a Ferry boat. I afterward lent this boat to a company and received half they made with her. I then went to Slate Range about 8 miles higher up with Sullivan. We both bought a claim for 50$ each. We worked that claim half a day (but) it did not pay me well enough and I left Sullivan and went to Foster's Bar. I worked at a race and got the river turned. I lent the Missouri Company 300$. The day the river was turned, I found the claim would not pay and left it.*

*I then went down the River again and worked at the old place some three or four weeks. I then had a row with Col Prentiss, through that I left and went to Foster's Bar. I then, with one other, made a garden (and) built myself a house. I did not work* any more at the mines. I had about 6$ per day for my boat. I had a claim I paid 300$ for. I allowed others to work it for me and received about 10 or 12 dollars per day for it. I then went into partnership with a man named Bernard Feller in a store. I did nothing for one week or more until I got tired of doing nothing. I then commenced building a house for boarders. I never finished the house. The Company I lent the 300$ to left and did not pay me.

Then a man named Dan Casey, lame & has a brother, sold out and I bought all they had in their house. In searching this house I found a trunk. The trunk was open, but full of clothes (and) I considered I had a right to them as I bought all there was in the house and took them. I wore these clothes while I was there. One night afterwards I went up to Mr. Dodge's house and played at Monte—I lost about 200$ that night and I thought I was cheated out of it and determined I would be even with him for it. So I stopped that night in a tent and saw him put his money in a large chest. I waited until all were asleep, then went in and took away the chest. On opening it I found I had about 4,300$. There were two specimens in it. One weighed 98 oz., worth 1,568$. The other piece was worth 723$. The balance was in dust and about 600$ in silver. I took all of this and secreted most of it in my garden. I then went to work as usual and worked about 10 days and was then apprehended for stealing this trunk of clothes formerly spoken of. I was admitted to bail for the sum of 500$. I deposited the money myself—3 days afterwards I was taken up on charge of stealing of Dodge & Co 4,300$. For this I was committed at Marysville. The mob this night wanted to hang me (but) the Judge swore in about 60 men to protect me.

Next morning Mr. Dodge came to me and said he would let me go if I would give him the money. I told him I would give him the money and gave it to him. I was afterwards told it was all there except 150$. I told him if it was not all there I must have lost part of it. I remained with the Sheriff till after dinner. We then called an auction and sold off the things, except the boat which I gave to a friend of mine. The things brought about 1,750$. The Sheriff, Edward Burr, kept the money. At night he went out nominally to collect the money. The cook came to me & told me if he were in my place he would go. I could not well go without my money, but still he advised me to go. I did think, & still do, think that Sheriff Burr told the cook to give that advice. I have never received the money from him.

I went away. I went about 3 miles that night & stole a mare. Next night I arrived at Sacramento—I sold the mare next day. I do not know to whom it belonged. I remained in Sacramento about 2 weeks. I got acquainted with three Americans & one Sydney man who lived by stealing horses & I sold them for them. The names of the men were Dab, James Peet & John Griffith—the last man was afterwards drowned.

The Cholera Morbus broke out in Sacramento. A boy, name unknown, told us that there was a Brig with considerable money on board—about 20,000$. We went on board and found about 1,200$. John Edwards, Jerry Brown, John Griffiths & self were concerned. We then came to San Francisco. John Edwards told us there was a vessel here with considerable money on board. Jim Burns, alias Jimmey from Town, came down with us. Jimmey robbed a Spaniard of about 30 oz. when we were coming down from Sacramento City. We divided the money between us.

The same night by information of Edwards we went on board the James Caskie and robbed her—we had hard fighting. The Capt. became desperate—we left him nearly dead. In the fight the Capts. wife came out with a sword. I took it from her. I acted as Capt. of our boys—we were all masked. I left my men in charge of the Capt. while I searched the vessel. Capts. wife gave me what money there was on board. She gave me one of Adams large 6 shooters. I gave the money and pistol to one of the men. I do not recollect which. Capts. wife begged of me not to take the Capts. life. I told her I did not want to do that if he would only be quiet. I then looked into the cabin and saw a splendid Gold Chronometer Watch. She begged of me not to take it as it was a gift from her Mother. I told her those being the circumstances I would not take it. The rest of my Company kicked up a row with me for not taking it. I told them they had made me master and I would act as such. I tied the Capt. I then told her not to speak a word for two hours as I should not leave the vessel before that time—I also tied a boy on board, then went on shore. We looked at the money and found only 170$ instead of 15,000$ as we supposed. I should have stated before that Capts. wife told me that all the money had been sent in the Steamer before we came on board. The following were engaged with me—John Edwards, Jim Bown, George Smith. I remained in San Francisco 5 or 6 days. I tried to rob the store of Grayson Guild & Co. I stowed away there all one night, but effected nothing—the safe was too heavy.

I then went to Sacramento by myself—left all the others here. I lived at a house kept by Mr. Moore in L street. I played cards most of the time. I sold a few mules and horses for the horse thieves under the name of Campbell. Moore, who kept the house, died and I bought out his wife for 150$. All the things stole in Sacramento City were brought to this house and I took care of them. The name of the boarders were John Jones, John Griffith, Wm. Nelson, a boy of about 17 or 18 years of age, Old Jack— these were all thieves. After a few days John Griffith was taken for picking a man's pocket of some 800$. On Monday morning is committed to take his trial before Recorder Washington. He was allowed bail in 1,500$. Straw bail was refused, so I hired a team & loaded it with stolen goods and started for Mormon Island & Salmon Falls. I sold all the goods at Mormon Island and Salmon Falls and went to Sacramento City. I went to the sheriff and got a pass to go and see Griffith. When I went on board the [prison] brig they told me he was drowned the night before trying to escape with his irons.

While I was gone to the mines, some one robbed my house. I did not think it worth while to open another, so I went to live by the side of the burying ground. A few days after I was arrested for house breaking. I employed Mr. Frank Pixley. He got me out of the scrape by the false swearing of Old Jack. He agreed to get me out of the scrape for 20$, but afterwards told me I must give him 50$ more, which I did. I told Mr. Pixley I was guilty of house breaking. About one week or 10 days afterward I was arrested for breaking into the house of Mr. Smith who kept a lumber yard. I was nearly shot there—one shot went through my hat. I was taken and committed on board the brig for trial. I forgot to state that previous to this I robbed a house corner of Front & K st.—a clothing store. I got about 800$ worth of property—no money. Mat Hopwood, a Sydney man, alias Big Brummy, was with me at this house. About two days after I was on the Brig again.

Employed Mr. F. Pixley and paid him 50$ and also paid Mr. Pixley 50$ for Big Brummy who had been robbing a woman. Two days after a constable came down from Auburn and identified me as the man who shot the sheriff at Auburn. Two or three hours another constable came on board from Foster's Bar. They go on shore to the office of Judge Sacket. Judge Sacket gave an officer a warrant to bring me on shore. I was taken to the office of Judge Sacket on J Street. Mr. Pixley appeared for me and would not allow the judge to examine me. I was again sent on board the Brig & Judge Sacket [gave] an order to the sheriff to take my body to Marysville.

The sheriff came for me the next morning. When he came Mr. Frank M. Pixley told him his warrant was not good or legal and he could not have me and he had to get another. I then gave Mr. Frank M. Pixley 600$ in gold dust and an order for 130$ which he told me he received and would pay me on the next day. The same night I made my escape from the Brig. I walked that day half way to Dry Creek, half way to Stockton. The next day I disguised myself as well as I could, got on a steamboat and came to San Francisco.

I then lived in Sydney Valley (this was in December last) at the house of Mr. Edwards. I went out at night—not often through the day. (Mr. Edwards did not know that I had escaped from any place). I went to the Port Philip House, corner of Jackson and Gould st....where I believe Mr. Jansen lived next door to at the time.

The first thing Whittaker got information of about 8,000 or 9,000$ in a meat market on Broadway near the foot of...st. I, John Edwards, Whittaker and George Adams took the safe out of the window and could get it no further. The next thing was Chas. Minturn's safe. Belcher Kay gave us the information. Kay had gone about 2 or 3 days before hand to ascertain what money there was. He was Port Warden at the time. I, John Edwards, Edward McCormick—or Teddy, Sam Whittaker, George Adams, Belcher Kay and Bob McKenzie [most, if not all, of these men were ex-Australian convicts] were in this scrape. We took a boat, a set of shears, a Feather Bed, augers, saws and all such tools to cut away with and we all went armed. We got inside and moved the desks and the safe about one foot or so and made a few auger holes in the *floor. Some one came to the door at this time and we had to run. McKenzie gave the wrong signal or we should not have stood for one man. We jumped out of the window and swam on shore every one for himself and made the best use of our legs.*

*The next place was one that Belcher Kay had examined and reported there was about 20,000 or 30,000$ worth of jewelry. I and Edwards went upstairs and thought it could not be done as there were several in the lower story. We would not mind one or so upstairs—we could soon stop them. Belcher Kay was with me. The next thing was one Belcher Kay discovered viz Macondray & Cos. He told us there was three safes and one vault and plenty of money. When it came the night to do it, one or two backed out and we gave it up. The night after Mr. Whittaker told us of Mr. Jansen's place. He told us that he saw Mr. Jansen move about 10,000 to 15,000$. We agreed to go and get it—I, with Jim Briggs, John Morris, Morgan, Sam Whittaker, Edward McCormick, alias Teddy, Billy Hughes, Belcher Kay and John Edwards. The above were all with us at Macondray & Co, & Jansen. Morgan and Briggs had been with us about 10 days—the rest had been with us for a long time. Morgan went in Mr. Jansen's store first.*

*We saw him go up. Whittaker & self stood at the window while he went in. I thought he was too long and so we went in to help him. I got about half way up when I heard Mr. Jansen asked Morgan what he wanted there. Morgan told him he wanted some blankets. He turned around and saw me—I told him I also wanted Blankets. He stepped about 2 yards to show me some blankets—(I forgot to state we had cloaks on as a disguise). I hit him on the heard with a slung shot and knocked him down. I then left Morgan to take charge of him while I searched the store for money. I looked about and opened a desk and took out a Shot Bag cont'g money. We then went out and went home with the money. I carried the money all the way. I then counted out the money (and) found 1,586$ in gold coin. I divided it into eights making 196$ ea. We then came down town as usual as though nothing was the matter, and went to Mrs. Hogan's. Stopped there for two or three hours and then went home.*

*The next day there was considerable fuss about it. We did not intend to do anything more until the parties arrested (Burdue and Windred) got clear of the scrape, as we did not wish to see them hung, as they had nothing to do with it. We all agreed on Sunday night that if they hung them to burn the town down.*

*The next night we agreed to rob Beebees & Ludlows & Co. Bank. The same party of eight with the assistance of Rob McIntyre and Andy McCarty, Police Officers. These Police told us any time we were ready to do it they would take the Police on station away. The same Police Officers came here to recognize me, but did not know me. We tried two nights—had a key to unlock the outside door. We watched two days and thought there was not money enough as we saw the porter go to Mess Argentis & Co. in the morning and bring the money from there, and return it at night.*

The next night we went to Mr. Young's Bank next to the El Dorado [a large gambling hall and saloon]. We got good information from Morris Morgan about the vault—he helped build it. We went down the steps of El Dorado and with forced keys we opened the door. We went in and found two beds in the place. We found it would take too long as these people slept in the lower floor of the El Dorado. Belcher Kay and the same party were with us. Next night we got a small safe from Emerson & Dunbars only about 24$ in it. Next night we went to Lawyer Whittemores and got a safe. We took the safe up in the sand hills and was discovered in breaking it open. Morris Morgan and Jim Briggs were taken in this scrape. We lost all our tools by this operation—tools worth about 500$.

We went to Mrs. Hogan's, except Billy Hughes. I did not like to see two men go to the Police Office. I wanted the rest to go with me and take them [Morris and Briggs] out by force. They would not do it—they thought Lawyer Parbut would get them out in the morning. Morgan was acquitted the next day.

Next day I left for Gold Bluffs [Humboldt County] in schooner B. L. Allen—27 days passage. First man I saw at the bluff was B. B. McKinsley, "Dab" (the horse thief) and James Peet. Came down from Oregon—Peet said that he and Dab had taken some 60 head of horses from Sacramento Valley to Oregon and sold them. Played cards with Dab and won some 300$. Came back and paid passage for Dab and Peet to keep them quiet. Dab threatened me and I gave him 50$. Went to Kitchen and got him to send a boat for my things on board Schooner. Dab had me arrested as I was going to Sydney Valley. Drew on policeman and then gave him 100$. Stopped that night at Kitchens—saw Mrs. Hogan. She said there was a warrant for Whittaker and Long Charley for robbery of some 1,600$. Thought it unsafe to stay in her house.

Went to a stable to hire a horse and rode to Monterey (using the name Carlisle). I was anxious to arrive in time for the trial of the parties concerned in the robbery [burglary] of the Custom House. All my things are not at Kitchens. Went and saw the prisoners as soon as I arrived there. Second night after my arrival my horse was stolen. Dick Osman was first put on trial. We all knew the parties were guilty. Although they took thirteen thousand dollars down from San Francisco, all that was robbed was eight thousand dollars, though Randall said he had lost thirty thousand dollars. The fact is that Parbut, McDonald and Judge Merritt were counsel for prisoners, and Col. Weller, Butts and Wallace for prosecution. There was a great deal of swearing falsely and bribery.

The sheriff of Monterey [William Roach] received $700 and a gold watch for packing the jury and other services; and Morrison, a juryman, received $100 from the prisoners, which was paid after the trial. Dennis McCarthy was constable. He received $100 for false swearing from prisoners. He first swore for prosecution and swore back in favor of prisoners. The judge knew nothing about it. Jim Carson, a juryman, held *out for guilty—he was bribed by the prosecution. All the money was taken from the prisoners; the court charges, amounting to one thousand dollars, was first taken out, and the balance of thirteen thousand dollars, say twelve thousand dollars, was equally divided between the prisoners and prosecuting counsel. The prisoners then paid their own lawyers. Randall got one-half and the prisoners the other half of the twelve thousand dollars. Morgan, Tom Quick and Ryan were in jail, but Osman was tried and consented to the division. Parburt told me to let the prisoners out of jail, and I broke the door down and let them out.*

*I went to the southern mines after seeing all friends off and walked to Mission of San Juan [Bautista]. Then took stage for San Jose. From San Jose found a tidy horse and started for the mines—got surrounded by some Mexicans near the (San) Joaquin and had my horse taken from me. We went back some eleven or twelve miles to Livermore's Pass—gave them my watch and chain for my liberty and started for Sonora. Went to Sullivans [gold camp in Tuolumne County, near Sonora] and worked about one week, then went to Mariposa and worked nearly three weeks there. Met two men who knew me and did not feel safe to stay where I was known. Came down to San Francisco. Arrived on Tuesday night and found Kitchen at the El Dorado. Then went to where K. formerly lived. Next morning went to Mission to meet a cousin and saw him there. I wanted to rob an old Spaniard—don't know his name. My cousin calls himself Stephens. Same one recognized by Mr. Ellis and Mr. Brinley. Did not know where the money was kept. Went in and looked at the safe and told him I would come and find some one and see him again. Was arrested doing nothing.*

*Str [steamer] Starr—Some time in Jany or Feby I rode down with Smith from San Francisco to San Jose and Santa Clara for the purpose of getting the gold and silver from the Churches. Could not find any golden images though I attended Mass regularly. Left embarcadero soon for San Francisco—boat got stuck on the bar. All hands called into the cabin to be searched—took my dust and that of one other passenger. Money stolen I know nothing of.*

*Jno. Edwards and Teddy McCormick went on board Str. Starr and opened the window and also the desk and took some 250$.*

The Committee at this point asked Stuart a series of questions, but the answers were either not recorded or were lost. He did, however, make some response in the following statement:

*Knew Jenkins; knew Windred; thinks he is gone out of the country; know Adams; does not know where he is now; know Nelson and Wilson, horse thieves in Sacramento City, when I landed from the J. Kaskie went to Edward's house; John Edwards has red* whiskers; is an Englishman; broke into Smith's lumber yard about 8 o'clock at night; Jemmy-from-town stole a trunk from Mr. A. J. Ellis' house; Jemmy-from-town robbed Dow's safe and blew it up with powder; gave Pixley an order for my money in the name of James Campbell; arrived at Foster's Bar about the middle of April; hired Sullivan, Hunt and Hews to work at Foster's Bar; never committed more crimes at Foster's Bar than I have stated; Dodge & Co. kept a gambling house at Foster's Bar; names of three Americans and one Sydney man, horse thieves, Dabb, Peet and another man name forgotten. I think I knew of every robbery committed in Sacramento when I was there; have worn a serape and rode on horseback in San Francisco. I generally board at Edward's house. Some of my friends have boarded at the Port Philip House. John Morgan is known here as John Morris and lives with Briggs; is 50 years old, large, stout fellow and weighs 15 stone. Have heard hundreds remark here that the day would soon come when this country would be taken by the Sydney people.

We have had an understanding with police officers McIntyre and McCarty for a long time. They were concerned with us in the robbery of Young's Bank, next to the El Dorado. Don't know who makes burglars' tools. Briggs makes some. Knew Otis [William Otis Hall], a horse thief, saw him arrested and saw him on trial. Knew [Salomon] Pico; did not know Fisher or Hill or Hull at Monterey. Ryan was the only one who robbed the Monterey Custom House that reaped any benefit. I gave Pixley an order for 113$ on Lowe; lives on Front street, Sacramento City; has a bay window in it; very pretty house.

Money stolen from Jansen was divided in Edward's house, near Clark's Point. A quarrel between Belcher Kay and Whittaker was caused because they did not equally divide the money. We should certainly have fired the town in three or four places, had the men arrested for striking Jansen been hung. The men who committed the jewelry robbery here were George Adams and Teddy McCormick. I have been to Angel Island; generally stop at Daniel Widler's house; think there are no robbers there. Mrs. Hogan's house is a crib for stolen property—she wears my daguerreotype; she knows all about our motions. Mr. Hogan is innocent.

Dawn was just beginning to break as Stuart finished his confession. The document is frequently confusing, often skips from first to third person and is poorly written, but it is a fascinating treatise on the versatility of early California criminals. We can probably assume most of it is true, although he left out the Moore murder and probably other crimes. He was gambling for his life at this point.

Most important, however, was Stuart's revelations concerning his partners in crime and the involvement of the local police. The confession was published in the local press and did much to justify the formation of the

Committee of Vigilance. Monterey Sheriff Roach and his friends protested against the accusations and the two San Francisco police officers asked for a hearing before the vigilance committee, but were refused. It seemed clear that the confession revealed a criminal organization of dangerous proportions and a dragnet was quickly put in motion to run down the criminals Stuart had identified.

The very day Stuart began his confession, Frank Pixley appeared before the State Supreme Court. He presented an affidavit complaining that Stuart was being unlawfully held by a body of men calling themselves the vigilance committee. Pixley obtained a writ of habeas corpus for the purpose of placing his client in the hands of the law the following morning at 11 o'clock. "The action of the committee," noted the *Alta*, "has already incited the Courts to a performance of their duty, and Stuart, if delivered into the hands of the law will doubtless meet with the same just punishment which he would from the Committee. It is hardly to be imagined that the Committee will disobey the order." But the *Alta* had miscalculated the resolve of the vigilantes!

Jacob Van Bokkelen, the vigilante police chief, who helped prosecute Stuart. From an 1853 daguerreotype. California Historical Society.

The committee felt strongly that abuse of the habeas corpus law was one of the prime reasons for their existence. They knew they were faced by a serious problem, however, since many members felt the highest court in the state must be respected. Rather than refuse to give up the prisoner, several members took turns hiding him at various points around the city. When Sheriff Jack Hays searched the vigilante rooms, no Stuart was to be found.

The many witnesses and the confession were ample proof of Stuart's villainies. In the next few months others of the gang were tracked down, while many fled the state, were shipped out by the vigilantes or just disappeared.

At 9:30 on the morning of July 11, 1851, the Monumental Fire Engine Company bell began tolling to signal a meeting of the vigilance committee. Selim Woodworth, a prominent local merchant, conducted the meeting during which it was unanimously voted that Stuart had not been totally honest in his confession and must die for his crimes. The time of death was to be that very afternoon. Colonel J. D. Stevenson was to make the announcement to the crowd outside. Stuart was then apprised of the decision and admitted into the presence of minister Flevel S. Mines for any last rites he might wish. The Reverend Mines' recollections of those final moments are most interesting:

"I," said he (Stuart), "have not thought of God for fifteen years and I cannot expect that He would think of me in the few moments that are left me now. If there are everlasting burnings," he added, "I expect to go to them, for I have led the life that must take me to them." I reminded him that…he might yet be saved. He said "it was too late; so great a work could not be done in so short a time." Besides, he hardly knew any longer, he said, whether the religion of his youth was true….

At first, like Jenkins, (Stuart) was vindictive, though certainly less sullen in his temper. At my second interview he promised that he would try to lay aside the feelings in which it was so unsafe to die. At the third meeting (having left him a space to his reflections), he acknowledged the justice of his fate, and declared he could die without resentment and in charity with all, and that, with the crucified malefactor, he could confess that he received the due reward of his deeds, and could trust only in the mercies of the cross for pardon.

Stuart refused Dr. Mines' offer to accompany him to the gallows. It was 2:30 in the afternoon when members of the committee came downstairs from their rooms and assembled three abreast in the street. The *Alta* reported "There were nearly a thousand of them, principally composed of our oldest, best known and most prominent citizens, merchants, bankers, mechanics and business men of every description."

Surrounded by a heavily armed phalanx of stern-faced vigilantes, the bound Stuart marched to his fate. Down Market Street they moved, surrounded by growing crowds of citizens who fully expected either a conflict with the authorities or Sydney men on a rescue mission. But nothing happened.

As the formation seemed headed for the wharves, there was a rush to secure seating, while the decks and rigging of nearby ships in the bay became clogged with spectators. The long, Market Street wharf was a solid mass of people surrounding the impromptu gallows of two uprights and a cross beam used for hauling freight onto the pier. As the vigilante formation pushed its way through the crowds, Stuart appeared perfectly cool and collected.

"How strange it appeared," wrote an eyewitness, "at the moment of execution that the vast crowd assembled should have, as if by one mind, uncovered their heads." In a moment the condemned man had the rope placed around his neck, but he still showed little emotion.

"He appeared to feel," noted the *Alta*, "as though he was satisfied with his sentence and did not desire to live longer. The resemblance between Stuart and Burdue was most striking and it is not at all strange that one should have been taken for the other. The immense crowd remained breathless, and Stuart, when under the gallows said, 'I die reconciled, my sentence is just.' The rope was pulled and in a moment he was dangling in the air."

Oddly enough, the coroner's examination produced a statement that "life was not extinct in Stuart for several hours after he was brought to the Station House." A prominent physician commented that if proper means had been employed, the outlaw could have been resuscitated. But this was all

*The hanging of Stuart on the Market street wharf was witnessed by huge crowds of people as evidenced by this contemporary engraving. Author's collection.*

academic. "English Jim" Stuart was dead.

With the hanging of two of the other leaders, Whittaker and McKenzie, the criminal presence of the Sydney convicts seemed to be effectively curtailed. Mrs. Hogan and other fences and criminal consorts were either scared off or shipped from the state. In Sydney Town, as early as June 18, 1851, the *San Francisco Evening Picayune* reported:

*The hanging of Whittaker and McKenzie. From a contemporary sketch in the Illustrated London News, Nov. 15, 1851.*

We were exceedingly gratified...to notice that a great number of the most notorious cribs have been closed. Dens, around the doors of which, but a week or two ago, great hulks of fellows with faces marked with traces of every species of crime, might have been seen lounging...are now deserted...and on the closed doors may be seen notices that they are for rent or sale....If the vigilance committee keep on in their present course for a few more weeks longer, the city will be cleared of the gang of scoundrels that has infested it for so long.

Although the 1852 San Francisco census showed some 1,339 Australian residents, most were families and few were probably of the criminal class. Crime was to be a problem for many more years in frontier California, but at least the plague of Australian convicts seemed to be curtailed.

*Captain Edgar Wakeman, said to be the hangman of Jenkins and Stuart. Author's collection.*

# Chapter Two / NOTES

The description of Stuart's demeanor while making his confession is from William T. Coleman's *Statement* in the Bancroft Library, University of California, Berkeley.

Sources of information on the transportation of English convicts in the eighteenth and nineteenth centuries can be found in several excellent works: Hughes, Robert. *The Fatal Shore.* New York: Alfred A. Knopf, 1987; Hawkings, David T. *Bound for Australia.* Phillimore, England: Chichester, 1987; Hawkings, David T. *Criminal Ancestors.* Wolfeboro Falls, NH: Alan Sutton Publishing Ltd., 1992.

Information on Stuart's early years is from various versions of his confession as published in Williams, Mary Floyd, editor. *Papers of the San Francisco Committee of Vigilance of 1851.* Berkeley: University of California Press, 1919 (hereinafter cited as Williams' *Papers*). This is a published collection of all the papers of this organization and is an invaluable resource for anyone studying this period of San Francisco history. See also Bancroft, Hubert H. *Popular Tribunals,* Vol. I. San Francisco: The History Book Company, Publishers, 1887. Useful also were the *San Francisco Herald,* July 18, 1851, and the *San Francisco Daily Alta California,* July 12, 1851.

Stuart's troubles at Foster's Bar were related by John Sullivan, George Mason and George F. Hunt who had known him there. See Williams' *Papers.*

Stuart's robbery of the *James Caskie* is described in the *Alta* of October 27 and the *Sacramento Transcript* of October 31, 1850.

The murder of Charles E. Moore and the subsequent tracing of his killers to Sacramento is recounted in the *Marysville Herald,* December 13 and the *Sacramento Transcript,* December 16, 1850. Also very informative is Ramey, Earl. "The Beginnings of Marysville," Part III. *California Historical Society Quarterly,* March, 1936. See also the *Marysville Herald,* December, 17, 1850, and March 25, 1851. The statement of John Sullivan in Williams' *Papers* provides additional data.

Stuart's capture while burglarizing an office is detailed in the *Transcript* of December 14, 1850. His escape is reported in the same paper of December 19, 1850. Sacramento's first prison ship was the 314-ton bark *Strafford* in April–June, 1850. When it returned to sea duty, the city purchased the 259 ton bark *La Grange* which served until it was sunk in high water in 1859. See Goodman, III, John B. *The California Gold Rush Fleet Encyclopedia.* Beverly Hills: Typescript, n.d., courtesy John Boessenecker.

The description of "Sydney Town" or "Sydney Valley" is taken from the *Alta*, July 29, 1851. The reference to a glass of rum costing "a rial," refers to the Mexican real, or rial, a standard circulating dollar coin in the U.S. at that time; see Webster LL.D., Noah. *An American Dictionary of the English Language.* Revised and enlarged by Chauncey A. Goodrich, Professor in Yale College, Springfield, MA: George and Charles Merriam, 1850, and Robert Chandler. The statistic of Australians in California is from Ricards, Sherman L. and George M. Blackburn. "The Sydney Ducks: A Demographic Analysis." *Pacific Historical Review*, February, 1973. Information on "Sydney Town" and its unsavory saloons, boarding houses and dives is in Williams, Mary Floyd, Ph.D. *History of the San Francisco Committee of Vigilance of 1851.* Berkeley: University of California Press, 1921; Monaghan, Jay. *Australians and the Gold Rush, California and Down Under, 1849–1854,* Berkeley: University of California Press, 1966.

The Jansen robbery is well described in Bancroft's *Popular Tribunals*, Vol. I, and, of course, in Stuart's confession. See also the *Alta* of February 20, 1851. Sam Whittaker was a principal leader of the Sydney convicts in early San Francisco. He was born in Manchester, England, about 1818 and sentenced to New South Wales for life in 1836. He claimed to have obtained a pardon in Australia, but at the time of his capture he had "lost" it. He arrived in San Francisco in August of 1849. See his confession as published in the local press and in the previously cited Williams' *Papers*.

The capture and trial of Burdue and Windred is related in Bancroft's, *Popular Tribunals*; Stewart, George R. *Committee of Vigilance: Revolution in San Francisco, 1851.* Boston: Houghton Mifflin, 1964 and Mullen, Kevin J. *Let Justice Be Done.* Reno: University of Nevada Press, 1989. See also Soule, Frank, John H. Gihon, M.D. and James Nisbet. *Annals of San Francisco,* San Francisco: D. Appleton & Company, 1854.

Sam Brannan's speech is quoted in Williams' *Papers*.

Some statistics of the San Francisco crime rate during this period are in Mullen, but they don't seem to reflect the true situation as recorded in Bancroft, the *Annals* and certainly the contemporary press. It wasn't just assaults and robberies that concerned San Franciscans, but also the fires, the poor criminal conviction rates that continually returned criminals to the streets and the poor performance of much of the police force. Later events showed that City Marshal Malachi Fallon and various police officers were actually in league with criminals and protected them.

The letter from "Justice" appeared in the *Alta,* December 16, 1850. It was in response to a fire reported in the *San Francisco Evening Picayune,* December 16, 1850.

The great fire of May 3, 1851 was described in detail by the *Picayune,* May 4, 5, 1851. A letter from Baker & Meserve, explaining how the fire couldn't have originated in their shop, appeared in the *San Francisco Evening Picayune* of May 5, 1851.

The story of the Lewis fire is reported in Williams, Bancroft, Mullen and the contemporary press. For the founding of the San Francisco Committee of Vigilance, see both volumes of Williams. A good account of the Jenkins robbery and hanging is in the *San Francisco Evening Picayune,* June 11, 1851.

Stuart's travels to Monterey and the mining country are noted in his confession. His capture while returning from the mission is documented by much testimony as published in Williams' *Papers.* Boatman John Sullivan's statement concerning his recognition of Stuart as a former employer is also among Williams' *Papers.* Sullivan's quote upon recognizing the prisoner is from the *Statement* of Vigilante George E. Schenck in the Bancroft Library.

The Pixley-Stuart confrontation in the vigilance committee rooms is reported in Williams' *History.* Frank Morrison Pixley was born in New York and arrived in San Francisco in the early days of the Gold Rush. His criminal law practice was apparently so lucrative that for a time he lived near the state prison in Marin County. He was also of a literary bent and was founder and publisher of the *San Francisco Argonaut.* He died in the bay city in 1895. Sibylle Zemitus, California History Section, California State Library, to the author, April 23, 1998.

There are many affidavits in Williams' *Papers* to establish the identity of Stuart. The *Alta* quote on Stuart and Burdue is dated July 7, 1851. Burdue's trial and presence in Marysville is reported in the *Marysville Herald* from March 25 to July 15, 1851. Burdue's monte game on Long Wharf is noted in the *Annals of San Francisco.*

The previously cited standard vigilante histories tell virtually the same story of how Stuart came to make his confession. He may or may not have had an agreement with the vigilantes that if he told the truth he would be turned over to the legal authorities. As Mullen points out, it didn't help his case much to have several of his victims sitting on the vigilante executive committee.

There are several versions of Stuart's confession. The one used here is from the original as published by Williams' *Papers*. I have edited it minimally to make it more readable—the punctuation consisting mainly of dashes. The version published by Bancroft in *Popular Tribunals* and the *Alta* and *Herald* have all been edited into a more readable state. Slight variations and amplifications in the confession, as printed in Williams, were apparently contemporary and added at various times to make it more understandable.

The confession enumerates more than a dozen robberies, accounting for nearly $9,000 in money, besides much personal property. Many of the raids, such as the *James Caskie* brig robbery, were quite violent in character. Some 25 fellow criminals are also named, along with two corrupt police officers, Captain Andrew McCarty and Assistant Captain Robert McIntyre. The suborning of witnesses and other antics by attorneys and public officials, as noted by Stuart, must have further stiffened the resolve of the vigilantes.

Lawyer Pixley's appearance before the California Supreme Court is reported in the *Alta*, July 9, 1851. The resulting concealment of Stuart by the vigilantes, his trial and sentence of death is covered in both Williams' works, as well as the other standard histories.

Reverend Mines' letter describing his talks with Stuart was published in Williams' *Papers*. Contemporary accounts of Stuart's hanging appeared in the *Herald*, the *Alta* and the *Picayune*, July 11, 12, 1851. The eyewitness quote is from Ham, Randall E. *A Buckeye in the Land of Gold, The Letters and Journal of William Dennison Bickham*. Spokane, WA: The Arthur H. Clark Company, 1996. The coroner's inquest on Stuart's body was reported in the *Alta*, July 13, 1851.

The 1852 census data is from the previously cited Ricards and Blackburn. "The Sydney Ducks."

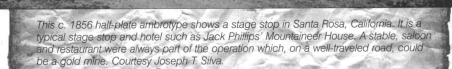

This c. 1856 half-plate ambrotype shows a stage stop in Santa Rosa, California. It is a typical stage stop and hotel such as Jack Phillips' Mountaineer House. A stable, saloon and restaurant were always part of the operation which, on a well-traveled road, could be a gold mine. Courtesy Joseph T. Silva.

Robert H. Paul went to sea as a young boy, reaching California in February of 1849 on a whaling ship. In Calaveras County he became a constable and deputy sheriff and by clever detective work and hard riding was one of the principals in breaking up the Tom Bell gang. Paul was later elected sheriff and became a noted officer in Arizona in the days of Tombstone and the Earp brothers. John Boessenecker collection.

# 3 "I have been most foully betrayed"

## Confessions of Tom Bell and Associates

Dolph Newton was a reported member of Tom Bell's gang and later associated with Rattlesnake Dick Barter. John Boessenecker collection.

The seven masked riders were scattered in groups along the road. It was hot in the Sierra Nevada foothills this 12th of August, 1856, and they could hear the stagecoach as it rattled along the dusty, rutted trail towards Marysville. The coach was preceded by an outrider named Rideout, a Camptonville gold dust dealer. Mr. Rideout was concerned about his large shipment of gold on the stage and was escorting it to the Marysville express office.

At a fork in the road, two of the masked riders halted Rideout and demanded his money at gunpoint. Replying that he had none, Rideout dismounted and walked towards the nearby stage which had now stopped. When the highwaymen called out that anyone on the stage who resisted them would be shot, the express guard immediately opened fire as the driver whipped his horses into a gallop. The coach dashed by in a cloud of dust and gunsmoke amid a fierce exchange of gunfire. Several passengers were wounded, while the startled robbers struggled to regain control of their horses and their composure. One of them was holding his bloody hand as they galloped from the scene.

The highwaymen's leader was an ex-convict named Tom Bell, and this was reported to be the first attempted stage holdup in California.

Thomas J. Hodges, who later adopted the name "Tom Bell," was born in Rome, Tennessee about 1823. He acquired some medical training before serving in the Mexican War, then went to California in 1849. He filed on a rich claim in Mariposa County, but gambled away his money as fast as he made it. Tom found himself broke when his claim ran out. A Texan named Wiley proposed stealing some mules and the two men made several successful raids, selling the animals in the Utah Territory at a good price.

His initial foray into crime was brief, however. Hodges was picked up and sentenced to state prison in early October of 1851, where he was admitted as prisoner number 24. Since there was no state prison building yet, Tom found himself in a cell aboard an old sailing ship of 268 tons named the *Waban*. The ship had been anchored near the shores of San Francisco for a time, but it was too easy for the prisoner's friends to make contact.

*A chain gang work party at San Quentin in the early 1850s. Gleason's Pictorial Drawing Room Companion, January/June, 1852*

In late 1851, the *Waban* was moored near Angel Island, in the bay, where Tom and the other prisoners quarried stone for a time. A dozen convicts managed to overpower the guards and escape in early January 1852. In May there was another escape attempt, but after a desperate conflict, the guards managed to maintain control. It isn't known if Hodges was involved in these incidents. Later, Tom and his fellow convicts helped prepare the site for the new state prison at Point San Quentin in Marin County.

On May 12, 1855, Hodges, Cherokee Bob Talbot, Jim Smith, Bill White, alias Bill Gristy, and several others escaped while on a wood-chopping detail. Taking the name "Tom Bell," Hodges utilized several of his escape pals as the nucleus of a bandit gang. The group was always a loosely-knit organization, with members coming and going as needed. One early-day lawman estimated Bell's gang at some thirty members at one time or another, and known members do indeed tally up to such a number.

Bell quickly recognized the importance of a lookout man to spot rich travelers as potential victims. An ideal location and an accomplice was found at a Placer County inn known as the Mountaineer House, on the road between Folsom and Auburn. Striking up an acquaintance with owner John H. "Jack" Phillips, Bell quickly established that they were of a like mind concerning larcenous undertakings.

The Mountaineer House was a favorite stopping place of teamsters, miners and other travelers. It was a typical roadhouse of the time, with rooms, stables, restaurant and bar presided over by Phillips and his attractive wife Kate, both of English origins. They were a curious pair. Kate, with a local reputation for being kind and helpful, had obvious good breeding, despite being illiterate. Jack, described as jovial, although "an ignorant and repulsive Cockey" with a broken nose and a body covered with scars and tatoos, was also unable to read or write. Their story was even more bizarre.

Kate Phillips was the only child of a British army major whose wife had died when their child was quite young. When she came of age, Kate fell in love with a young lieutenant, but he was quite poor and her father had other ideas. A captain in the same regiment was also interested and since he was well off, Kate's father insisted she marry him instead of her poor lieutenant. The captain, however, was a notorious gambler and drinker. Kate determined to avoid her situation and looked about desperately for a way out. She found her salvation in Jack Phillips.

Jack had been an orderly to her father and as part of his duties often accompanied Kate on rides into the countryside. In their conversations she had seen something more than the ignorant soldier and Jack lent a sympathetic ear to her dilemma. Having recently inherited 100 pounds, Jack was planning to desert the army and go to America. He now offered to elope with Kate, saying he had been an admirer for some time. They were married in London and in time emigrated to Australia, according to their story. It may well have been, however, that Jack was shipped to Australia as a convict. In any case, they sailed for California in the early days of the Gold Rush.

Bell had no sooner made arrangements for the Englishman to tip him off on traveling victims than he sent a written note asking for help in a particular matter. Phillips refused to accept the message. When Bell castigated him for it later, the innkeeper flipped a pistol ball in the air.

"That is the only messenger I will recognize," he growled. "I am not going to be caught by any written message."

Bell appreciated the logic of Phillips' comment and from then on gang members were required to carry a pistol ball with an "X" marked on it for recognition.

Enlisting the cooperation of Mrs. Elizabeth Hood who operated another inn on the Sacramento road, Bell and his gang plundered travelers, teamsters, stores and peddlers on the mountain trails. A typical robbery was described by David Lash who was stopped by Bell and an accomplice on the Sacramento road in late July 1856:

> First saw them on the road between 4 and 5 o'clock; they presented pistols to my head and told me to stand and deliver and

*Teamsters hauling supplies to the mountain villages were prime targets of Bell and his gang. When the wagons returned to Sacramento or Stockton, the drivers had money for a new load and were again in danger of being robbed. California State Library.*

give up my money;…they took me one-half or three-fourths of a mile off the road; after I got there they overhauled my things; they then asked me how much money I had, and Bell put his hand in and took all my money. I told him I had $40; he counted it and said it was right; the value of goods they took was $200 or $300; they took 30 or 40 yards of black silk, embroidery collars, &c., they took my horse, saddle and bridle;…they tied me to a tree and told me to stay there till after dark, and then I could get away.

A peddler named Rosenthal was robbed and murdered near the Mountaineer House, but Bell is reported to have bandaged the wound of a man shot in the leg during another robbery. The newspapers were full of his exploits and the California legislature discussed the establishment of a state police force to go after the outlaws.

On August 12, 1856, Bell, Bill White, Jim Smith, Montague "Monte Jack" Lyon and three others laid in wait for the Camptonville stage as it carried a reported $10,000 in treasure and passengers to Marysville. After stopping the stage, Bell demanded the gold bullion be thrown out, calling forth a dose of hot lead from the express messenger instead. In the resulting battle, some forty shots were exchanged. The *Marysville Herald* reported:

The robbers finding themselves so stoutly opposed, retreated, leaving the passengers masters of the field and treasure.

The driver, Mr. John Gear, was shot through the right arm, above the elbow. Mrs. Tilghman, wife of a barber of this city, was shot in the head, the ball entering over the right eye and penetrating the brain. Mr. John Campbell, another of the passengers, received a glance shot over the eye. Another passenger was shot through both legs...one white man and four Chinamen, passengers, left and ran back on the road which was passed over.

As stirring as was the defense of the coach, it was hardly justified considering the casualties. Mrs. Tilghman was reported to have kept "her senses" and could converse, but was blind. There was little hope for her recovery.

Lawmen were quickly on the trail. Charles DeLong, a member of one of the posses noted in his journal:

Wed. 13,—...Heard of the robbery of the Stage returned home, went to Campton[ville]. got up a party to pursue the robbers

Thu, 14,—Started out 7 strong went to Keystone[,] Dobbins; and Ramirez. Shot Ramirez for resisting our searching his house, left there struck the river at Ohio Bar, got parted all made the Oregon House in the night

Returning on the 16th, DeLong complained of being "used up pretty badly." J. M. Ramirez was one of the wealthiest merchants in the county, having a mill and roadhouse above Marysville. Ramirez's wound was apparently slight, The *Herald* reporting on the 15th that "a party wishing to search the premises of Mr. F. (*sic*) Ramirez for Monte Jack, who it is known, has been about there some days, shot Mr. Ramirez.... Whether the wound is dangerous we could not learn."

Three of the bandits' horses were found, one of them having a bloody bridle. It was later learned that one of the outlaws had indeed been shot in the hand, and this was his animal. Two days later Bill White and Juan "Spanish John" Fernandez, both members of Bell's gang, were arrested at Knight's Ferry after robbing several teamsters. In grilling Fernandez, Calaveras County Deputy Sheriff Bob Paul learned of the marked bullet and the Phillips connection. While White was making a full confession to T. W. Lane, one of his captors, Deputy Paul headed for the Mountaineer House to see what he could discover. White's statement is quite enlightening as to the state prison, the personal lives of the outlaws, and their methods of operation:

*Confession of Bill Gristy, alias Bill White*

*I was of the party in the attack on the Camptonville stage. Our object was to take all the treasure from the Express houses at Downieville and Camptonville. We were about three weeks on the lookout for this, all of this time we were staying at the California House, 25 miles from Marysville on the road to Camptonville. The house is kept by Madam Cole, formerly of the Golden Gate, Downieville, and John Gardiner; this house was in with us—it was one of our stopping places. Our party at this time consisted of Thomas J. Hodges, alias Tom Bell; Ned Convery, alias Ned Conner; Montague Lyon, alias Monte Jack; Jim Smith, Bob Carr, alias English Bob, Juan Rocher, alias Juan Fernandez, and myself—seven in all. Our plan was to send Smith Sutton, a miner living near the California House, to Camptonville to spot the treasure as it came down. He was faithful to his promise and came down as far as the California House on the stage the day of the attack and reported everything all right. I went to John Gardiner and borrowed his rifle and we then all started for the place of attack. You have already read an account of the fight, published in the newspapers, which in the main was correct. I fired the rifle one time, and my pistol three times. The party, with the exception of Bell and myself, ran after the first fire. Bell acted throughout very cool. It was not our intention to have fired a shot, had we not been fired on by the Express Agent, Dobson.*

*As we failed in this affair and the country was too hot for us, we concluded to go South and drop a part of our company, Jim Smith and Montague Lyon, as they would get drunk occasionally, and we wanted none but sober men. Our plan was soon arranged. We went down to the hog ranch kept by Mrs. Hood, on the Nevada and Auburn road, one of our places of rendezvous; got the old woman and her three daughters, and started for the junction of Tulare Lake slough with the San Joaquin River. Our plan was to locate a stock ranch at this place and steal stock to put on it. Some of our party, the more timid, were to engage in this branch of the business, while Tom Bell and myself, assisted by one or two others were to take to the highway for cash to keep up our expenses on the ranch. Accordingly, I left on the 9th of September with the Mexican, Juan Fernandez, leaving the balance in camp; we traveled north as far as the Stockton and Mokelumne Hill road, before we could find any person to rob. We noticed that almost all the teamsters travelled in large companies.*

*The first two we robbed were Mr. Sarlee's two teamsters; we got about fourteen* dollars. That night we stole two horses at the Tremont House, same road, and then made our way back towards the Sonora road. Our plan was to have gone clear through to the California House, but the Mexican got scared at the idea. We concluded to operate between the Merced and Mokelumne rivers. We were arrested the day after we turned back, at Knight's Ferry.

The robbery of Rosenthal near Folsom.

We were all concerned in this robbery. At the time, we were staying at the Mountaineer House, owned by Jack Phillips, a Sydney man, seven miles from Auburn on the Sacramento road. When Rosenthal passed on his way to Folsom, Jack Phillips spotted him for us and we followed him. Tom Bell rode up to him and asked where he lived. He said at Chips Flat. Tom then said, I believe you have very rich diggings up there and that he was going there to mine. By this time he had arrived two miles below the Franklin House. We took him about one hundred yards from the road, and found on his person twelve hundred and fifty dollars. We then took his sash and tied him to a tree, and told him if we did not come back before night, to halloo for help and then some person would come to his assistance. About six days after this, we learned by the papers that he was missing. We then all went back to look for him, but he was gone. I did not know what to make of this. The day he was robbed we all noticed that Tom Bell remained behind a few minutes. We came to the conclusion that he had killed the man, or else he had got loose and circulated the report of his death in the papers so he might come on us and be able to identify us. We then went back to the Mountaineer House, and gave to Jack Phillips about one hundred and fifty dollars. This house is a stage house, and all the hostlers and every person around it knew us and our business.

The Gold Rush town of Auburn in Placer County was in the heart of Tom Bell country. California State Library.

*I was sent from Placer County to the State Prison in the year 1855 for ten years for stealing three horses from the Girard House. I remained until May, 1855; at that time there were six or seven others besides myself escaped. I can only recollect the names of Tom Bell, Ned Connor and Jim Smith. The manner of our escape was this; I was told by one of our guards that his captain wanted to see me at the office. I went, and he told me he wanted to get rid of a portion of the prisoners then in prison. His plan was for me to take the party composed as stated above out on the next day (and the guard with us would be posted as to his part in the matter) ostensively to chop wood, and when the first tree fell, we were then to break and run. I was to expose myself more than the rest. The guards were to shoot blank cartridges at me. I accordingly spoke to Bell and told him my plans. He did not approve them at first, but when I told him the party could run one way, and I would expose myself to be shot at, he seemed to admire my courage, and agreed to my plans (as he thought) for our escape. Bell ever after this overrated my courage. I told him that they might shoot at me as I did not care to live. It was a good chance for me to convince him of my bravery, as there was really no danger.*

*At the time the tree fell, I run down in front of the guards, and they fired at me. The other party did as directed, and we made good our escape. There really was no danger. A further account of this affair was published in the newspapers at that time. Although the officers of the prison were very kind to me during the whole of my confinement, I have thought there was something behind the scenes more than this to lead to our escape. It is generally known that Gen. Estell made a bad contract with the state to keep all her convicts, and he was very anxious to be relieved of said contract, but could not do so. My opinion always has been that he adopted this course to make the contract system so odious with the people so he could be relieved of a bad bargain.*

*Tom Bell, Ned Connor and myself have been together ever since our escape. We have been concerned in various highway robberies and stealing. One case I now think of is that wherein Tom Bell is said to have taken up an artery in a man's leg that was shot by us. Now, this is not correct. The facts of the case are these; at this time we were carrying on our operations between the forks of the Yuba, and as far north as the south fork of Feather river. We were travelling along and overtook a gentleman and we immediately concluded to "put him up."*

*I rode up to the side of him and introduced our business; he refused to give us his money, was frightened and I saw he intended to run. I told him if he did I would shoot him. That I did not want to do. He put spurs to his horse and started at full speed, and I did the same; at about fifteen steps I fired my pistol at his thigh and hit my mark. He still continued to run, and I tried to shoot him in the other thigh, but as my horse was after him at full speed, I found it difficult to hold on to my mark. I was* afraid to shoot as I did not want to kill him. I then closed up on him and caught him. By this time Tom Bell came up. After taking all the money he had, Tom took his pocket handkerchief and tied up the wound. There were no arteries hurt. By this time a teamster drove up. We stopped him and found he had about two hundred dollars on his person. He objected to giving it up at first, but one threat was sufficient. We afterwards saw in the papers that he had $1200 in his wagon. We did not believe it and thought the statement was made to tantalize us. After robbing the teamster, we put the wounded man in the wagon with instructions that he should be well treated.

Tom Bell and myself could not agree well together in our operations. We frequently quarreled, and on several occasions I have had to draw my pistol on him. The fact is, we would have separated long ago, but I could use Tom and he thought he could use me. We generally traveled separately from each other. He wanted to make us all do as he pleased. The following is a description of:

Tom Bell—About six feet high; has long auburn hair: thick, light-colored beard all over his face, blue eyes, flat nose, which had been broken when a boy; complexion light, slender made; weight 145 pounds and age thirty three years.

Fred Farnsworth—Stays with the family at the mouth of the slough; age thirty-five years; five feet, nine inches high, weight 175 pounds; blue eyes, black hair and whiskers. The family is composed of an old woman named Elisabeth Hood, and her three daughters; she is a large, fat woman, has red hair and a red face, and was born in St. Louis County, Mo. The three daughters are nine, eleven and fourteen years old. The oldest, Sarah, is kept by Tom Bell as his mistress.

Pierre Ridge was a lifelong thief and outlaw and claimed to have belonged to Bell's gang. He may have done so under an assumed name as he used many aliases during his life. This photo is from an 1870s Sacramento police mug book. Author's collection.

Warren Farnsworth—Escaped from jail at Nevada, during the time of the late fire. Age thirty, weight 140 pounds; round shoulders, long black hair, heavy goatee, and dark blue eyes.

English Bob—formerly hostler at the Mountaineer House; weight 140 pounds; light hair, complexion the same; age thirty-two years.

Ned Connor—Escaped convict; weight 150 pounds; dark brown hair, red *whiskers all over his face; he is five feet eight inches high, blue eyes, and of Irish descent. He is shot on the inside of the little finger of the right hand and through the second finger. This was done in the attack on the Camptonville stage, and is not well yet.*

*Jim Smith—Is a German; he ran away several times from the State Prison, but finally served his time out; weight 175 pounds; is five feet ten inches high, has light hair, gray eyes and looks wild out of them. On the back of one of his hands is painted in Indian ink the initials of his name, with a star between: a crucifix is also on one of his arms.*

*Montague Lyon served twelve months in the State Prison; is six feet high; age twenty-five years; cross-eyed, with auburn hair and light whiskers.*

*This confession is made with the promise that you will do all in your power to have me pardoned out of the State Prison. If all I have told you is not true, you are hereby released from your promise. I think what I have done and said will be of great advantage to the people of this State, and it is my intention to leave it, if pardoned.*

Bell's organization was rapidly falling apart. As Bill White was being escorted back to San Quentin, Deputy Bob Paul called on Jack Phillips about three in the morning on September 28. Pretending to be an outlaw, he gave Phillips the bullet he had taken from Fernandez and explained he had been sent to ask Tom Bell for aid in getting his men out of jail. Phillips fell completely for the ruse. He told Paul of receiving messages from Bell by letter before, but he had refused them for fear of being deceived by lawmen. Holding the bullet in his hand, he commented, "There is nothing like these fellows."

Phillips talked about the outlaws and promised to pass on Paul's message if he saw Bell first. When the deputy left, he knew the power of the outlaws had been broken. Phillips was arrested the next day.

On September 30, Placer County Sheriff William T. Henson received a message from a shady character named Charley Hamilton. Working undercover as a member of Bell's gang, Hamilton was a black outlaw who had been promised immunity if he tipped off the lawmen on Bell. He proved true to his word. He telegraphed Henson that Bell was camped in a ravine near Folsom, and by nine o'clock that night Henson, deputies John Boggs, B. F. Moore and several others were galloping towards the Bell camp. On the road they met Hamilton who offered to guide them to the camp.

Boggs and Hamilton were riding in advance of the others as they neared a hotel called the Franklin House shortly after midnight. When a group of riders passed them, Hamilton suddenly realized it was Bell's party and told Boggs who called back to the others, "Here they are!" Dismounting, the sheriff called out for the desperadoes to surrender, but Bell had no intention of giving up.

John C. Boggs came to California with the Gold Rush and was a noted Placer County lawman. John Boessenecker collection.

The outlaws were now caught between the two parties of officers and flashes of gunfire and clouds of gunsmoke quickly filled the air. It was over nearly as quickly as it began. One of the lawmen's horses was wounded, and Ned Convery was found sprawled dead alongside the road. Bell and Perris "Texas Jack" Owen, apparently a new gang member, galloped off and were pursued for some distance, but were finally lost in the darkness and chaparral.

Edward H. "Ned" Conver, usually called Convery, was an ex-stevedore from New Orleans. He had been convicted of grand larceny in Stockton in July 1853 and entered San Quentin on August 3 for a three-year stretch. After his escape with Tom Bell and others, his bandit career was to be short and he would wind up now in a muddy potter's field, his parents never to know the end of their wild, redheaded boy.

Bell stole a horse and headed south, while Texas Jack apparently headed for Sacramento. Posses were fanning out over the countryside and the *San Francisco Herald* of October 6 reported the almost complete break up of the gang:

> Arrest of Several of Tom Bell's Gang—Our County Jail now, says the Calaveras *Chronicle*, contains five of Tom Bell's freebooters. On Tuesday last, Deputy Sheriff Shuler arrived in the Sacramento stage having in charge Jack Phillips, said to be a harborer of Bell's gang, and a gatherer of information for their special benefit. On Thursday the Sacramento and Stockton stages brought each two more of the highwaymen....So far, six of the gang have been arrested, and others soon will be. Near the junction of the Tulare Lake Slough and the San Joaquin river, they came upon the winter quarters of the banditti, and arrested two brothers named Farnsworth, the only persons there at the time...Two prisoners named Gardner and Sutton

arrived on the Sacramento stage. They were arrested at the California House...by Sheriff Clark, Deputy Sheriff Paul, and Constable McCormick....

*Summons for witness David Lash to appear at the trial of Jack Phillips. John Boessenecker collection.*

But Tom Bell was already dead. On October 4, 1856, he had visited a ranch he had recently established on the San Joaquin River, but found the inhabitants gone. He didn't know that Mrs. Hood and the two Farnsworth brothers had been picked up by a posse led by Calaveras County Undersheriff Daniel L. Mulford. They had no sooner sent their captives north to Stockton than another impromptu posse arrived, commanded by Judge George Belt, a Merced River rancher. Together, the two groups kept watch on the area hoping Bell or others of the gang might show up. Finally, Mulford's group gave up the vigil. Belt's group, however, decided to stay awhile longer.

As he was leaving the area on October 4, one of Belt's party noticed two horsemen talking among some trees along the river. The judge was informed of the suspicious strangers and the posse closed in and presented shotguns and navy pistols at the surprised riders. After a brief parley, Tom Bell admitted his identity and both he and the *vaquero* he had been conversing with were tied and taken up the road to a spot near Andrew Firebaugh's ferry on the San Joaquin River.

It was late in the afternoon by now. One of the possemen had been sent to bring back Mulford's posse, but it was decided not to wait and Bell was informed he was to be hanged immediately. He took the news calmly, asking that he be allowed to write several letters. One was to his mother in Rome, Tennessee. He read this to the posse, hoping it might influence his fate. It didn't. The second letter was to Mrs. Hood who had also served as an informer. It was written in "a bold, elegant style," and was also obviously slanted to soften the hearts of his captors:

*Firebaugh's Ferry, Oct. 4, 1856*

*Mrs. Hood—My dear and only friend now in this country. As I am not allowed the liberty of seeing you, I have been allowed the privilege to write you a few lines, as I have but a few moments to live. I am at a great loss for something to say. I have been most foully betrayed. Bill and John have told things that never took place. I am accused of every robbery that has been committed for the past twelve months, which is entirely false. I never have committed but three highway robberies in my life—but still I am to blame, and my fate is sealed. I am to die like a dog; and there is but one thing that grieves me, and that is the condition of you and our family. Probably I have been the instrumentality of your misfortunes. In my last moments I will think of the many favors you have done me, and if I had fifty kingdoms to present, you should have them all. But alas! I am poor, and my fate is sealed. I would like to give you some advice, but I fear you may think me presumptuous. What I would say is this; That you had better send the girls to San Francisco to the Sisters of Charity. There, they will be educated and taken care of. Tell all the girls farewell!—tell them to be good girls, and to be very particular to whom they pledge themselves to for life. All the money I have is ten dollars which I have given to Mr. Chism for Sarah. If you ever see Edward S., tell him of my fate. I must come to a close, for the hounds are thirsting for my blood. Goodbye, forever.*

*Thomas J. Bell*

And so Thomas J. Hodges, alias Tom Bell, passed into history. Despite the fact that his gang was rounded up quite neatly after the disastrous Camptonville stage attack, few of his gang members did hard time for their crimes. Ned Convery was dead, but Monte Jack, English Bob Carr, Texas Jack Owen and several others were still at large. Bill White was returned to San Quentin, while the Farnsworth brothers and Smith Sutton were being held for arraignment and later apparently released for lack of evidence. Juan Fernandez was held to testify against Jack Phillips whose trial was scheduled for the first of the year.

On October 30, 1856, Sacramento Police Officer William Wilson walked down the gangplank of the coastal steamer, *Orizaba*, in San Francisco. In his custody was "Texas Jack" Owen. Wilson had tracked Owen to San Francisco and was certain he was leaving for the Atlantic states aboard the steamer *Golden Age*. The ship was clearing port on the 20th and Wilson barely had time to search the vessel before the final whistle blew. Although his quarry had not been located, Wilson still felt sure Owen was aboard, so he booked passage, also. On the third day at sea, the officer spotted his man on the promenade deck and the outlaw was quickly in custody. When the steamer

*Orizaba* approached on its return trip to San Francisco, it was signalled and Wilson and his prisoner went aboard.

Reportedly the son of a wealthy rancher on the San Joaquin River, Owen was ultimately released since there was little hard evidence against him.

Jack Phillips was another matter. The law had a good case against him for sheltering fugitives and receiving stolen property, and both Bob Paul and Juan Fernandez told credible and damning stories. The trial commenced in the Placer County Court of Sessions on February 19, 1857, and concluded the next day. Bob Paul testified for the prosecution first, followed by Juan Fernandez:

### Testimony of Juan Fernandez

*Juan Fernandez sworn—My name is Juan Fernandez. I knew Tom Bell, I knew Ned Convery, I knew Bell, White, Monte Jack, two men (brothers) by name of Farnsworth. I knew these men, Farnsworth, in June 1856, and Convery, White and Monte Jack at same time. I first knew Tom Bell in 1847, first knew him in Tennessee. First knew the others in this state. Knew Jack Phillips and was at his house with Tom Bell, Ned Convery and Bill White. Was there first in July last. White and myself started for Mokelumne Hill, Tom Bell and Convery left but I did not know where they went. I and these men went to defendant's house on the 21st of July and left on the 24th, and returned on the 25th. We did not go to Mokelumne Hill, but turned back. I know that defendant was acquainted at that time with Bell, Convery, White and all but Monte Jack, and I then got acquainted with defendant. Tom Bell also returned on the 25th July. Self and White returned first. Bell and Convery afterwards. Self and White returned between 6 and 7 o'clock on the evening of the 25th. Bell and Convery about 9 or 10 o'clock at night of same day. I slept there that night and ate there. When Bell and Convery returned, Bell had a strange horse, a small roan colored horse. Convery was riding a small, dark brown mare, fat and in good order. The roan horse Bell was riding was in tolerable condition, not very fat. There were saddles on the horse, did not notice them particularly. That morning Bell rode away on a large sorrel horse, horse in good order, but a little lame behind.*

*Ned Convery was not as tall as Mr. Mills, (District Attorney) but heavier, about five feet and maybe one or two inches. Should say he was four or five inches shorter than Mr. Mills. He had whiskers at that time, Bell was about 6 feet and one or two inches in height, slender built, straight, had light hair and wore mustache. Both these men had pistols, six shooters, and Bell had a knife. Ned Convery had some goods tied on his saddle behind him, in a piece of India rubber cloth and tied with leather straps. I saw these goods. I saw a black silk dress, two woolen dresses, think of green and red color, some ladies shoes, perhaps 2 or 3 dozen, can't tell how many,*

To his Excellency:

Hon. John B Weller,

Governor of the State of California.

        Your petitioners would respectfully represent that sometime during the summer of 1856. an escaped convict known as William White, convicted at the June term of the Court of Sessions (10ᵗʰ June 1853) of Placer County, of the crime of Grand Larceny, and sentenced to ten years imprisonment in the state prison, was re-captured in the vicinity of Knights Ferry San Joaquin County on sus- picion, That while said White was de- tained at Knights Ferry, he manifested a desire to, and did confess to Thomas W. Lane, O. P. Calloway and others that he had escaped from the States Prison, and promised to divulge further secrets, and impart such information, as would lead to the detection of the notorious robber Tom Bell and his gang of desperados, on condition that the under signed would intercede in his behalf, to obtain his pardon and send him out of

A page of Bill White's pardon application. California State Archives.

some were cloth and others leather gaiters. Saw some ladies belts, silk thread, ladies collars, wristlets and bosoms. The cloth in which the goods were packed is the same as that now before me, (package of goods exhibited to witness—witness picks out goods and recognizes most of them as being the same seen by him with slight differences). The roan horse and brown mare were put in the stable by Bell. The goods were opened upstairs in defendant's house, the Mountaineer House, some 6 or 7 miles from Auburn. Mr. and Mrs. Phillips were present when the goods were opened, also Tom Bell, Bill White, Convery and myself. There were two other persons present, that belonged to the house. White opened the goods.

Q. Was there any conversation between Bell and Phillips concerning these goods?

[ Question objected to by defendant—objection overuled. Defendant excepts to what Bell may have said.]

A. There was. After they opened the goods, they told Phillips how they came by them. Bell told him. He said they had found a pedlar on the road, that he told Ned Convery to go and stop him; that Convery obeyed his orders; that he, Ned Convery, told pedlar to stop. After he had stopped, Ned asked him for his money, that after he gave up his money they took him one side of the road and took his pack off his horse. They took some of his goods and tied the man and told him to stay there till night and that they would come and untie him. Then they rode off. One of them dismounted and turned back to see if the man was loose—found he was loose and came back and told Bell he was loose. They both went back and tied him again hand and foot. They tied his feet about a foot apart, so he could not walk too fast. This is the conversation that passed between them.

[All this conversation was objected to by defendant.]

Bell was also making fun of Convery for shooting at the man and not to hit him, this was also in presence of defendant. They said that they tied him the first time so that he could walk, and walk slow. They said they took $250 from him.

Some of the goods were given to Mrs. Phillips in presence of defendant. These were 3 pairs ladies shoes, 3 belts, 1 ladies collar. (Witness picks shoes, collar, chimsettes, etc., from the pack in Court like those taken by Mrs. Phillips.) Ned Convery took the balance of the goods away. A pocket handkerchief was given to another man in the house. I knew what was done with the money. $50 was given to Mr. Phillips. Bell and Convery each gave $25.00 to Phillips. All four of us started that night. Went to the Hog Ranch on the road from Sacramento to Nevada. Returned afterwards to Phillips again.

I knew of the stage robbery on the Camptonville and Marysvile road. It took place on the 13th August. They went from that place Hogg Ranch, on the 14th August, from there to defendants on the 16th. They stopped at that time back of defendants field about 4 or 5 hundred yards from the house. Staid there about two hours. Defendant brought us something to eat in a shot pouch, he had a rifle on his shoulder. We heard a noise and defendant made a motion to Bell's party that somebody was coming. Defendant then left. In a few moments a man came along. He remained about 20 minutes. We went back to the Hogg Ranch. A week or ten days after that time we came back to defendants house and remained some 3 or 4 days. We then staid back of the field and slept there. White went to the house to get some provisions. Phillips brought some. We ate at defendants house once after the robbery of the pedlar.

After the stage robbery while we were eating in the house, a pistol fired in the road. We did not know who it was; thought it might be officers, and Bell's party got up to go out of the house, but Phillips pushed us back and said he would first see if anybody was around the house. He came back and said nobody was around the house and we all left. We were only at defendants house once after the robbery of the pedlar, which was at the time of the above described occurrence. On the night of the pedlar affair, defendant kept Bell's party concealed upstairs. I was usually called by this party "John." I am from the city of Mexico.

Defendant gave Bell a bullet. I was present when it was given, it was in July. I think it was after the pedlar affair. This was on account of a letter Bell had sent to Phillips by one of the Farnsworths, and defendant would not take or read it because he did not know but it was a trap by the officers to catch the defendant, but he gave him a bullet marked so that he could not be trapped, I saw the bullet. It has holes, crosses, etc. ( Bullet in Court is like it.) I told Paul about it and gave one to him like it, in the Sheriffs office in Mokelumne Hill. I told him after the robbery of the pedlar. Defendant told Bell that some of the officers from Marysville, Mr. King and others, and from Auburn, had been to his house; that their warrants were for Tom Bell and Ned Convery. While stopping back of the house of defendant, we slept on blankets. Some of them were furnished by defendant. Some were our own. When we were at defendant's house we were concealed upstairs. Defendant told us all the news. That strangers stopped there frequently with blankets, but he knew they were there for the purpose of discovering whether Bell and party were there. Tom Bell was known by the name of Tom Hodges in Tennessee.

Cross-Examines—I knew Tom Bell in Tennessee in 1850. We both lived at Rome, Tennessee. He did not rob or steal then, neither did I. I first knew him in this country in 1852; he was then packing to Shasta. I was then working in Sacramento city, and continued there until the last of 1852, then went at mining near Coloma where I continued until 1853. I then mined at Volcano until 1855. Do not know what Bell was doing then. I then went to Sonora and staid five months, then went to Jackson and mines two weeks, then went to Sacramento city in August '55, then went to Marysville.

Kept a restaurant in Marysville nine months in company with a Spaniard named Phillips, then went to Nevada [city]. All this time I did not know what Bell was doing. I staid there about one month. Went then to Jackson to mine, and thence to West Point about four months. Up to that time did not know Ned Convery or Bill White. I had a quartz lead—had no other business.

Next went to Nevada and staid about fifteen days, went to see a family I was acquainted with. Returned to West Point and staid about 29 days. Went again to Nevada, a third time, and stayed about twenty days, went to see the family before spoken of. I then saw Tom Bell for the first time since 1852. The first night at Nevada, while at a public house, Tom Bell came in. This was 1856. He knew me. I asked him what he was doing. He said he was gambling. After that I was one of Tom Bell's party. I went with him to the Yuba and there first saw White at Cal. house. Bell hired a horse to leave Nevada. I rode behind him on his horse. We left in the evening. It was about 20 days after I saw him there. We went to see a man named Gardner, not that I wanted to see him, but Tom wanted me to go. He forced me to go and said if I did not go he would not give two cents for my life—I went under these circumstances.

We stayed there one day and I there first saw White, but did not then know Convery or Phillips. Bell introduced me to White. We then started for Hogg Ranch. I went because Bell brought me there, This was in June. We all rode back, staid there one day and then went to Mokelumne Hill, were four days going. We did nothing on the road. I then sold my claim. White and Bell went with me to make me sell it. The claim was 16 miles from Mokelumne Hill. I was there about 5 days. We then went to Hogg Ranch and staid two days, did nothing on the road. Then went to California House and staid about five days—did nothing. This was from June 1856 to July.

We found Ned Convery in July 1856. I did not then know what Convery was doing. I staid there till 19th July. They (Bell, Convery and White) left the house about 4 or 5 days after we arrived, I staid there with the man Gardner. I staid because I could not help it, Bell told me if I left the house and he came across me, he would show me how to obey his orders. They did not leave Gardner as my guard, but he took charge of me.

About 16th July, Bell, Convery and White returned and left again on the 19th. Gardner was keeping a hotel, We returned to Hogg Ranch, were about 11 1/4 days travelling the distance. We staid there until the 21st and then came to Phillips' home, don't know the distance. We all four went together. Up to that time I had done nothing wrong, nor had they that I know of. In May, 1856 I was not in Marysville keeping Restaurant. It may have been nine months that I kept in Marysville.

I first saw defendant at his own house on the 22nd July, 1856. We left Hogg Ranch at 10 or 11 o'clock in the morning, staid that night, the 21st, about one mile from here. Did not, that I recollect, come to Auburn, only knew the direction of the *place. We camped out. Did not know of any robberies up to that time. Got to Defendant's house next day (22nd), can't tell the time of day, it was in the day time. Saw Phillips and hostler there, was not introduced to him, but heard him called by that name. Staid all night in the woods about 50 yards back of the house, Bell and White slept in the house. Staid part of the next day. During that day Tom Bell and Ned Convery rode off. Can't tell how many men I saw in defendants house. I staid there all day. After Bell and Convery returned (same day) White and I went off. We all staid back of the house except White, who staid in the house.*

*On the 24th we all left. White and myself started for Mokelumne Hill, I did so for the purpose of leaving White. We rode pretty much all day, don't know how far. About dark, being tired, we stopped in the woods, got something to eat and slept all night. I don't know what county this was in. In the morning returned to defendant's*

*Jail, left, and the Placer County courthouse in Auburn where Jack Phillips was tried and convicted. Author's collection.*

*house. White did not want to go farther. I went back because I did not want to get shot. Bell had told me to go with White. White's business was stealing. I did not know what it was, but had heard so. Did not get back until evening of 25th, about 5 or 7 o'clock. Bell and Convery were not then there—Phillips was. We went back into the woods and put our horses in the stable ourselves. There were three hostlers. On this last trip we crossed a bridge. We did not steal anything that I recollect. White may have stolen. I had no more money than when I left. I did not pay any money out. The pedlar's horse is up at Mokelumne Hill. The sorrel mare is called Kate. The goods were kept on the night of the 25th back of the field. The next day took them back to the house when that took place, which I before mentioned. I knew nothing as to where these goods came from, except what was said at that time. I have never had any* conversations with the pedlar, but have with Paul. I was examined before the Grand Jury and before the Justice of the Peace at Mokelumne Hill, but not outside of Court.

It was between 10 and 11 o'clock at night that Convery brought the goods up stairs. The rest of the goods were taken to the Hogg Ranch and given to Widow Hood. I got no goods or money. I got no money except three or three and a half dollars which Phillips gave me. I got one of the ladies belts, which I swapped off. The money was shown by Bell and Convery. Each gave Phillips $25. The other men upstairs were called Dave and Joe at the time the goods were distributed. Did not leave till next day.

I saw the robbery or attack upon the Camptonville stage. I was there. I was riding with Bell, Convery, White, Monte Jack & Smith. This was Tuesday, Aug. 13, 1856. Up to that time I had seen nothing except what I have stated. I was away from Bell and Convery about four days after the 2nd July. Up to the third time of seeing defendant, from 26th July, Bell and Convery were not at defendant's house. Was there third time at or about the 16th of August last, about eight or ten days after. When we heard the pistols at defendant's, it was the fourth time. It was down towards Folsom. It might have been eight or nine o'clock at night. Me and Tom Bell left that same night; White and Convery stayed back. I came to this state in 1850.

Re-direct—When they rode away on the 26th, they got the brown mare from defendant. Don't know what they did with those that were left, except one was turned out. At the California House, the night before the attack on the stage, I attempted to get away, but the cook told Bell and as I was going out of the house he asked where I was going; I told him nowhere; he said, well, and if I did he would shoot me if he ever came across me; and the next morning he told me to get on my horse and go with them, and thus I came to be with them when the attack was made. Bell was by my side when we came upon the stage. I did not fire. Bell asked me why I did not shoot and said he would shoot me if I did not. I then shot twice, but not so as to hit the stage. I never was with them willingly after I knew what their business was.

Later Fernandez was recalled briefly by the prosecution:

I think it was on Friday that the robbery of the Pedlar occurred. I am not certain of it. It was on Friday night the goods were brought to the house. I judged the day was Friday because we reached the Widow Hood's on Sunday afterwards.

I know the witness first called for the defense at the Mountaineer House. I saw him on the 25th July last. He knew Tom Bell, Ned Convery, Bill White and myself. He was present when the goods were opened upstairs. He received some of the goods. Bill White gave him a pocket handkerchief while in the room. I don't think he was present at the conversation I detailed at that house. The other witness for the defense *was at the Mountaineer House and he knew these men, except Bell. I don't know whether he knew Bell or not.*

The extent of Spanish John's guilt in all this was difficult to ascertain, both then and now. In a Knight's Ferry "people's court" hearing after his capture with White, Fernandez had plead guilty to the horse stealing charge. His cooperation as a prosecution witness against Phillips, however, was apparently enough to gain him immunity from other charges and he quickly faded from sight.

Two other prominent members of the gang were still at large. English Bob Carr apparently had sense enough to get out of the state, but Monte Jack was still around. Montague Lyon had served a one-year term in San Quentin for attempted murder in Sierra County. He was discharged in October of 1854, but was unsuccessful on the outside and joined up with Tom Bell when the opportunity presented itself. In mid-September of 1856 he wrote a letter to the *Marysville Herald* in which he wailed about injustice and enemies who conspired against him:

*California Mountains, Sept. 17, 1856*

*Mr. Editor—You will please do me the favor to allow these few lines to be published in your paper. Now I expect you all think Monte Jack had left the country, but he still is here and is bound to have that revenge which is due him before he dies for those slandering villains which has predjudiced the public against me. It is not me they have been hunting, it is that name which some of my enemies have titled me to, for I assure you I never gave myself that name.*

*Now, I ask the public, previous to the time M. J. Kohler and two more men came upon me, on the road leading from the New York Ledge to the Debbins' Ranch, for what purpose of greeting me which I did not know at the time when they came upon me what they wanted, for they was within ten feet of me, and never spoke to me at all. I passed off the trail to rest myself, allowing them to go by, as I was in no hurry, when going to the ravine, some fifteen yards from the trail to get a drink of water, the first thing I knew was they commenced rolling rocks down upon me. They then stopped that game, and come down in the ravine where I had remained in mystery, wondering what they had meant by such proceedings.*

*When Mr. Kohler came down he must have seen me, but he turned round to go away, when I asked him what he was looking for, if he was hunting me, and what for. He made a reply, "Oh no, no, I do not want you," and at the same time putting his hand upon his pistols, when having my pistols in my hand, I said if you do not want* me what are you hunting, and the same time I was speaking to him he was drawing his pistols. Now I knew something was the matter when I presented my pistol upon him and fired. He run and jumped a few paces, then stopped, fired one barrel and snapped another barrel at me.

Now I did not know what they wanted of me, whether they wanted to rob me or whether they all three had come to whip me, or what they wanted of me. I had been in Camptonville just an hour or so before, and I knew I had done nothing wrong. I spoke to Mr. J. Kohler just previous to my leaving Camptonville about some money matters, and he appeared to be friendly enough. Now when they came upon me I could not make out what they were after. I could see they had some hostile motives in view by their actions. I since learned that they wanted to arrest me on suspicion, thinking I knew something about some stock which had been stole.

Now I want to ask on what ground, what right, or what foundation did they have to come and try and arrest me. I can answer for them, for they had none, which I suppose they are now satisfied of. They had no proof that I had done anything wrong, for the time some of the stock was brought on this side of the river I was up at Moore's Diggings, and had been up that way for over a week, which I could prove by a dozen men.

You will no doubt recollect a piece published in the Inquirer, headed Moore's Diggins, near Rabbit Creek, dated May 20th, describing the digging. The article was signed George. Now, I was the man sent that piece to the Inquirer. That was the time which some of the stock was brought on this side of the river, which the ferryman will tell them the same. I think I suffered enough being arrested on suspicion, the time they was after Bell and Green for stealing some cattle. They arrested me because I had been ranching some stock for them, but that was through one of the officers going before the Grand Jury and swearing to a lie, which two of his brother officers could testify that he had done so, that cost me all the money that I had worked hard for during one whole year, and what redress did I have to get my money back. None. I could have sent that policeman to prison for perjury, for they was a dozen men could prove that he perjured himself, but that would not have paid me my money back. I had to appear at two different terms of court with my witnesses, when they could find no proof against me.

Now that was the first track to set my enemies a talking, and because I was not in business right away again, my enemies commenced slandering me as a bad man, and how I could afford to live and keep a horse to ride, without working. They made up in their minds that I must be stealing, and any stock that was missing around, the poor fools would whisper to themselves, I will bet Monte Jack knows something about them animals.

Now these gentlemen, which was down upon me, dared not to come forward and tell me so. The only way they could injur me was to backbite me, and excite the public saying I was a notorious character, publishing me as a cattle thief, and authorizing people to shoot me down if they saw me, or they should hang me if they could catch me. There has been a devil of a bellow about me. What have I done previous to the time Mr. Kohler came upon me. I tell you honestly, I do not know myself, as I had done anything out of the way, without it was to defend myself when imposed upon or insulted, for neither of those things would I allow any man to do to me, without resenting it. I once was in a scrape for shooting a man in self defense, but as for being dishonest previous to this fuss, I never heard of anyone doubting my character with regard to honesty.

Now I have seen enough to satisfy me where the people are prejudiced against anyone as they are against me, that they would not be satisfied without they sent him to the State Prison. Before I will go there I prefer death, which I expect sooner or later, for no man shall ever arrest me.

I understand Mr. Langston thinks I was in the crowd that tried to rob his express, but he is mistaken. Had I have been, that treasure would never have reached Marysville.

Now let some of you Grand Jury men go round to men that has known me for five or six years and enquire about my character. I do not think they will find anything very serious against me, except this outbreak, which was got up by men who are down upon me. From this time out, I am floating under the Black Flag, and I will yet strike terror to the hearts of those miscreants who have abused me. Let them watch and pray, for they know not the day nor the hour when Monte Jack will come upon them.

I remain yours,
Monte Jack

In mid-October Bill White's confession was widely published in the newspapers naming Monte Jack as one of the gang who attacked the Camptonville stage. Later Juan Fernandez corroborated White, and Monte Jack's claim of innocence suddenly had a decidedly hollow ring. Monte Jack wasn't heard from again.

Jack Phillips was easily convicted of being an accessory to robbery and was sentenced to two years at San Quentin. After his trial he told Undersheriff Ben Moore, one of the officers who had killed Ned Convery, that it was fear of the gang that had made him cooperate with them.

"His wife," Moore later wrote, "who was active nearly all the time for a pardon, personally besought me at Dutch Flat for my signature to her petition, and it required all the moral courage I could muster to deny her. Had it been nearer the end of his term I would have signed, as she exemplified a character of womanhood really praiseworthy. I have not heard a word of the family since the pardon, but would like to as my respectful admiration for the wife and daughter is sincere and abiding."

Tom Bell's attack on the Camptonville stage is widely regarded as the first such attempt in California, but that may, or may not, be true. George Skinner, alias Walker, alias Williamson, alias Reelfoot Williams, is reported to have stopped the first coach near Illinoistown in April of 1852. He was sent to state prison in November on a grand larceny rap and was killed in 1856 after the robbery of a gold train in Shasta County. George was too early in the game and the confusion of his many aliases kept him from being seriously noted in California road agent history. The Illinoistown stage robbery is mentioned in several early sources, notably in Harlow, Alvin F. *Old Waybills.* New York: D. Appleton-Century Company, 1934. To date, no documentation for this robbery has been found, although George Williamson entered the California state prison in November of 1852 from El Dorado County. See *List of Convicts on Register of State Prison at San Quentin,* Sacramento, J.D. Young, Supt, State Printing, 1889. For information on Williams and his brother Cyrus, see Secrest, William B. *Lawmen & Desperadoes* Spokane WA: The Arthur H. Clark Company, 1994. Robert Chandler, historian for Wells Fargo Bank, knows of no California stagecoach holdups earlier than 1856. There were many express companies and stage lines in those days, however, and earlier robberies may have escaped notice. Chandler to the author, March 15, 1998. The Stockton *San Joaquin Republican,* September 6, 1853, reports the theft of $20,000 from the back boot of a stagecoach as it traveled from Sonora to Stockton. This did not involve stopping the stage, however, and was more of a sneak theft.

Information on Thomas Hodges and his origins can be found in the *Nevada* (city) *Democrat,* October 15, 1856 and the *San Francisco Daily Evening Bulletin,* October 16, 1856. For Hodges' escape from San Quentin, see the *San Francisco Daily Alta California,* May 14, 1855. There is some information on Jack Phillips in Moore, Benjamin F., "Early Days in California," manuscript in Wells Fargo Bank History Department. See also, McDonald, A.D., "Rattlesnake Bar on the American River," *San Francisco Chronicle,* February 2, 1896, for Kate Phillips' early history.

The *Waban* was built in Westbrook, Maine, in 1836 and named after a noted, local Indian chief. It sailed from New York with twelve passengers and much cargo on September 1, 1849, destination California. There were numerous stops and delays, but it arrived in San Francisco on June 8, 1850. After a voyage to South America, the *Waban* returned in poor shape for further sailing and was purchased as a storage facility, then by the city of San Francisco as a prison ship. In December 1851 it was towed by the tug *Firefly* to Angel Island where convicts were quarrying stone. Goodman, III, John B. *The California Gold Rush Fleet Encyclopedia.* Beverly Hills: typescript, n.d., courtesy John Boessenecker.

Information on Mrs. Elizabeth Hood, or Cullers, can be found in the *San Francisco Bulletin*, October 13, 1856. David Lash's testimony is from the *Placer Herald*, February 28, 1857. The Rosenthal robbery and murder is described in the *San Francisco Bulletin*, October 18, 1856 and in Bill White's confession in the same paper, October 22, 1856. See also the *Marysville Daily Herald*, October 25, 1856, for the story of the man who found the body.

The attack on the Camptonville stage is graphically reported in the *Marysville Daily Herald*, August 13, 15, 1856, and the *San Francisco Daily Herald*, August 16, 1856. See also the *Sacramento Times*, August 15, 1856. Charles E. DeLong's journal was edited by Carl I. Wheat and published as "California's Bantam Cock," in the *California Historical Society Quarterly*, March, 1930. The Ramirez shooting was reported in the *Herald*, August 15, 1856. The arrest of White and Fernandez at Knight's Ferry is noted in the *San Andreas Independent* and the *San Francisco Bulletin*, September 24, 1856. Deputy Robert Paul's investigation of Jack Phillips is detailed in his courtroom testimony as published in the *Placer Herald*, February 28, 1857.

Bill White's confession was taken from the previously cited *San Francisco Bulletin*, October 22, 1856. It was published in various other papers also. What can be checked in his story is quite accurate, as it would be since he was bargaining for his freedom. Mrs. Hood, however, complained bitterly about White's remarks concerning her young daughters. White was returned to San Quentin, but was pardoned as a result of his cooperation with the law on November 2, 1858. Governor's Pardon Papers, California State Archives, Sacramento, California.

Pierre Ridge was a curious character whose account of his life appeared in the *San Francisco Examiner*, February 23, 1892. He claimed to be eighty-two years old at the time and told a story of forty years of crime in California, which is certainly indicated by his prison records. Parts of his story are undoubtedly true and can be verified. He mentions being associated with Tom Bell, Black Jack Bowen and many other early criminals.

The fight near the Franklin House is best described in the previously cited memoir of Benjamin F. Moore, "Early Days in California." See also the *San Francisco Bulletin*,

October 3, 1856. Information on Edward H. Conver, alias Convery or Conway, is from Boessenecker, John. *Badge and Buckshot*. Norman: University of Oklahoma Press, 1988. See also the *San Joaquin Republican*, July 23, 1853, and *List of Convicts on Register at San Quentin*.

Bell's capture and death are reported in the *San Francisco Bulletin*, October 8, the *San Francisco Herald*, October 12, the *Daily Alta California*, October 12, the *Nevada Democrat*, October 15, 1856, and most other newspapers in the state. Bell's letter to Mrs. Hood is quoted from the *San Francisco Bulletin*, October 13, 1856.

The capture of Texas Jack is from the *Sacramento Daily Union*, November 1, 1856. Juan Fernandez' testimony is taken from the *Placer Herald*, February 28, 1857. Montague Lyon's prison record is from *List of Convicts on Register at San Quentin*. His letter appeared in the *Marysville Herald*, September 23, 1856.

Jack Phillips' prison record, giving his description and noting that he was once a sailor, is from the *List of Convicts on Register at San Quentin*. Various records, including documents of his wife, are in the Governor's Pardon Papers, California State Archives, Sacramento, California. Ben Moore's comments are from his previously cited manuscript, "Early Days in California."

Jim was quite familiar with the leg irons used in both local jails and the state prison. *Calaveras County Museum.*

*"Old Jim"* Smith spent most of his adult life in California locked up in San Quentin state prison, shown below as it appeared when he was a resident in the 1860s. *California State Library.*

# 4 "We all had good guns, pistols and knives"

*Old Jim Smith's Story*

James P. Smith, whose mild appearance hid a character as crafty and desperate as Jesse James'. Author's collection.

The officers always called him "Old" Jim Smith, but he was merely "old" in criminal experience. Born in Prussia about 1831, few have heard of James P. Smith (probably Schmidt), although he was as colorful as he was unsuccessful as a bandit. Various nautical tatoos on his body indicated that he had been a seaman and had probably jumped ship at the time of the 1849 California Gold Rush. His first conviction was for grand larceny at Sacramento in September of 1851. He was sentenced to a two-year term in the California State Prison.

At this time there was really no prison at all. The twenty-acre site, at Point San Quentin on the bay just north of San Francisco in Marin County, had recently been purchased for $10,000. The old bark *Waban*, anchored offshore, was used to house the prisoners until cell blocks could be constructed on shore. Jim found himself back aboard ship, but under less than ideal circumstances.

Listing himself as a baker by trade, Jim may have been put to work preparing the bread, potatoes, meat and soup that constituted the convicts' main diet. The thirty or forty other prisoners were kept busy quarrying stone on nearby Angel Island, gathering firewood, filling in swampland around the prison site or leveling the ground. Prison life was mostly working out in the open and there were few complaints until they were herded below deck on the *Waban* at night.

The lower deck of the old ship had been divided into a series of eight-foot-square cells with four or five convicts occupying each cell. It was blistering hot in summer and cold and damp in winter. Toilet facilities consisted of a bucket and the smell of the place by morning can well be imagined. Worse, in bad weather the men might be cooped up for days, the stench becoming so unbearable the guards refused to go downstairs until the place had been aired out.

Perhaps it was the housing conditions that fed Jim Smith's determination to break out, which he did on January 5, 1852. It was less than four months after his term had commenced. He promptly resumed his career of larceny and was captured near Gilroy, a few miles south of San Jose, by a posse of citizens who demanded he tell where some stolen property was hidden. When Jim refused, he was hanged from a tree limb until he was gasping for breath. Still, he refused to talk. This was repeated until he was half dead, and he finally told the possemen what they wanted to know, as well as implicating his partners in crime. Jim later swore to kill some of that posse for their actions.

When he was returned to prison in March of 1854, Jim found his old home had been improved considerably. Although there were now more than two hundred and fifty prisoners, a commodious stone building contained forty-eight cells, each housing four prisoners. The old *Waban* was still in use for the overflow. Brick-making machinery had been installed near the wharf where some 70,000 bricks per day could be turned out. The bricks were used in constructing various prison buildings and also sold in the San Francisco market. A surrounding wall and more outbuildings were to be constructed next.

Jim and a crew of convicts had been quarrying stone on nearby Marin Island for some time when they began laying plans for a new escape. At night they were placed in their cells on the *Waban* and soon had smuggled tools aboard with which to cut their way out. When a violent storm swept through the area on the night of April 12, 1855, the conspirators quickly decided to make their move. Notice of the break appeared in the *San Francisco California Chronicle*:

When Jim Smith served his first term, there was no San Quentin Prison yet, just sleeping quarters in the prison ship, Waban. This is the plan for the first prison building which was too expensive and had to be modified. California State Archives.

## Another State Prison Exodus

A party of eight State Prison convicts broke away from Marin Island on Thursday night last. It is the custom there to shut up the convicts in the prison brig over night, fasten the hatches down and keep a guard on deck. Thursday night was very stormy and the guard was probably not very vigilant. By some means not explained, a party of eight of the convicts got a saw and cut a hole through the deck or side of the brig, got out and swam to the island. There they found a whale boat and rowed to the mainland. Whither they went is not known, but a boat belonging to a farmer of Marin County, near where they landed, is missing....

John "Black Jack" Bowen was a Rhode Island sailor, highwayman, and burglar and few California jails or prisons could hold him for long. Author's collection.

Besides Jim Smith, the escaping prisoners were John W. Kelly, John Campbell, John "Black Jack" Bowen, George Wright, John H. Hammond, Barney C. Smith and L. W. Dray. Both Bowen and Hammond were sailors also, and with a good head start on any pursuit, the convicts quickly piloted their small craft across the bay and disappeared. The convicts split up and went their own way, George Wright being recaptured the next day.

Jim Smith, still smarting under his hanging treatment at Gilroy, John Kelly and one of the other convicts made their way south towards San Jose. Jim's two compatriots agreed to help him settle with the Gilroy possemen who had previously made him confess. Two other escaped convicts joined the group, one Henry Smith and a Mexican. Camping near Gilroy, the group watched for a chance to ambush Jim's enemies, but when their Mexican comrade left the group it was feared he would turn them in. Stealing some horses, the men left for the mining country. Jim and two others made their escape, but Jack Kelly was captured by Stanislaus Deputy Sheriff J. S. Clarke and returned to Gilroy. He was lynched late one Sunday night.

Within a few weeks Jim Smith was also recaptured, grateful to have escaped the lynch mob that had hanged Kelly. Back behind bars, he was soon plotting yet another escape with a group of the most desperate convicts in the prison. This time the prisoners were apparently aided in their escape by the authorities themselves who wanted to be rid of some of the more troublesome inmates.

As noted in the previous chapter, a pivotal figure in the escape was convict Bill White. He was called into the office of Captain Asa Estes who made a startling proposal. White and a group of other prisoners were to be sent out on a wood-gathering expedition and at a signal, the convicts were all to break and run. There were various reasons for the scheme. Captain Estes simply said he wanted to get rid of some of the more dangerous prisoners, while White himself reasoned that General James Estell, who held the state contract for the prison, was seeking excuses to back out of an unprofitable situation.

Also, there were some twenty-one disgruntled guards at the prison who were paid a mere fifty dollars a month. At this time they hadn't received any pay at all for some time. Turning some of the more dangerous prisoners loose might have seemed like a good idea.

On the morning of May 12, 1855, Lieutenant John M. Gray, on horseback, led White and a group of other convicts into the nearby woods. Members of the detail were "Cherokee Bob" Talbot, Ned Conver, alias Convery, Thomas Hodges, Jim Smith, Asa Carrico and a man named Stewart. All must have

An early stagecoach rumbles down a California mountain road. Yosemite Natural History Association.

been nervous. The first tree that fell was the signal and White ran into a clearing drawing the fire of Gray, as the other convicts fled. White was gratified to hear no bullets zipping around him and knew the guard was indeed firing blanks. He quickly dodged into the forest after his comrades.

Gray later claimed he had been instructed to let the men escape, but didn't know his weapons contained blanks. "I fired six or seven shots with the pistol and gun, ineffectually. The men laughed at me, and said something to me in a jeering way which I did not perfectly understand. The prisoners succeeded in escaping unharmed. I then examined the barrel of my pistol and found that what had the appearance of a bullet was only a very thin piece of lead, covering some dirt and powder mixed together."

Conver, White and Jim Smith stayed with Hodges who proposed forming a band of highwaymen. Adding Montague "Monte Jack" Lyon, "English Bob" Carr and others to the gang, Hodges assumed the alias

The early San Quentin cells were wooden benches with straw mattresses. This is a cell in the original cellblock, some years later. San Quentin Museum Association.

"Tom Bell" as they began their raids on teamsters, travelers and isolated stores. The following year the gang made their ill-fated assault on the Camptonville stage in which a Mrs. Tilghman was dangerously wounded, along with several others. With irate posses tracking them throughout the region, the gang broke up into small groups. Conver was killed in a gunfight with officers, Bell was lynched and most of the gang was captured.

White, in his confession, noted that after the stage attack Jim Smith and Monte Jack had been dropped from the gang since they liked their liquor too much. Perhaps Jim was glad to be out of such a wild bunch anyway. He, too, was soon picked up, however. Tried for a robbery in Amador County under the name William Ellis, Smith found himself back in San Quentin on October 12, 1856, as prisoner Number 1014.

Having long since forfeited the privileges of being a cook at the prison, Jim now found himself working the brickyard. A private contractor named

Johns was head of the California Manufacturing Association which operated the facilities manufacturing bricks for the recently completed wall and various other prison buildings. Jim kept his mouth shut and did his work, all the time waiting for another escape opportunity. It was nearly four years later when he saw another opportunity.

On May 14, 1860, Smith broke out once again, but his freedom was short-lived. By the end of July he had been picked up for robbing a teamster outside of Folsom. The robbery had netted only three or four dollars and he was soon back behind the walls of San Quentin.

Convict Charles Mortimer saw the breakout attempt in early 1866 and later fingered Jim as one of the ringleaders. Author's collection.

Smith was reported as being a prominent member of the last big escape from the prison in July, 1862. Some 300 convicts broke out, Jim and several others taking along Warden John F. Chellis as hostage. Most were recaptured after heavy causalities among the escapees.

Returned to his cell, Jim never stopped plotting to escape. In mid-January 1866 Smith and others jumped Captain James Fitzpatrick as he was ushering a line of convicts into the large mess hall. As Fitzpatrick yelled and fought off his attackers, a convict cook ran up with a knife and defended the officer. Both the guard and the cook barely made it out the door to safety. The rioting prisoners were then locked in the mess hall as nervous guards were held back from firing through the windows. Outside, the night was stormy and black and the prisoners hoped to sneak out of the building and go over the wall. They saw the hopelessness of their situation, however, and the break soon fizzled out. Plot leaders were quickly captured and heavily ironed.

Convict Charles Mortimer later wrote that Smith and several others were suspected of turning in some of the ringleaders: "There were three or four of the leading spirits in the plot accused of treachery by their comrades. Their names were Snell and Jim Smith, fourteen years each; Snell was pardoned out some months afterward. Smith was pardoned six years after, but began to look for a pardon at the time Snell got his....I have no doubt of the correctness of the charge of treachery."

Jim's motive for his betrayal was, perhaps, fear of the whipping post. The following day the plotters were lashed in position and flogged with a four-foot cowhide lash. "I... saw the victims writhe and their muscles quiver as the keen rawhide fell upon and sank into their flesh," wrote a witness. "Some of those men's backs and sides were masses of corruption for months after," wrote convict Mortimer. After fifty lashes, one of the convicts was ironed and thrown into the dungeon for several weeks. When finally taken to the hospital, his back "was alive with maggots. "That night, four others scheduled for the whip the following day, tunnelled through their cell walls and made their escape.

*Sketch of the whipping post as depicted in* Thirteen Years in the Oregon Penitentiary *by Joseph Kelley. Author's collection.*

Smith seems to have lost interest in escape after this. He applied himself to his work and was discharged on March 16, 1867.

Trying his luck in Placer County this time, Jim was picked up on another robbery charge just over a year later. As Number 3849, he walked through the San Quentin gates again on July 9, 1868. He was indeed an "old con" by this time and again he settled down and kept his nose clean. After serving out his term, he was discharged on December 16, 1875.

He had met Charlie "The Shoemaker" Pratt while in prison. Pratt, who had served five terms at San Quentin and earned his nickname there, had been discharged in October and perhaps the two felons had set up a meeting. Jim had only been out of prison a few weeks when he and Pratt held up the Fiddletown stage in Amador County on January 10, 1876. Taking another ex-convict named George "Texas" Wilson into their select group, the three stopped the Georgetown to Auburn coach a week later. Wells Fargo detectives and other lawmen were already on their trail and on January 29, 1876, the *Sacramento Bee* reported the capture of Smith and Wilson:

*Detective Leonard Harris helped arrest Jim for stage robbery. Author's collection.*

Stage Robbers Captured—In Folsom yesterday morning, aided by Len. Harris, Steve Venard and Constable Kimball, detective Hume captured two desperadoes who are wanted for various stage robberies. The fellows were taken completely by surprise or they would never have surrendered without bloodshed, for both had declared their determination never to be captured alive.... They were brought to this city last evening and will be kept here until the officers have arranged the evidence against them and determined where to bring the first actions. Their chances for long terms across the bay are very good....

Texas George Wilson. John Boessenecker collection.

Pratt was nabbed a short time later. All three road agents plead guilty to one of the robberies and were sentenced to twelve years "across the bay." Jim must have been philosophical about his ongoing relationship with San Quentin. It was "home" to him now and the good old days of relatively easy escapes were a thing of the past. There were more than 1,200 convicts now, with only 400 of them regularly employed. Convicts roamed the yard and could smoke and talk, at will, even to the guards and officials. Many wore the prison stripes now, although some wore hickory shirts or coats. There were three cell buildings, a fountain and flower gardens brightening up the yard and surrounding staff buildings and factories.

Charles Pratt joined Jim in several 1876 stage holdups. Pratt served five terms in San Quentin and died there. Author's collection.

Jim was put in charge of the brickyard and his hard work impressed the guards and officials. He was pardoned by Governor William Irwin in September 1879 on the condition that he leave the state and lead an honest life thereafter.

On the outside again, Jim quickly reverted to a lifestyle that only a prison could make him give up. Under the heading "A Checkered Career," the *Sacramento Bee* of November 30, 1879, reported the closing scenes of Jim's freedom:

*A heavily-laden Concord stagecoach prepares to leave Virginia City, Nevada, in 1865. Such coaches often carried gold bullion from the mines, and Jim and his pals couldn't resist attempting to stop them as they came over the mountain passes. Bancroft Library.*

### The Shingle Springs Robber Proves to be an Old Offender

Mention was made in last evening's *Bee* of a highway robbery on Thanksgiving morning, at an early hour, near Shingle Springs in Amador County. The robber was arrested and from reliable authority the following particulars are learned: His name is James P. Smith, alias "Old Jim Smith."...On his discharge the state paid Smith a considerable sum—up in the hundreds—with which to again start life outside of this state. One week ago last evening as the 9 o'clock train was coming into Sacramento, J. B. Hume saw a man get off the cars with a bundle in his arms and slip into the darkness at the depot. Hume went up to the man and found that it was none other than his old friend Smith, who said he was broke and had a ticket to Roseville only; also that he wanted to get out of the state, in accordance with the conditions of his pardon, but guessed he would have to walk to Virginia City. He also told Hume that he would never trouble Wells Fargo & Co. again, but as he was a little broke he thought he would have to do a little "work" to meet his present necessities. Hume advised him to quit his bad habits altogether and procured passage for him to Reno, for which place Smith started on the evening train. On his return to this city from Reno, conductor Allen reported to Hume that Smith had left the train at Colfax, from whence he doubled back to this city, and then went to where he committed the robbery. Old Jim Smith will now have to go to the State Prison for life, as his former convictions will be alleged in the indictment against him, and the Judge can exercise no discretion in the matter.

Jim's whimsical side is nowhere more apparent than in a prison interview he gave in July 1884. There are no dates or locations offered and any kind of chronology is lacking, but the piece is particularly enlightening as to just why he spent so much of his life behind bars. It is a fitting epitaph to a failed criminal lifetime of rowdy high adventure:

### Yarns by a Highwayman

*It is enough to make a 49er's blood boil to hear about the operations of these sneak thieves who are now working these little country roads. There ain't one in fifty of them that has the sand in him to hold up a thoroughbred. I've pinched members of Congress, Judges of the Supreme Court, ex-governors, argonauts and big men generally more'n once, but these fellows don't know anything about men of that quality—only to dodge them. Staging ain't what it used to be anyway. When the overland stages were running it took a good man to stop them. In the first place they were driven by the most reckless men you ever see, and the men inside of them were true Americans. If they gave up it was because they had to—that was all. The chumps who travel nowadays ain't got the spirit of '49 or these fellows who are in the business now never'd get a color.*

*I remember once early in the sixties I went out in Calaveras County with two partners to see about a stage that was due just about then. We all had good guns, pistols and knives and we got them ready to use for in those days things of that kind were not carried for ornaments. The overland didn't show up as early as was expected—some accident had happened to it in the mountains—and when it did come it took a little too sudden. We'd been fooling around for several days and got a little careless, I must admit.*

*One day it was warm and sunny and we all got scattered, though we had an understanding that wherever we were, we were to keep an eye on the road all the time and if any of us discovered the stage, the one doing so was to fire a shot or two as an* alarm signal. Along about the middle of the afternoon I heard a gun, and a minute later there came another report that sounded like a volley of musketry. It puzzled me a little, but I grabbed my shooting irons and made for the road. I had just got into a good position when I heard another shot a little nearer, and then another volley, a good deal louder than the other. Then came the clatter of horses and the roll of wheels. It was the stage.

I could see her acoming. You don't see driving like that these days. She was on two wheels half the time and when she got near enough to me and the dust lifted a little I could see the gunbarrels a-sticking out of her like quills on a hedge hog. The driver—a hard man that I knew mighty well—had the lines for his leaders in his teeth and those for the wheelers he had tied to the brake and he had a pistol in each hand. I never saw a grander sight in my life. I wanted to stop that outfit single-handed, just for the sake of seeing who was in it, but she had got up a tremendous momentum by the time she came abreast of me, and as she fairly shook the earth when she zipped past where I was hiding, I just ducked my head and let her go. I knew by the way she acted that there had been trouble up the road and I didn't care to make matters any worse just then. She was full of men and they all had guns.

When the dust had settled a little and the noise died out, I crept to the roadway and walked along slowly for a mile and half where I found one of my partners with about a pound of lead in him. A little further on I came upon the other one. He wasn't hurt, but he was scared within an inch of his life. He'd never been on the road before and he said if that was what I called stopping an overland, he had had enough. He said there was no stop to them. He hadn't enlisted to fight a man-of-war with a double gun deck and he wanted me to understand it. Well, he came pretty near getting into trouble with me, particularly when we came along to where the other fellow was, but I pacified him after awhile by telling him that it was all our fault. We hadn't ought to have separated. In those days there were just as tough men inside the coach as any you could recruit for the outside, and anybody who got away with them had to be a good one.

Just after the war I got information to the effect that a number of the boys were going back to the States and as I knew they had a good deal of dust I made up my mind that I would have to levy on them. The night before they started they drank heavily and when they came to get aboard they were all in a helpless condition. I was the first man to discover this peculiarity of homeward-bound passengers and it stood me in a good many hundreds of dollars. You could always get away with a stage a good deal easier during the first ten or twelve hours of its trip than at any other time. I made no mistake as to the coach I am speaking of.

Finding out when it would start, I took a couple of friends and went out on the road as far as we could get comfortably. Toward evening we heard her a-coming, and *we laid low. When about near enough, we jumped into the road and covered the driver. He was a little bit heavy, like the rest of them, but he was smarter than they were. When he saw us he reined right up, and sat there perfectly still while one of my men kept watch of him and the other one and myself interviewed the passengers. They were thoroughly surprised and those who were not too drowsy to resist, were too sick. We got half-a-dozen bags of dust, some watches and a few bills, and then left them. There was a treasure box aboard, which we pried off and undertook to carry away with us. It was mighty heavy and we didn't make much progress with it before nightfall. Feeling rather tired, we went to sleep, never dreaming of harm; but at daylight when we awoke we heard a racket in the road and looking out from behind the shrubbery we saw the passengers whom we had robbed the evening before. They were evidently on the warpath for us.*

*I was just motioning to my men to keep still when one of them, a clumsy cuss, lost his balance and in trying to recover himself made a noise which attracted the attention of the passengers. They were after us in a minute. We had to abandon the treasure box and after a while they got so hot on our trail that we had to drop the bags of dust, too. They fired about a dozen shots after us, but when they found the plunder they seemed to conclude that it wasn't worth while following us any further. This little episode taught me another important lesson in my business—that when you get anything from a drunken man that you want to keep, you must get out of his reach before he sobers up. That was the case in the overland days, anyhow.*

*I came upon a stage once that had a woman in it—a big-boned, red-faced woman. The other inmates showed fight and it took a shot or two from my party to keep them quiet. We had got just about all there was to be had and had ordered the driver to go ahead when the woman threw herself out of the vehicle yelling "I'm one of you." "No you don't," says I. "Why not?" says she. "Because," says I, "I don't know you and maybe you ain't what you seem." She then went on to tell me all about herself, and in half an hour she made me believe that she was a born robber who had been wishing all her life for a chance to go into the highway business. I rather liked her style, and in a day or two I had come to the conclusion that she might be made useful in overhauling stages.*

*She and I were alone on the road one day, my two partners having fallen behind us a little, when she got to chaffing me about shooting at a mark. She said she could shoot better than I could. Just for fun I pinned a piece of paper on a tree and let her take one of my pistols. She fired at the mark, but didn't hit it. Then I fired and I missed. Then I loaded her pistol again and handed it to her and was just going to load mine when she says, "Look here." She was pointing the weapon at me. Says I, "Don't do that, it might go off." "I know it," says she, "and maybe I will want it to go off. Stop loading that pistol or this one will go off and I know it." I thought she was* fooling for a while, but when she gave me the order to march I knew I'd been nabbed. That there woman run me into Frisco and I did three years time on her account.

I've been caught a good many times, but I never was really ashamed of myself except the last time. I got into bad company and ought to have been lynched right on the spot. I had just got out and had heard a good deal about the fellows who are stopping coaches now without any guns or anything of that kind. I found one of them and told him he was a chump. Then he said it was cowardly to use firearms when moral suasion would do just as well. He claimed that he could put on a look that would frighten the passenger more than a dozen rifle shots. I had never thought of it in that light before, and not wishing him to think me a coward, I accepted his challenge to go up in the mountains near the Oregon line for an experiment. We had pistols, but we agreed that we were not to load them. I was a little nervous, but he seemed so confident that I began to feel that perhaps stage robbing had been improved along with many other things.

We stopped a coach and the driver smiled and kept still, just as my friend said they always did. I was to keep him covered with my empty pistol while the other fellow ordered the passengers out and stood them up in a row preparatory to going through them. My friend had got pretty well down the line and I was admitting to myself that the science had certainly made some progress since my day, when one of the victims hauled off quick and knocked my partner down, jumped on him, took his empty revolver away from him and began snapping it at his ears. It didn't go off, of course, but in a minute the others were on him holding him fast and the man with the revolver levelled it at me with the order "Throw up your hands!" I had always been used to loaded pistols in my day and while I was painfully conscious that mine was empty, I forgot for a moment that the other was also, and up went my hands. Just then the idiocy of the thing popped into my head, but it was too late. They were on top of me in a minute and they soon had us both tied up with hitching straps and ropes.

Now, that was a nice pickle for a 49'er to be in, wan't it—hunting coaches with empty guns and then being captured with one of them? I wouldn't have blamed the Judge much if he'd made it forty years, instead of twenty.

But it didn't matter any more. Shortly after this interview Jim began showing signs of disorientation. There are no existing records of his case, but at that time state policy towards mental illness was quite liberal. One authority of the time stated that "nearly every form of mental infirmity and impairment, in persons who are indigent and become burdensome, is called insanity, and the subjects thereof are committed to the insane asylum. Hence we have counted as insane mere simpletons, epileptics who are simply troublesome, senile dements, methomaniacs [those with a craving for alcohol], and so forth."

In other words, most poor and indigent citizens of California, at that time, whose family couldn't care for them, were warehoused in the insane asylum. Whatever Jim's actual diagnosis, in October of 1884, he was transferred to the state insane asylum at Napa, California. He died there on March 13, 1886.

*Jim Smith's final days were spent at this Napa, California, state insane asylum. History of Napa County, California.*

## Chapter Four / NOTES

Background information on Jim Smith is from *List of Convicts on Register of State Prison at San Quentin*, Sacramento. J. D. Young, Supt. State Printing, 1889. See also *Report of Jas. B. Hume and Jno. Thacker, Special Officers, Wells, Fargo & Co's Express, Covering a Period of Fourteen Years, giving losses by Train Robbers, Stage Robbers and Burglaries, etc.* San Francisco: H.S. Crocker & Co., 1885.

An account of Smith's first prison break is in the *San Francisco Herald*, January 6, 7, 13, February 3, 1852.

For information on the early history of San Quentin and conditions on the *Waban*, see Lamott, Kenneth. *Chronicles of San Quentin*. New York: David McKay Company, Inc., 1961. See also the *Sacramento Democratic State Journal*, December 31, 1853. State legislative journals for the Senate and Assembly for 1855–56 also contain various committee reports on prison conditions and affairs, statements of guards and officials, prison food and work details and equipment at the site.

For Smith's April 1855 escape see the *California Chronicle* and *San Francisco Daily Alta California*, April 17, 1855. For Jim's hanging experience and his revenge attempt, consult the *San Jose Semi-Weekly Tribune*, May 22, 1855. The escape with Hodges, Cherokee Bob, Bill White and others is detailed in the *San Francisco Daily Evening Bulletin*, October 22, 1856, and the *Alta*, May 14, 1855. Guard John Gray's testimony was given before a state legislative committee and published in the *Sacramento Daily Union*, February 6, 1857. Gray had come to California in company with James M. Estell, the first lease holder of the state prison. In speaking of Gray, General James W. Denver stated "that a braver man never lived," yet at the prison he was constantly drunk and was reported to have cohabited with women prisoners. When Estell lost his prison lease, he saw to it that Gray was hired at the Tejon Indian Reserve where he was killed in a drunken fight with one George Hodges *Los Angeles Star*, December 10, 1859. See also California State Assembly. "Report of Committee Relative to the Condition and Management of the State Prison." In: Assembly Journal Appendix, Document Number 26, 1855 session. Sacramento: B. R. Redding, State Printer, 1855.

Jim's various prison escapes and returns are all noted in his prison record. His 1860 capture is reported in the *Placer Herald*, July 28, 1860. The big prison break on July 22, 1862 is reported in the previously cited Lamott, *Chronicles of San Quentin*, as well as the contemporary San Francisco press. The mess hall escape attempt was reported in the *San Francisco Bulletin*, January 15, and the *Alta*, January 16, 1866. The eyewitness account of the flogging appeared in the *Bulletin* of January 17, 1866. Charles Mortimer's recollections were published in his autobiography, *Life and Career of Charles Mortimer*, Sacramento: William H. Mills & Co., 1873.

The capture of Smith and Wilson is reported in the *Sacramento Bee*, January 29 and the *Placerville Mountain Democrat*, February 5, 1876. Charles Pratt's long prison record is noted both in the San Quentin "Prison Register," and the previously cited Wells Fargo "Robbers Record." Pratt died in prison in March of 1883. For data on the prison condition and grounds during the 1870s, see *Appendix to Journals of Senate and Assembly of the Nineteenth Session of the Legislature of the State of California, Vol. III*, 1872. Sacramento: California.

Jim's work in the brick factory at San Quentin and his pardon, lapse, and recapture are all reported in the *Sacramento Bee*, November 30, 1879. The old convict's recollections appeared in, of all places, the *New York Sun*, July 13, 1884. The dispatch was sent in by a California correspondent datelined San Francisco, July 7. It is difficult to check Jim's stories, but his levity suggests he may have livened them up for the reporter's benefit. The reader hungers for Jim's version of his many escapes from prison.

Smith's death date at the Napa State Insane Asylum was reported in a letter dated January 16, 1987, to the author from Sharon Hosler, Assistant to the Executive Director, Napa State Hospital, Napa, California. For the handling of the insane in the late nineteenth century, see Fox, Richard W. *So Far Disordered in Mind: Insanity in California, 1870-1930*. Berkeley, Los Angeles, London: University of California Press, 1978.

*Niles Searles prosecuted Dorsey and Collins at their Nevada City trial. Nevada City Historical Society.*

*The Nevada County Courthouse, where the Cummings murder trial was held, is at the top of the hill. The saloon in the foreground had the unique distinction of being able to advertise—"Go to Blazes." And during trial recesses, no doubt everyone did. Pat Jones collection.*

# 5 "There's nothing in stealing"

## Charles Dorsey's Story

*The murderous stage robber Charles Dorsey as he appeared at the height of his criminal career. Author's collection.*

"**H**is face is one of a thousand," noted a reporter in describing Charles Dorsey. "High cheek bones, lantern jaws, stiff and stubby gray mustache and sunken cheeks, all give him a repulsive yet strangely attractive expression. The eyes, though, are the greatest feature. They are almost coal black and very deep set. They appear to be constantly on the alert for some approaching danger, and are never at ease."

His eyes were indeed Charley's most prominent feature. When a *San Francisco Examiner* reporter saw a mug shot of the convict in 1892, he cooked up a fictional news article in which Dorsey hypnotised his fellow convicts to do his will. Dorsey, the reporter fantasized, had hypnotised George Shinn to assist him when the two men made their noted escape from San Quentin in 1887. With a headline reading, "Hypnotism Helping Crime," the article was a typical, irresponsible *Examiner* headline in the tradition of the supermarket tabloids of today. Aiming to expand circulation and garner advertising, publisher William Randolph Hearst never let the truth get in the way of a good story. The article did, however, emphasize the public interest in Dorsey.

He was a burglar, stage robber and murderer, yet in his last years there were those who lauded him for his reformation, hard work and integrity. His story is fascinating. He died in obscurity, at the age of ninety-three, yet remains one of the most enigmatic and desperate criminals of old California.

Dorsey himself told what little he wanted known about his early life to a *San Francisco Chronicle* reporter in 1890:

*I was born in Kentucky in 1841. My parents were well-to-do people. From my birth I was a victim of circumstances, a creature of fate, a victim for other people to* *make money on. I was a boy on my father's farm when the war broke out and entered the rebel army with a gang of raiders. After serving four years, during which time my two brothers were killed and my father's home broken up, I came to California in 1865 without a trade, money or friends. I ran around the country, fell in with an ex-convict named Brown, and for stealing $60 out of a room in Grass Valley I was sent up for two years. I used the names Charles H. Thorn, Charles Dorsey and A. D. Moore. In Chicago I was known as Charles H. Lee. My true name I have never divulged.*

*After I served my two years I got into trouble again in El Dorado County and was sent up for four years for robbery. I was next sentenced from Stanislaus County for ten years for robbery. Three men were sent up for that crime. I was innocent, and knew nothing of the robbery until two days after it occurred. I was given a new trial and my sentence was increased to fifteen years. I never served the time, however. It little matters how I got out of it, but I did not escape.*

Using the name Charles Dorsey, he had been convicted of robbing the home of M. L. Marsh in Nevada County, entering San Quentin on August 30, 1865. Although the prison had three large buildings housing cellblocks at this time, officials still struggled with overcrowding. Many convicts were engaged

*San Quentin, California's state prison, as it looked when Dorsey sojourned there in the 1860s. California State Library.*

in work at the prison, however, as reported in the *Yreka Weekly Union*, November 24, 1866:

> State Prison—There are about 700 convicts. From 100 to 150 are employed in the care of the prison. The following are at work at thirty to thirty-five cents a day: Carr & Co. have 125 brickyard hands employed, Kimball 25 in the wagon shop, Stone & Hayden 150 in the saddle and harness shops, G. K. Potter 80 in the boot and shoe shop, the Mission Woolen Mills Co. 70 in the clothing department, and James Dows 40 to 50 in the cooper shops....

As number 3092 Dorsey served most of his two year term and was discharged on May 10, 1867. Under the name Charles Moore, he was convicted of a robbery in Stanislaus County and again admitted to San Quentin on March 13, 1873. This time, as number 5528, it was a fifteen year term.

Dorsey found the prison still overcrowded, some 931 inmates being housed in 444 cells. In the next few years he became particular pals with horse thieves Ben Frazee and Jim Crum and a burglar named John Collins. The men exchanged tales of their larcenous activities and as their terms neared an end, looked forward to getting together on the outside. It was yet another example of San

Banker William Cummings, killed by Dorsey during the Eureka stage robbery. California State Library.

Quentin's reputation as a "school of crime" and a conspirator's paradise.

When Dorsey's sentence was commuted on October 29, 1878, he joined Jim Crum and Ben Frazee at the latter's ranch in Nevada County. That winter the trio stole horses and spent their money in saloons and card games. When John Collins was released in June 1879, he joined Dorsey and Crum in robbing a stage in Tuolumne County. Further robberies were planned, but Crum became uneasy and went his own way. Dorsey and Collins then proceeded to Frazee's ranch in August where they plotted another stage holdup.

On September 1, 1879, the Eureka stage rattled down through the Sierra Nevada mountains in Nevada County. After leaving Eureka, the coach passed through Moore's Flat and was about three miles northeast of Nevada City when it was stopped by two highwaymen who stepped out of the bushes alongside the road. As John Collins directed the passengers to get out, Dorsey waved a shotgun alternately at both the travelers and the driver.

After robbing the passengers, Dorsey directed Collins to throw all the luggage and the express box out into the road. When this was done, the valise of banker William F. Cummings was discovered to contain two bars of gold bullion. When Cummings saw that they were taking his gold, he rushed forward and tried to seize it from Collins, who resisted fiercely. As the two men struggled for the valise, they fell to the ground. Cummings managed to get back on his feet first, but Dorsey, seeing his opportunity, shot him in the neck and killed him instantly. With the dead banker sprawled in the road, the two bandits gathered up their booty and ordered the stage driver to move on.

The two outlaws lost no time in fleeing the state in a wagon and traveled overland to Prescott, Arizona. Selling their wagon, the two outlaws made their way to Kansas City, then down to New Orleans. Here one of the gold bars was melted down for coin, while the other was shipped to the Philadelphia mint where it was also converted to coin and sent to Louisville, Kentucky where Dorsey and Collins reclaimed it. They had made nearly eight thousand dollars in the transaction and after dividing their ill-gotten gains, decided it was safer to separate.

Collins took up with a woman and made a tour of the East until his money ran out. He was soon back at his old burglary trade.

Drifting to Union City, Indiana, Dorsey posed as a man of means, once presenting a thousand dollar bill to the local bank. He had an affable nature and after acquiring a good reputation in the town, he had no trouble investing in several businesses. By mid-1882 he was a partner in a thriving lumber company.

In December 1880, Collins was picked up on a burglary charge in Saint Louis. He was tried and convicted, but immediately began filing appeals. Still in touch with Dorsey, he now wrote to Union City asking his old partner to come up with an alibi for use in his appeals. The ever resourceful Dorsey faked two affidavits, signing them in the names of two Union City businessmen named John Rigger and John Smith. Sending his own letter along with the declarations, Dorsey signed it as "C. H. Thorne, Agent and Attorney." It was a bad mistake.

The depositions "proved" that Collins was in Union City on the night of the burglary and were enough to convince the jury. In describing his trip from Union City to Saint Louis, however, Collins noted that he had traveled from Memphis to Saint Louis in twelve hours. Marshall McDonald, the prosecutor, slipped out of court at this time and returned shortly with a railroad official who testified that such a trip would take twenty-two hours. "On this slight discrepancy," reported the *St. Louis Republican* with a touch of sarcasm, "Mr. Collins was convicted and sentenced to the penitentiary. He was afterwards indicted for perjury."

An incredibly serendipitous occurrence now took place. As Collins was walking in the jailyard one day, he was surprised to see Roger O'Meara, an ex-convict he had known in San Quentin. Collins asked him about California news, particularly the investigation of the stage robbery in which banker Cummings was killed. When told the robbers had not been caught, Collins smiled and confessed that he and Dorsey had done the job. He told O'Meara all the details of the incident, little knowing he was talking to someone who was desperately looking for a way out of his own burglary rap.

In California, the Eureka stage robbery investigation had indeed gone nowhere, and despite large rewards being offered, finally petered out. The most promising clue seemed to be that two ex-convicts, Dorsey and Collins, had been seen in the area prior to the murder and robbery. They seemed to have disappeared into thin air, however.

The case was all but forgotten, until San Francisco Police Chief Patrick Crowley received a letter from his counterpart in Saint Louis. Collins' confession to O'Meara was given for what it was worth, along with a mug shot of the prisoner. Crowley and his chief of detectives, Isaiah W. Lees, scanned their own mug books and exchanged knowing smiles when they found Collins' portrait.

Wells Fargo Detective Charles Aull had previously been a San Quentin official and had known Collins. Lees and Aull were promptly on the train for Saint Louis where they arrived on September 26, 1882. They easily identified Collins as the man they were after. In talking to O'Meara

*Charles Aull (above), a Wells Fargo detective, and San Francisco Detective Captain I. W. Lees brought Dorsey and Collins back from their sojourn in the Midwest. Folsom Prison Archives.*

and District Attorney McDonald, the two detectives began assembling clues as to Collins' recent movements. When McDonald showed them the two affidavits and the accompanying letter from Union City, Aull recognized Dorsey's handwriting and the two were soon on their way to Indiana as noted in the *Union City Times*, October 7:

*Dorsey's partner, Collins, was hanged for the Cummings murder. Author's collection.*

Quite a furor was raised in our usually quiet city last Monday morning at the arrest of Chas. Thorne, partner of Moses Murphy, by two strangers....They found Charley eating his breakfast at Branham's restaurant and walking up to him the arrest was made without any resistance on his part. He was taken to St. Louis on the Excursion train....

Lees and Aull deposited Dorsey in jail, then began backtracking the two outlaws based on information obtained from O'Meara and Collins' attorney. At New Orleans they located the mint official who had handled the gold bar. At Louisville they found the saloon keeper who had kept the other gold bar, then traced the shipment to the Philadelphia mint through the Adams Express Company. On October 17 the *San Francisco Chronicle* noted:

### Arrival of the Stage Robbers

The overland train brought to this city yesterday Captains Lees and Aull, who had in custody John C. Patterson (Collins) and Charles Dorsey, notorious criminals against whom are pending charges of robbing a stage...and killing William C. Cummings....Captain Lees remarked to a *Chronicle* reporter last evening that the trip from the East was tiresome and tedious in the extreme, and was rendered more so by the ceaseless vigil kept over the prisoners night and day.

The two stage robbers were lodged in the county jail at Nevada City, California. Lees, Aull and other lawmen had put together an airtight case for the prosecution, bringing in witnesses from around the country to establish the travels and activities of the two outlaws. The Nevada County *Grass Valley Union* reported:

The history of this crime, the disappearance of the criminals, and their discovery after three years of time, is a strange chapter of criminal history, and the manner in which the case has been worked up by Aull and Lees is one of the most creditable pieces of detective skill of the time.

Dorsey was tried first, his trial lasting some eleven days. He was convicted, but given a life sentence because several jurors believed he might have been in Union City at the time of the robbery and murder. Dorsey himself later told a different story: "There is still a mystery about that affair to clear away....I escaped in this way: One of the jurymen was a soldier with me in the rebel army and he held out against the other eleven jurors and thus saved my neck."

Ironically, Collins was hanged, even though it was proved that Dorsey had done the shooting. Dorsey himself was quoted by the *Grass Valley Union* as saying that "the verdict was wrong, as the evidence showed that he should be hanged for murder or was entitled to an acquittal."

On March 15, 1883, Dorsey again entered the cold walls of San Quentin as number 10760. Always stoic and reticent in manner, he nevertheless frequently remarked that he would never spend the rest of his life in prison. As the years rolled by he made few friends, his restless eyes seemingly always looking for the slightest chance of escape. He was seen on occasion with the notorious Charles Boles, the famed "Black Bart." Another acquaintance was a trusty named George Shinn who had tried to rob a train by wrecking it. Apparently he considered these men of sufficient stature to warrant his association.

Isaiah W. Lees, one of the great detectives of the nineteenth century, helped capture Dorsey and Collins and build the case against them. Author's collection.

When Charley became ill in October 1885, he was sent to the hospital to recuperate. With a convict named Martin Tracy who was working as a nurse, Dorsey soon hatched an escape plan. Acquiring the aid of several others, the two convicts obtained crude saws and began cutting through the bars on the windows. Progress was slow, however, and Dorsey soon developed a better plan. In an adjoining room there was a closet. Removing the back from the closet exposed a brick wall and the men began chiseling out the mortar and removing the bricks. The time spent by the convicts waiting for a foggy or particularly dark night, however, gave prison officials time to get wind of the plot. Caught in the act, Dorsey and his pals were heaved into the dungeon and taken out and questioned separately. Under the heading "A Desperate High-wayman," the *San Francisco Chronicle* reported:

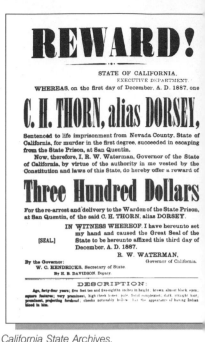

...Dorsey was taken out afterwards, and when questioned took the whole blame upon himself for leading the others into the scheme. He exonerated Sullivan of any participation in the proposed escape and then sullenly sat down on a bench in the room. He bitterly said that he was tired of living, as he had no hope of ever being released, and he preferred being killed while attempting to escape to serving out his sentence until death

*California State Archives.*

came to his relief. He suddenly sprang from his seat and made a threatening gesture as if intent upon attacking the officers who were in the room. The officials saw that the hostile movement was made in the belief that some one of them would shoot him, and Dorsey was disappointed when he was led off to the cell.

But if Dorsey's spirit was broken, he quickly recovered. His trusty pal, George Shinn, was in charge of the garbage wagon hauling trash out through the prison gates. The two men conspired to take advantage of this routine to make their escape and waited until December 1, 1887, a black and rain-swept night.

With Dorsey hidden under some canvas and garbage in the bed of the wagon, Shinn waved at the guard as he drove past the gatekeeper and into the night. At the wharf the two convicts pushed a rowboat into the stormy waters and headed across the bay to Contra Costa County. Dorsey later told the story to a Sacramento newsman:

*I would have died in those hills had not George begged me to keep up heart and fight it out. I wanted him to go on and leave me to die alone. I told him to take what money I had and make his escape. I felt that I could never pull through, and did not want to jeopardize his chances. But he would not listen to the proposition and said that if I stopped he would stop. So I took heart again and trudged bravely on. George stood it better than I did, because I became sick.*

*Hardships! Let me tell you, young man, nobody can conceive, nobody knows, or ever can know, what we suffered. It was in winter when we effected our escape, and it was storming fearfully at the time. We left San Quentin prison in a boat and landed on the Contra Costa shore drenched to the skin and numb with cold. We struck out immediately for the hills. We had to hide in the brush by day and travel what little we could by night. It rained all the time, yet we did not dare to build a fire to warm ourselves. We were nearly famished and ate raw vegetables and whatever we could lay our hands on. It was only the mental strain and excitement that kept us from giving up entirely. Every now and then we would see the mounted officers searching for us and that did not add to our peace of mind. I was sick and tried to persuade Shinn to go on and look out for himself, but he wouldn't do it. I was well acquainted with the country over which we were traveling, but never did it seem such a vast and endless wilderness. Finally, however, we reached Benecia, and could hardly drag one foot after the other. We took the train there to Sacramento, and upon arriving there had our first square meal.*

*Well, resumed Dorsey, we camped for some time near Sacramento, in a little cabin near Perkins, and pretended to be miners. Then we pulled up stakes for the East. We got down in Arizona next and worked at various things—all hard work.*

A stagecoach in the mountains in the days when Dorsey and Shinn were active as road agents. California State Archives.

*We located at Colorado Springs next, and there Shinn left me and went to Denver for a while, but came back and joined me later on.*

Eventually the two desperadoes went to Chicago where they engaged in odd jobs and in some burglaries. Yearning for more excitement, they returned to California where, in July 1889, they initiated a series of holdups, but added little to their pockets. They pulled off a few muggings and stickups around Chico and Oroville, then held up a saloon near Marysville. Disappointed at their take, the two outlaws held up the Sonora-Milton stage on July 31, but the express box was empty and they netted only about $50 from the passengers.

On September 10, they stopped the Quincy to Oroville stage, securing a gold bar worth nearly $800. They hid out in a secret cabin on the American River near Sacramento where they were joined by an ex-con named Mickey Delaney. The three outlaws then attempted the holdup of M. G. Dandried's Sacramento saloon. The job blew up in their faces when the owner ran for his rifle in a back room. Dorsey followed him and managed to shoot him several times before fleeing with his pals into the night. Dandried followed and fired at them, but his aim was bad due to his wounds.

The outlaws engaged in another series of petty robberies, then in early April 1890 they stopped the Forest Hill stage. When a passenger refused to be robbed, Dorsey stepped forward and would have shot him if Shinn hadn't interfered. Continuing their depredations, the outlaws abruptly decided California was becoming too hot for them when Shinn narrowly missed being nabbed by the Sacramento police. In late June the two highwaymen returned to Chicago.

George Shinn, the convict who broke out of San Quentin with Dorsey in 1887. From an old Wells Fargo mug shot in Author's collection.

In the Windy City the two desperadoes set up a carpet cleaning business as a ruse for locating likely burglary prospects. George Shinn later recalled that they had committed some twenty-odd "jobs" when fate again interfered in an incredible way.

By some mind-boggling coincidence, Roger O'Meara had turned up in Chicago and spotted a familiar face on the street. On July 3, 1890, he wrote of his experience in a letter to the *Nevada City Daily Transcript*:

Dorsey's mug shot upon his recapture and return to San Quentin in 1890. California State Archives.

Editor Transcript—Dear Sir—You may be surprised to learn that I met Charlie Dorsey and a companion today at about 11 o'clock on Lake Street of this city.

He appeared to recognize me at the first glance as he passed me, but could not restrain himself from turning and sizing me up....The cruel eyes so well remembered of the fugitive murderer looked fiercely and fearlessly at me, though a policeman was on the corner (Clark and Lake) within easy call.

Dorsey and his companion had evidently but recently arrived in this city. They were dressed each in a new ready, made suit of dark clothes. They were tanned by the sun, no doubt having traveled much under its rays. Dorsey was clean shaven with several days growth of beard.

After ruminating about how his services were unappreciated for his Saint Louis work and how the officers always got all the credit for what others did, O'Meara closed by remarking that he let Dorsey go his own way rather than turn him in to the authorities. But he should have known the California detectives had caught criminals on far less information. When Wells Fargo Special Officer James B. Hume got wind of the letter, he obtained a copy and was quickly on the train for Chicago.

Enlisting the aid of Pinkerton detectives, Hume directed the hunt for the two fugitives. It was nearly two weeks before they were located. Shinn was trapped at his boarding house and later that evening Dorsey was called from his supper and walked into the arms of the detectives.

"I guess it's a groundhog case," commented the outlaw. "Come on, I'm ready."

Shinn's wife had reportedly been with him, but she had disappeared. Dorsey had also been living with a woman at various times, but she too could not be found. Putting chains and heavy, metal Oregon Boots on the two outlaws, Hume wired San Quentin officials and asked that officers be sent with requisition papers to meet him in Chicago. When Captains Edward Reddy and C. N. Fish arrived, the party was on the next train to the coast.

They reached Sacramento early Sunday morning, October 26, 1890. The two fugitives were soon back in their cells at San Quentin.

The outlaws were repeatedly sought by reporters, Dorsey being interviewed by a *San Francisco Chronicle* representative at San Quentin on October 28. Back in prison stripes behind the terrible walls of prison, he now fully realized his situation:

*I have now nothing left on God's green earth but a bad name. I have no money, not even a ten cent piece to rattle on a tombstone. They charge me with the Pixley train robbery, when I am not even familiar with the case. They can take me out and hang me for this crime, for it is the easiest matter in the world to convict a man if he's got a bad name. I'm an old man now, and all broke down; I'm buried. Life at best is not worth living, and when you get down to the lowest, as I have done, it's about time to shuffle off. Get me out of here and give me a two hours start, and I could not get away. There is such a thing as fate, and you can't get away from it. Here they will keep me in a solitary cell, just as if I could fly over the wall. There's nothing in stealing. Of all things that is the poorest. I learned the truth only too late in life. By the gods, a man once down in life is down for all time, and nothing can stem the tide of fate that's turned against him.*

But Charlie didn't stay down for long. Before a year had elapsed he was deeply involved in a much more elaborate escape plot. His old pal Mickey Delaney was back in prison also and he too was immersed in the scheme.

Convict C. C. Sullivan had a brother living in Watsonville. Over a period of time he brought five pistols to the prison in a desperate attempt to free his kin. The weapons were delivered to a trusty named Welles who was allowed outside the walls every day to serve as an aid to the prison physician. Welles hid the guns in a bucket of milk and in this way smuggled them into the prison.

The pistols were then given to convict Abe Turcott who worked in the prison carpentry shop. In the shop's privy Turcott had discovered a trap door leading to a narrow passage under the building. He had hidden the weapons and some 300 rounds of ammunition at the end of the passage as he and the other six conspirators waited for the moment to make their break.

Although those involved were careful not to tell other convicts of their plan, by September 1891, Warden William Hale and Captain John Edgar knew that something was in the wind. Putting an outsider in stripes and having him mingle with the convicts soon established that an escape attempt was imminent and that hidden guns were involved. Warden Hale was now forced to act.

Seven convicts were isolated as the leaders and one by one were queried about the plot. Charles Dorsey denied any knowledge of such a plan, as did Abe Turcott, Sullivan, and Delaney. Burglar George Ross and stage robbers H. W. Hanlon and Charles Manning also played dumb. Each of the convicts was strip-searched, locked in solitary and placed on bread and water. Told this was to be their fare until someone talked, the convicts still refused to say anything.

Mickey Delaney, a notorious burglar and highwayman, was Dorsey's pal inside prison and out. Author's collection.

When Sullivan's brother was arrested in Watsonville, the plot quickly began to unravel. Only when Welles came forward and confessed were the prison officials certain that guns were indeed actually hidden on the prison grounds. Although Hale now had good reason to flog or hang the prisoners by their thumbs til they confessed, he refused to do so. And his patience paid off. Turcott called Captain Edgar and confirmed that the pistols had been hidden under the carpentry shop. The convict led Warden Hale and Edgar to the trapdoor in the shop privy, then wriggled through the narrow passage and retrieved the weapons.

"TURCOTT CONFESSES," shouted the headlines in the *San Francisco Chronicle* on September 26. Another escape plot had been foiled and Warden Hale could relax until the next rumor surfaced. C. C. Sullivan, regarded as the leader of the plot, was shipped to Folsom to separate him from the other convicts. Dorsey and the balance of the conspirators were all long-termers and there was little to be done to them. Charley probably resigned himself to his fate at this time.

In 1907 John E. Hoyle took office as Warden. A thoughtful, kindly man, the new warden exemplified the so-called "New Penology" which gave men like Dorsey hope they could cling to. A California parole law had been enacted in 1893 and after the turn of the century new, more modern cell blocks were constructed to ease the overcrowding. Hoyle introduced segregation of prisoners, inspirational speakers to address the convicts and various other innovative programs. Although he had his detractors, Hoyle would later be characterized as a man who, if he were superseded by Jesus Christ, "the majority of the convicts would find fault with His administration."

Charley mellowed over the years. Escape was no longer an option in the old man's mind. Prison was a way of life. He would die in San Quentin. Still rough and crude by nature, he was recognized as one who could be depended upon and as he grew older he was given easier jobs.

Fremont Older was editor of the *San Francisco Call* in the early 1900s. Liberal in principles, he sought to correct society's ills by pointing out the excesses of big government and capitalists of the time. Gradually Older came to admit, however, that if you "take the money from the rich and give it to the poor, the poor would be as unbearable as the rich are now." Still, he remained socially conscious to the extent that he had an overwhelming curiosity about lawbreakers. Why were they criminals? Could help and kindness turn them around? Did society mold them, or were they born villains and their course charted from the moment of birth? He could never make up his mind about such matters, but for years he had a string of ex-convicts working at his ranch as a sort of way station until they got their feet on the ground.

Older made many trips to San Quentin where he met and talked to prisoners. When a convict impressed him, he would work to secure him a pardon. Sometimes he would publish their stories, but he was always sympathetic. On one trip he was shown the scaffold and was given a recital by the convict in charge, explaining the details of how a hanging was carried out. He was struck by the convict's rather singsong spiel, as if he had given the talk many times.

He asked Warden Hoyle about this man and was told, "That's Charley Dorsey. He's in for life for murder. He was a stage robber, one of the most desperate men among the criminals of California. He's been here twenty-nine years."

Without knowing the details of his crime, Older was shocked that the old man had never been paroled.

San Quentin Warden John Hoyle. Author's collection.

"I wish you could get him paroled," replied Hoyle. "He's a fine character. I would trust him to go around the world with a million dollars. I know he would keep his word and return when he said he would, with every dollar intact."

Older talked with other convicts about Dorsey and became convinced he would make good if he were paroled. Dorsey told him of his criminal career, but rather than admit to being a murderer, he blamed the killing on his partner, John Collins. He probably didn't think he could get a pardon anyway.

The editor went to work. He had a hard time in Nevada County where feeling still ran high against Dorsey for the Cummings murder, but in time he obtained the required signatures on his petition. Governor Hiram Johnson granted Charley's parole on December 21, 1911, as a Christmas present to Older. It was a fine present for Charley, also.

That night Older and his wife took the old convict to dinner at the Fairmont Hotel in San Francisco. Later in their rooms, Charley told them of his escape in 1887 and his life in Chicago. He also told them of the girl he had

*The gallows at San Quentin where Dorsey entertained visitors to the prison. San Quentin Prison.*

been living with there just before his capture, although Charley kept his tale virtuous. They had planned to marry, he said, and had bought a lot on which to build a home. After his capture he had given her the lot deed and some $800 they had saved. Upon his return to San Quentin, they had corresponded for eleven years. Finally he had stopped writing, cautioning her that the relationship might cause trouble when she met some good man she might want to marry.

Charley took a well-handled card photograph from his pocket. "Course she doesn't look like that now. She's probably an old woman now. That was thirty years ago. I wish I knew what has become of her." Older later recalled that "it was the picture of a gentle, sweet-looking girl."

The next day the trio drove down to Older's fruit ranch in Santa Clara County. Charley was seventy years old at the time, but he went right to work, revelling in freedom, fresh air and sunshine. "He plowed from daylight to dark," Older recalled, "never seeming to tire. He ran everything connected with the ranch, made all the purchases, paid all the bills. He was perhaps one of the most exacting men in the way of honesty that I ever encountered." The old outlaw was eventually made foreman of the ranch.

Dorsey had strict ideas about the ex-cons who worked on the ranch. He always ate at the bunkhouse, although the Olders had extended a standing invitation for him to dine with them at the ranch house. One day Older brought home an ex-con who had served a short term for petty thievery. That night when Charley showed up for dinner with the Olders, they asked him why he had changed his mind. He growled: "Well, you know I can't eat with that fellow. He's a low-down thief; he's not in my class. You know, over in San Quentin there are just as many classes as there are outside, and more, too. I can't associate with a fellow like that." He was probably recalling his prison friendship with the noted Black Bart.

When Charley grew too old for ranch work, Older secured him a job in San Francisco's Golden Gate Park. He received a full pardon about this time and when he retired at age eighty-three, there was a small pension from the

San Quentin as it appeared when Charley Dorsey obtained his pardon and went to work for Fremont Older. Author's collection.

city. Charley made money also on a few small investments, but he still kept busy, working in restaurants and raking leaves. He was ninety-three years old and living with a niece in Los Angeles when he died in 1932. He was able to leave several thousand hard-earned dollars to those who cared for him in his last illness.

"He had character and great ability," remembered Fremont Older, "qualities that might have made him a very successful man, but they were offset by a violent temper and an independent and rebellious spirit. I doubt if he would have been able to live a life without violence."

## Chapter Five / NOTES

Dorsey's description is from the *Sacramento Daily Union*, October 27, 1890. The hypnotism article was published in the *San Francisco Examiner*, October 24, 1892. Dorsey's recitation of his life story is from the *Nevada City Daily Transcript*, October 30, 1890, as reprinted from the *San Francisco Chronicle*.

The Marsh robbery is recalled in the *Grass Valley Union*, March 2, 1883. Dorsey's first entrance into San Quentin and his later commitments are in the "Register and Descriptive List of Convicts under Sentence of Imprisonment in the State Prison of California," California State Archives, Sacramento, California.

For the number of prisoners at San Quentin in 1873, see *Appendix to Journals of Senate and Assembly of the 20th Session of the Legislature of the State of California, Vol. IX*, 1872, State Printing Office, Sacramento, California.

The story of Crum and Frazee can be found in the trial testimony in the *Grass Valley Union*, February 20, 1883 and the *San Francisco Chronicle*, November 30, 1883. For more of Crum's activities, see Dugan, Mark and John Boessenecker. *The Grey Fox*. Norman: University of Oklahoma Press, 1992. Crum led his own gang of horse thieves as noted in the *Sonora Union Democrat*, November 18, 1871.

For an account of the Cummings murder and robbery, see the *Grass Valley Union*, September 2, 3, 1879. Dorsey and Collins' travels afterwards are traced by a long article in the *San Francisco Chronicle*, August 10, 1882. Collins' Missouri trial is covered in the *St. Louis Republican*, October 10, 1882. For the whole story of the Collins and Dorsey capture and Lees and Aull's fine detective work, see the *St. Louis Republican*, September 27 and October 10, 1882, the Indiana *Union City Times*, October 7, and the *Indianapolis News*, October 3, 1882.

The *Grass Valley Union* quote is dated October 24, 1882. Dorsey's trial is fully reported in the *Union* during late February and early March of 1883. Collins' execution is the subject of a long article in the *Union*, February 2, 1884.

Dorsey's chumming with Charles "Black Bart" Boles while in San Quentin was recorded by James B. Hume, the noted Wells, Fargo detective; Dillon, Richard. *Wells, Fargo Detective*. New York: Coward-McCann, Inc., 1969. Hume once referred to Dorsey as "the worst man in all the 1,200" in San Quentin.

Dorsey's 1885 San Quentin escape attempt is detailed in the *San Francisco Chronicle* and reprinted in the *Nevada City Daily Transcript*, November 1, 1885.

Dorsey's own story of his and Shinn's escape was reported fully in the *Sacramento Daily Union*, October 27, 1890. Their Chicago and California crimes were detailed by Shinn in his later confession as published in the *Union*, November 2, 1890. See also the *Nevada City Daily Transcript*, December 4, 1887.

Roger O'Meara's letter in the *Nevada City Daily Transcript* appeared on October 18, 1890.

Dorsey and Shinn's capture in Chicago was reported in the *Nevada City Daily Transcript*, October 18, 19, 1890. See also the previously cited Dillon, *Wells, Fargo Detective*. Turcott, Hanlon and Manning were desperate characters who had escaped the previous August with guns smuggled to a spot near the prison. They had wounded one guard in the arm and shot another guard's horse out from under him as they fled the site where they had been working outside the prison walls. Cornered by a large contingent of guards and others, the men refused to surrender and hastily threw up a log fort. After a night-long gun battle, the convicts asked to confer with a local sheriff to whom they finally surrendered. See Boessenecker, John. *Badge and Buckshot*. Norman and London: University of Oklahoma Press, 1988.

Dorsey's *San Francisco Chronicle* interview was reprinted in the *Daily Transcript*, October 30, 1890.

For Dorsey's 1891 escape plot, see the *San Francisco Examiner*, September 6, 10, 26, 27, 1891 and the *San Francisco Chronicle*, September 26, 28, 39, 1891.

Information on San Quentin Warden John Hoyle can be found in Lamott, Kenneth. *Chronicles of San Quentin*. New York: David McKay Company, Inc., 1961. See also Ford, Tirey L. *California State Prisons, Their History, Development and Management*. San Francisco: The Star Press, 1910.

Fremont Older's contact with ex-convicts and his friendship with Charles Dorsey are detailed in Older, Fremont. *My Own Story*. New York: The Macmillan Company,

1926 and Wells, Evelyn. *Fremont Older.* New York: D. Appleton Century Company, Inc., 1936. The story of Dorsey as the San Quentin gallows "spieler" is from an undated Fremont Older newspaper column in the author's collection.

Dorsey's death notice is from the *California Death Certificate Index* in the California State Library, Sacramento, and the *Los Angeles Times*, September 14, 1932.

Final mementos of a ruthless desperado; the tie Tiburcio Vasquez was wearing when he was hanged, a section of the rope and the beads and medals of his faith. *California State Library.*

Monterey was an idyllic-appearing adobe village by the sea, but it housed many desperate characters during the youth of Vasquez. *California State Library.*

# 6 "I always avoided bloodshed"

## The Dangerous Days of Tiburcio Vasquez

Tiburcio Vasquez was California's most desperate outlaw for many years. California State Library.

"When we had the Nightstalker—Richard Ramirez—at our jail," recalled San Francisco Sheriff Mike Hennessey in 1997, "you couldn't believe how many people wanted to talk to him or interview him." More than one hundred years earlier, in 1874, another Hispanic outlaw sparked a similar interest. Long lines of people visited the cell of Tiburcio Vasquez after his capture, as though he were a colorful celebrity, rather than a murderous bandit. Some things never change.

One of the most colorful of the early California bandits, Tiburcio Vasquez is second in prominence only to Joaquin Murrieta and Black Bart. He was a sympathetic figure to many of his countrymen who overlooked his larcenous and bloody exploits because he primarily robbed the Americans whom they believed had "stolen" California by treaty after the Mexican War.

Many among the Hispanic population knew the real Vasquez, however. Jose Jesus Lopez, who aided in his capture, recalled that "Vasquez was a man of no principle at all. When he was not robbing some honest, hardworking person, he was busy seducing some wife or a young girl, not sparing even his own niece."

According to the 1850 Monterey County Census, Tiburcio Vasquez was born in 1835, a descendant of the earliest settlers of Mexico and California. He had three brothers and two sisters. All attended school in Monterey and Tiburcio learned to read and write both English and Spanish. Their home, situated directly behind Colton Hall, still stands in the coastal city.

The young Tiburcio was initiated into crime at an early age. A particular crony was a Monterey thug named Anastacio Garcia, and in 1854 the two were involved in a saloon brawl resulting in the death of a local constable. Vasquez and Garcia fled, while a pal named Jose Higuera was lynched the following day. The nineteen-year-old Tiburcio's feet were firmly planted upon the Primrose Path.

In July 1857, Vasquez was picked up for horse theft in Los Angeles and found himself on his way to San Quentin for a five-year stretch. He escaped

*A woodcut in the* California Police Gazette *depicts the bloody 1859 prison break in which Vasquez was involved. Some ten convicts were killed or wounded. Most were quickly recaptured, but Vasquez and a few others made good their escape. California State Library.*

during the big break of June 25, 1859, but was soon recaptured on another rustling charge as reported in the *California Police Gazette* the following July:

> The two Mexicans arrested for stealing horses at Jackson, prove to be two escaped State Prison convicts. One of them is Jesus Mindosa, who was sent to the State Prison from Los Angeles, a year or two since, for stealing horses, and the other is Teburzo Baskes (sic), who was sent from the same county for the same offense. Both escaped from the State Prison, June 25th.

Back in prison, Tiburcio kept his eyes open for another opportunity to escape. He didn't have long to wait. In late September, Vasquez and some twenty other prisoners were unloading wood from the schooner *Bolinas.* After the noon meal, the convicts were marched back to the wharf to begin reloading the schooner with bricks. Suddenly, several of the prisoners seized guard

A. D. Moon and quickly rushed him aboard the ship. As convicts hustled the schooner's captain and mate below decks, others frantically hoisted the sails and prepared to cast off.

As the schooner's sails caught the wind and it began to move, the ship had barely turned about when it suddenly stalled in the water. The convicts had forgotten the ship was moored to a buoy. Before they could figure out what happened, the nearest guardpost opened fire with a cannon burst of cannister shot. Several convicts were wounded as they thrust guard Moon to the front as a shield. Prison policy, then and now, dictated that guards must fire on escaping convicts even if they had hostages.

As rifle fire and more cannister ripped into the schooner and the convicts, Moon's left arm was broken by a shot, and wounded and dying convicts dropped around him. Completely demoralized, the prisoners now sought shelter below decks or dropped over the side into the water. As the cannister and rifle fire continued, a white flag was suddenly seen being waved from the ship. Several boats manned by guards now signaled to cease firing as they rowed toward the torn and punctured schooner.

Boarding the vessel, the guards quickly rounded up the sullen convicts and supervised loading the wounded in the boats. Convict A. B. Winchell was found dead, riddled with rifle and grapeshot. John Dixon was shot in the chest and died a short time later. Seven other prisoners were injured, several with what were thought to be mortal wounds. Eleven of the would-be escapees were unhurt, among them Tiburcio Vasquez.

Back in the prison, the wounded were hospitalized, while Vasquez and the others were heavily ironed and thrown in one of the dungeon cells. A week or so later Tiburcio managed to write a letter to his mother in which he complained of his treatment:

*Beloved Mother: Perhaps you are not aware of the difficulties that I have to surmount and overcome every time I feel inclined to open my heart to you by way of a few badly written lines, but I hope you will overlook the little faults and mistakes of your unfortunate son.*

*A month ago I wrote to you and sent the letter by A. S. Berreyesa, which gentleman was here visiting sone cousins of his…but I have received no answer to the same yet. The contents of said letter was to give you information of an unfortunate affair into which I was led. I left the place during a riot, and was arrested a month after in the San Joaquin Pass, and very near to you, by a party of armed men, who took us (my friend and me) by surprise, and brought us back again here, and after two months of close, hard confinement in prison they put me again to hard work.*

*A party of Americans one day took possession of a small vessel, and I went with them, but by being unused to working a vessel the guns and rifles from the shore soon put our craft unmanageable; and out of fifteen men on board three were shot on the spot, and five badly wounded....I came out without a scratch, although being like the rest in the midst of the shot and the grape....I, therefore, now most earnestly beg you to come and see me, as I am overloaded with irons, and, without any cause, cruelly ill treated.*

*Courage mother, do not lose your spirits for me. Your son was born to suffer, and the Supreme Being shall assist him in all this time of distress until he may again go to serve his mother once more.*

Vasquez had lied to his mother, implying he was on his way to visit her when he was captured in the Pacheco Pass the previous July. Actually, he was captured in the Gold Rush country on the other side of the San Joaquin Valley. It is difficult to understand why he would want to worry his mother by describing two desperate attempts to escape prison, but he undoubtedly had an ulterior motive in doing so.

Tiburcio gave his letter to a man named S. T. Bee, thought to be a cousin, who promised to post it to his mother. On October 15, 1859, the *Sacramento Daily Union* reported the theft of three saddles from the village of Lafayette, in Alameda County. A posse was quickly formed and three Mexican thieves, thought to be riding stolen horses, were tracked to their camp in the foothills of Mount Diablo:

> The camp was immediately surrounded, and the Spaniards called upon to surrender; upon which they broke for the brush. The pursuing party fired upon them, wounded one, when the two others immediately surrendered. They were carried to the Walnut Creek House, where the wounded man died this morning....

On the dead outlaw's body was found a letter addressed to "Sra Dona Guadalupe Cantua," the mother of Vasquez. She probably never received her son's letter.

Tiburcio served out his term this time and was released in August 1863. The following year he was again in serious trouble. Vasquez and a cousin, Faustino Lorenzana, were suspected of the murder of a butcher in Santa Clara County, but Sheriff John H. Adams could find little evidence and the killers quickly disappeared. After an unsuccessful store burglary in Mendocino

County, Vasquez found himself back in San Quentin in January 1867.

When he was released from prison in June 1870, Vasquez returned home to Monterey. He soon drifted over to San Juan where he had an affair with the wife of his friend, Abelardo Salazar. Leaving with the woman, Vasquez soon tired of the dalliance and abandoned her. Unexpectedly accosted by Salazar one night in San Juan, Tiburcio was badly wounded in the resulting gunfight. He escaped into the Coast Range mountains where he recuperated at a hideout in the Cantua Creek area.

*Abelardo Salazar repaid Vasquez' treachery with gunsmoke. From the 1865 San Francisco Police mugbook. John Boessenecker collection.*

Women were a constant distraction for Vasquez. This continual skirt chasing resulted in shootings, alienation of friends and gang members and ultimately his downfall.

On August 17, 1871, Vasquez, Narciso Rodriguez, and Francisco Barcenas stopped the Visalia stage between San Jose and Pacheco Pass. They robbed several other travelers at the same time and lawmen were quickly on their trail. A posse led by Santa Cruz Sheriff Charles Lincoln trapped the outlaws in the Lorenzana family barn at Branciforte, near Santa Cruz. When Barcenas

*Street scene in old San Juan showing the Plaza Hotel in the days when Vasquez had his shootout with Abelardo Salazar. San Juan Bautista Historical Society.*

was flushed from the barn, a deadly gunfight took place as recounted in the *Santa Cruz Sentinel* of September 16, 1871:

> ...Haynes leveled his gun—a double barrel shotgun—and snapped three caps, while the revolver of his desperate assailant cracked away at him, it also being a miss shot, by about two inches, rendered such by the deadly aim of Majors who fired at him the ball striking him square in the mouth thus making his aim unsteady. Not 'til he had received another shot which entered below the right eye and penetrated the brain did he drop, and even then in his death struggle, he grasped for his revolver, now useless in his hands. Another shot from the pistol of Majors put an end to the desperado's earthly career....

Barcenas was killed, but Vasquez managed to escape, although badly wounded. Rodriguez was arrested the next day and was soon on his way to San Quentin. After recuperating at his Coast Range hideout, Vasquez began assembling a new gang, initiating the series of raids that soon made his name a terror throughout the state.

Picking Clodoveo Chavez, a San Juan resident, as his first lieutenant, Vasquez recruited Abdon Leiva, Teodoro Moreno, Romulo Gonzales and others for his new gang. He often recruited for particular jobs and always had his eye out for a promising young bandido. Victor Gardenas was a muscular, orphaned teenager doing ranch work when several of the Vasquez gang approached him:

> When I was fourteen years old the Vasquez gang came to the Sotelo ranch and they urged me to join their group. I hesitated, knowing their reputation. They talked with me for about an hour with Vasquez astride his horse a short distance away.
>
> Finally Vasquez drove up and told his men to leave me alone. He then gave me the advice I shall never forget when he said, "My child, it is very wise of you not to follow our gang because this is a sad life. Sometimes you don't eat or sleep, always waiting for the enemy to overcome you."

*Henry Miller, prominent cattleman and land owner. Author's collection.*

Not one to heed his own advice, Vasquez planned a raid on the payroll of cattleman Henry Miller at the small settlement of Firebaugh's Ferry on the San Joaquin River. Using Abdon Leiva's ranch house as a staging area, Vasquez

Like most ferry operations, Firebaugh's contained a store, saloon and stage stop. Such isolated locations were tempting targets for roving outlaws. Elliott's History of Fresno County.

promptly seduced Rosaria, Leiva's wife, while plotting the robbery.

Tiburcio and four men appeared at the ferry just after dark on February 26, 1873. The $30,000 payroll didn't arrive as planned, so the bandits proceeded to rob and tie up twelve people in Hoffman's store, then plundered the safe. When a stagecoach pulled up in front of the station, it too was ransacked. After the robbery, the outlaws scattered and laid low, resulting in a rumor published in an April edition of the *Fresno Weekly Expositor:*

A San Jose dispatch of the 17th inst. says: A letter received by the Sheriff from his deputy at Gilroy states that Basquez, a notorious road agent, was killed last week by one Castro, at Cantour, a point about thirty miles below New Idria. Basquez was a young Californian, a trim built, active fellow, daring and desperate, a professional gambler and a complete outlaw. He led the gang which attacked a stage at Firebaugh's Ferry. Sheriff Adams, of this county, has been looking after him for a long time with a bench warrant. There is much rejoicing at the news of the death of this desperado.

Any celebrating was premature. Whether Vasquez actually had a scrap with someone named Castro is not known, but "Cantour" obviously refers to the Vasquez hideout in the Cantua Creek area. A Jorge Castro was one of the early Cantua area settlers of the late 1850s and this may be the "Castro" referred to in the above article.

Vasquez was soon planning new raids. When a train robbery fell through in late July 1873, he robbed the Twenty-One Mile House, a hotel and restaurant on the rail line near Gilroy. The gang next slipped into the tiny settlement of Tres Pinos on August 26, and while robbing Snyder's store, they shot and killed three innocent bystanders. Packing all the plunder they could carry on eleven stolen horses, the outlaws fled south. A posse led by Santa Clara County Sheriff John H. Adams was quickly on the bandits' trail. Trailing the fugitives south to Los Angeles County, Adams' posse had a brief shootout in Rock Creek Canyon and even captured some of the stolen loot, but the outlaws managed to escape.

Leiva's wife had accompanied the outlaws in their flight and at this time Abdon discovered his wife and Tiburcio in a compromising situation. He immediately fled to blow the whistle on his treacherous, erstwhile boss.

On November 10, Vasquez struck at an isolated ferry crossing on the San Joaquin River. Located some two miles below the village of Millerton, Jones' store was a typical Vasquez scenario. Nearly a dozen men were in the place that evening, six or eight playing cards at two tables, while several others watched. Smith Norris, the clerk, was busy behind the counter. It was about six o'clock in the evening when both the front and rear doors burst open and six Mexicans, flourishing pistols, yelled "Put up your hands!"

John Bugg, Walter Brown and John Berry looked up with the others in startled surprise. Everyone was told to get down on the floor on their faces. When they did so, their hands were quickly tied behind their backs. John Bugg recognized the dark-skinned Mexican who ordered him to the floor. "You damned, black bastard," Bugg snarled as he dropped to the floor, "if I had my six shooter, I'd show you whether I'd lie down or not!"

All the men were robbed, then Norris was made to open the safe from which some thousand dollars was extracted. While two lookouts held the horses outside, the bandits stayed for an hour and a half, drinking at the bar and stealing whatever goods struck their fancy. Finally, with a salute of "Adios,

Ysidro Padilla was with Vasquez on the Kingston raid, then later led his own gang. He died in prison. John Boessenecker collection.

Caballeros," the outlaws swaggered outside and in a moment disappeared into the bitterly cold night. The Chinese cook untied himself and a patron, Captain Fisher, then the two quickly released the others.

Fisher headed for Millerton to alert Sheriff Scott Ashman, while Bugg headed home to arm himself. He joined the sheriff's posse the next morning, but it was a fruitless chase, the bandits vanishing into the fastnesses of the Coast Range.

On December 26, Vasquez and his men suddenly appeared some miles to the south at the small village of Kingston, on the Kings River. Vasquez had recruited a large force at this time, consisting of Blas Bicuna, Ramon Molina, Ysidro Padilla, Manuel Gomez, Ignacio Ranquel and three or four others. Tying their horses, the bandits walked across the toll bridge and entered several stores. They tied up and robbed some thirty-five victims, then pilfered every safe they could find. When local rancher John Sutherland was alerted to the bandits, he opened fire, forcing them to flee across the toll bridge and out of town. Several of the raiders were wounded, Clodoveo Chavez taking a bad shot in the leg, while others were captured.

Lawmen and impromptu posses were quickly scouring the countryside. Mexican settlers and vaqueros at Las Juntas and the California Ranch were threatened and roughed up to the extent that Governor Newton Booth received a horde of complaints. Booth telegraphed Sheriff Ashman at Millerton insisting he must protect the innocent. The *Fresno Weekly Expositor* reported that rumors were everywhere:

Ramon Molina, a Cantua Creek hardcase as indicated by the scars covering his face and body, rode with Vasquez in several raids. California State Archives.

We could fill the entire local department of the paper this week with the thousand-and-one rumors floating about. Rumor says one of the members of a party now hunting Vasquez found a gold watch belonging to himself in the possession of a suspicious-looking Mexican....'Tis said that a Mexican has been suspended from a limb....Rumor has hanged two Mexican thieves near Kingston.

The gang scattered while Vasquez hid out in Southern California. By late February, Chavez had rejoined his old commander with another recruit and on the 25th they held up the Bakersfield stage at Coyote Holes in the Mojave Desert.

But time was running out on the now famous bandido. Not only were various sheriff's posses and others scouring the California wilderness for him, but Governor Booth had commissioned a party of manhunters under Alameda County Sheriff Harry Morse to track down the outlaws. Besides

*Kingston was originally a ferry site on the Kings River. A new bridge, seen at far right, had just been completed when the outlaws crossed over to rob the village's hotel and shops.*
Elliott's History of Fresno County.

many county rewards, the state now offered $8,000 for Vasquez alive and $6,000 for him dead.

After several other robberies, Vasquez separated from his men, seeking to hide out in the cabin of an old camel driver named Greek George Caralambo near Los Angeles. While there, he was reportedly betrayed by the family of his niece whom he had seduced and made pregnant. Informed by Sheriff Morse of the bandit's hiding place, Los Angeles Sheriff William Rowland dispatched a posse that captured him on May 13, 1874. Vasquez was wounded slightly with a shotgun blast. The news was headlined across the state and in Los Angeles large crowds gathered to see the most feared bandit since Joaquin Murrieta.

One of the first interviews with the noted outlaw was conducted by a local newspaper editor who visited Vasquez in his cell:

*"Greek George" Caralambo. Author's collection.*

Los Angeles, May 15—Through the politeness of Sheriff Rowland, J. M. Bassett, editor of the *Herald* of this city, was today permitted to visit Vasquez and held a long conversation with him. Vasquez is still weak from loss of blood, and quite sore from his wounds. In appearance he is anything but the ferocious red-handed brigand his reputation has given him. He is a man of about medium stature, with a well-knit, wiry figure. He does not weigh over 140 or 150 pounds. His complexion is much lighter than the ordinary Mexican. His features are clear-cut, with an intelligent expression. His eyes are rather large and a light grey or blue in color. His forehead is high and his head well-shaped. In manner he is frank and earnest, with no disposition to make himself a hero. His general demeanor is that of a quiet, inoffensive man, and but for his calm, steady eye, which stamps him as a man of great determination and firmness, no one would take him for the terrible Tiburcio Vasquez.

Mr. B. introduced himself to the bandit by stating that he represented the Associated Press and desired to know if he wished to make a statement that should go out to the world in his own language. He replied that he did wish to make such a statement, but was too weak to do so today. After some further conversation he expressed a willingness to go over the history of his life up to the date of his capture. He understands English very well, but speaks it imperfectly, and the greater portion of the appended statement was obtained through Sheriff Rowland as interpreter.

*The cabin of "Greek George" Caralambo where Vasquez sought relief from the searching posses on his trail. California State Library.*

**Conversation between Vasquez and the Reporter.**

Vasquez lay upon a cot in one of the front rooms of the jail and turning his face towards his questioner, he answered every

No. 1.

# The Western Union Telegraph Company.

The rules of this Company require that all messages received for transmission, shall be written on the message blanks of the Company, under and subject to the conditions printed thereon, which conditions have been agreed to, by the sender of the following message.

JAS. GAMBLE, General Sup't, San Francisco.    65    WILLIAM ORTON, President,    G. H. MUMFORD, Secretary,    New York.

Los Angeles Cal May 16 1874

Received at Sacramento, _May 16 1874 410 P. M._

To His Excellency Newton Booth
I have the honor to report the Capture
of Tiburcio Vasquez alias Ricardo
Cantous on the fourteenth inst in
this County have delayed announcing
the Capture until his identification
could be more certain. The nature
of his wound fully ascertained
and his statement reduced to
writing — His wound are not
necessarily serious He has been
identified by at least one hundred
persons and his Confession places
his identity beyond all doubt

First page of the telegram from Sheriff Rowland announcing the capture of Vasquez to California Governor Newton Booth. California State Archives.

question in a prompt, unhesitating and apparently truthful manner. The following conversation took place:

B.—*What you shall say to me will be telegraphed to the Associated Press and published in the San Francisco papers and those of the East. You will not say anything that you don't wish published, or that may injure you on your trial. Vasquez—I have nothing to conceal and will make a straightforward statement.*

B.—*Commence then with your boyhood days, and tell me what you recollect of the first fight or difficulty in which you were engaged.*

V.—*I was born in Monterey County in this state, in 1837. I am now thirty seven years of age. The first years of my life were spent in the county of my birth, in the usual manner of the young of my life and class. My first difficulty occurred in a ballroom in Monterey, when I was fifteen years of age. I was engaged in a fight, but no blood was shed.*

*Spring Street Los Angeles as it appeared at the time of the Vasquez capture. No longer a village of adobe haciendas and shops, the town could boast many brick and frame structures rivaling San Francisco. Los Angeles Public Library.*

*B.—After the fight, what did you do?*

*V.—I went to work, but the officers came to arrest me. I resisted. A fight ensued and I escaped. No one was killed.*

*B.—Have you ever taken human life?*

*V.—No Sir. I have tied up and robbed many men, but I have never shed blood.*

*B.—After you escaped from the officers in Monterey County, where did you go?*

*V.—I took a few cattle and went into the hills near Ukiah, Mendocino County. The officers soon learned where I was and again attempted to arrest me, but after another fight in which no one was killed, I escaped.*

Although he was not present, Sheriff William Rowland's posse captured Vasquez.

*B.—What time intervened between your fight in the ballroom in Monterey County and this last attempt to arrest you in Mendocino County?*

*V.—Not more than seven or eight months.*

*B.—Where did you go after leaving Mendocino County?*

*V.—I went to my mother in Monterey County and asked for her blessing, and I told her I was going out into the world to suffer and take my chances.*

*B.—What did you mean by "suffer and take my chances?"*

*V.—That I should live off the world and perhaps suffer at its hands.*

*B.—Is it true that you were driven to outlawry through injuries inflicted by white men?*

*V.—To a certain extent, yes. When I lived in Monterey County I kept a dance house and sold liquor. The Americans used to come in and beat and abuse me and mistreat my woman.*

*B.—Is the story true that your wife was debauched by a white man; and were some of your relatives killed by Americans?*

*V.—I was never married in my life. I have had women when I wanted them, but I never had a wife.*

*B.—Do you think a woman had anything to do with your capture or in placing the officers on your track?*

*V.—(Laughing) No. I never trusted one with information that could harm me.*

*B.—You say you have never killed anyone?*

*V.*—No; I always avoided bloodshed, and always urged my people not to kill or hurt those they robbed.

*B.*—In what part of the state have you committed your robberies, or most of them?

*V.*—In Santa Clara, Monterey, Fresno, and Los Angeles counties. I have committed many robberies in those counties, but don't wish to name them or give details. I robbed Firebaugh's Ferry last November, and it was my party who robbed the bank in Fresno and created the terrible commotion there some months ago.

*B.*—Were you posted on the movements of Morse and party?

*V.*—Yes; I knew every movement Morse made. I have been around his camp night after night, but have never been near enough to Morse to recognize him and should not know him if I met him on the road. I know Sheriff Cunningham of San Joaquin County. He is a brave man; I could have killed him several times. I never had Morse in a sure place.

*B.*—Did you ever have Sheriff Rowland where you could have killed him?

*V.*—Yes, several times. He has taken more risks than any of them. The pursuit after the Repetto robbery was very close. Rowland passed within ten yards of me as I lay in the brush after abandoning my horses in Lajunda Canyon. I had by my side two Henry rifles and two revolvers.

### The Tres Pinos Murder

*B.*—Now, give me your version of the Tres Pinos murder.

*V.*—I will tell you the truth, and in order that you may hereafter know that what I say is true, I will give you the names of my party. If these men are captured they will substantiate what I say. At Tres Pinos my party consisted of five men, all told. Adon Lava [Abdon Leiva] acted as my lieutenant, and when I sent a party he went as chief. I remained some distance away from Tres Pinos and sent Lava with two men into the place with instructions to drink and smoke, but to draw no weapon nor do any violence until I arrived. Chavez remained with me. We soon followed the advance guard, and when we reached Tres Pinos we found the murder already committed. I scolded the men for disobeying my orders, and said to the lady whose husband was tied that if she did not give me that money I would kill him. She gave me the money. I did not kill him.

*B.*—How much money did she give you?

*V.*—Oh, very little. The whole amount didn't exceed $200. The goods were taken from the store after my arrival.

*B.—Who committed the murders?*

*V.—Lava shot the man in the stable and at the store door. Romulo killed the man inside the house. (Here Vasquez gave, under seal of secrecy, the names of the four men who were with him, and also stated that two friends of Chavez whom he didn't know were of the party.)*

**Subsequent exploits**

*B.—After leaving Tres Pinos, where did you go?*

*V.—The two friends of Lava left us and went away immediately after leaving the scene of the murder. Shortly after, two of my party separated from us and remained in the upper counties. Chavez, Lava, and myself traveled south without molestation until we reached Rock Creek.*

*B.—Tell me about the affair with Lava's wife.*

*V.—A criminal intimacy had existed between myself and Lava's wife long before we left the ranch in Monterey County, but Lava never suspected us. At Rock Creek he caught us in Flagrento dilecto. Then he turned against me and sought to have me captured. Lava had been with me a long time prior to the Tres Pinos murder.*

As soon as his health permitted, the bandit chieftain was put aboard the steamer *Senator* in custody of Under Sheriff Albert Johnson and several other officers. It was seven o'clock on the morning of May 27, 1874, when the steamer arrived at the San Francisco wharf. Despite the early hour the party was met by a crowd of several hundred persons. A hack whisked them off to breakfast at the city prison, then, escorted by Chief of Police Theodore Cockrill and the Los Angeles officers, he was taken to the studios of Bradley and Rulofson where several photographs were taken. A large crowd had been gathering outside and when the group emerged from the gallery a near riot occurred as the mob tried to get a glimpse of the famous prisoner. Vasquez and his escort were rushed into another hack, the crowd rushing after it shouting, "Vasquez, Vasquez."

Back in the city prison Vasquez was besieged by reporters and other visitors. Those clamoring to see the famous outlaw were so numerous that Chief Cockrill was said to have actually considered placing a group of Vasquez impersonators in separate cells so as to move the crowds through more quickly. A *San Francisco Bulletin* reporter was one of the first to obtain an interview with the outlaw:

There is nothing particularly striking in his features, and he would hardly be taken for the bloodthirsty villain which he has proved himself to be. In the course of our reporter's conversation with him, however, something was said which visibly fired him up, when his eye glittered like a cat's and he looked far more capable of doing a desperate deed than when his face is in repose. He greeted the reporter very cordially and to an inquiry as to his health replied that he felt very weak yet, and was unable to sit up long at a time, but was improving as well as he could expect considering that he had had eight buckshot lodged in him not two weeks ago. He showed his various wounds and made a remark to the effect that he thought it rather cruel to shoot an unarmed man who was only trying to make his escape. The reporter then asked:

This is one of the Vasquez photographs taken by Bradley and Rulofson in San Francisco. California State Library.

*"Where are they going to take you now, Vasquez?"*

*"I don't know," was the reply.*

*"And I suppose you don't care much now, do you?"*

*"Oh, well, that is not for me to say. I am not my own master now," (with a shrug of the shoulders).*

*"Perhaps they will try you on account of your connection with the Tres Pinos affair. How do you think you would get through that?"*

*"Well, all I know is that I never shot a man in my life. I have had plenty of chances when I have had over five, ten or twenty men tied hand and foot, but I never wanted to shoot anybody."*

*"Vasquez, people supposed that you would never be taken alive, that you would fight to the death when they got you cornered. But it seems that you did nothing but try to get away. How is that?"*

*"Yes, I tried to run away."*

*"I know, but why didn't you show fight? Couldn't you get hold of your arms?"*

*The prisoner would not answer this question, but only replied again that he tried to run away....*

"Why did you remain so near to Los Angeles at the last? Didn't you think it was very dangerous to do so?"

"I don't know why I did. I see now that it was a bad mistake" (smiling sorrowfully).

"What were your plans previous to your capture? Did you intend to go on raiding and robbing without limit?"

"No, I expected to go down into Mexico in a couple of months or so."

"Were you waiting so as to get together more plunder before leaving?"

"Oh no, not that, (reproachfully), I would have gone sooner, only I was afraid I would be cut off if I tried it then."

"Now, Vasquez, you don't really mean to say that you never shot a man in your life?"

"Yes, I do; I never shot a man."

"Do you like your robber life?"

"No, not at all. Of course a man would not like to be hunted all the time like a dog."

"Why did you live such a life, then? Wasn't it your own choice?"

"No, I was obliged to."

"What do you mean by that?"

"I mean that when I tried to settle down anywhere and tried to get a living, they came and drove me out. They wouldn't give me any peace."

"Who are they?"

"Why, the Americans—the officers."

"If you behaved yourself they wouldn't meddle with you, would they?"

"Oh yes, they would; that didn't make any difference."

"Vasquez, were you in that party that rode through Santa Cruz one night about two years ago, firing at people as you went?"

"Yes."

"I suppose you know that your party wounded two men at that time, don't you?"

"Yes," (doubtfully).

"How long is it since you have been in San Francisco before this time?"

"I haven't been here for two years."

"Then you wasn't here last Winter, as was reported?"

(Laughing) "Oh no, not at all."

*"Do you know where your lieutenant, Chavez, is now?"*

*"No, he is off somewhere—I don't know where."*

About this time a mining entrepreneur from the Mojave Desert country appeared at the window of Vasquez' cell door. It was Mortimer Belshaw who had been robbed by the bandit at the Coyote Holes station. Belshaw asked for his watch back, stating he would be glad to pay for its return. The bandit was pleased at the remembrance of those halcyon days, but said he didn't have the watch and that Chavez might have it. In a later conversation the *Bulletin* reporter was told by Belshaw that "he knew that Vasquez was the man who did the shooting at the Coyote Holes affair. Mr. Belshaw's opinion of him, based on personal observation, is that he is 'a miserable, lying dog, but withal as courageous as a lion when fairly aroused.'"

Despite the weariness of the prisoner, Vasquez was put aboard the train for San Jose the next day. He was scheduled to be tried in Salinas for the Tres Pinos murders, but the jail there was considered risky and he was housed in the Santa Clara County Jail in San Jose. A change of venue from Salinas to San Jose was obtained by the bandit's lawyers and he was scheduled for trial on January 5, 1875.

While locked up in San Jose, Vasquez continued to be a big attraction. On one day alone he received 673 visitors, 93 of whom were ladies. He was interviewed by a *San Jose Daily Patriot* reporter on the morning of July 25, 1874:

On entering the cell, Vasquez arose and greeted our reporter with his usual Colfaxian smile. Sheriff Adams accompanied us...

*Reporter—I have come to see you this morning for the purpose of obtaining your version of some matters connected with your past life.*

*Vasquez—I have nothing to tell. I have told you before that I know nothing (smiling).*

*Reporter—I do not wish to have you say anything that will criminate yourself.*

*Vasquez—I know nothing (stubbornly).*

*Reporter—You mean that you don't want to tell anything? Shall I go away empty-handed?*

*Vasquez—Yes, that's what other newspaper men have done.*

*Reporter—(seating himself) Well, I will ask you one or two questions and then I will go. You needn't answer if you don't want to.*

*Vasquez*—I have nothing to say to you.

*Reporter*—We'll see. Let us go back to 1852. You have been accused of having had a hand in the murder of the Constable of Monterey? Your version of that affair has never appeared in print. How did it happen?

*Vasquez*—No, I had no hand in that. The boys had a fandango one night. I was there with Anastacio Garcia. During the evening Garcia got into a quarrel with Jose Guerra [Higuera] and while they were fighting, the Constable came in. There was a great uproar, and the Constable was shot through the heart. The next morning Jose Guerra was hanged by the Vigilantes for the crime. Garcia was caught shortly afterwards in Los Angeles, tried and executed for the same murder.

*Reporter*—How did it come about that you were suspected?

*Vasquez*—I will tell you. I was then running with Garcia, and was engaged to marry Garcia's sister. Many persons thought for these reasons that I was concerned. That night I slept in the house of Chona Garcia. I did not run away.

*Reporter*—How did you first get into San Quentin?

*Vasquez*—I was down in Los Angeles County in 1855. A friend of mine stole some horses and pawned them. The officers got after him, and as I was with him when they came upon us, they arrested me also. When in jail I told him to make certain statements which would clear him. He did so and got free, and I was sent to the State Prison for five years. I didn't intend to convict myself, but made a fool of myself and got nipped. I was wholly innocent.

*Reporter*—The prison register shows that you escaped. How was that?

*Vasquez*—Well, one day three or four of us prisoners made a rush for the carpenter, George Leigh, and the gatekeeper, John Spell, and overpowered them. We got the keys, rushed out of the gate on the hill and got away. I traveled on foot, with one companion, through Solano, Napa and Sacramento counties until we came to Jackson,

John H. Adams, the hard-riding sheriff of Santa Clara County who almost captured Vasquez after the bloody Tres Pinos raid. Author's collection.

Amador County. There I stole two horses, one for myself and one for my friend. I was arrested for this on the San Joaquin, and about two months after my escape I found myself back in San Quentin. I served my time out.

*Reporter—You left prison the last time in 1871. Shortly afterwards the Soap Lake stage robbery was committed. Who were the participants?*

*Vasquez—Myself, Narciso Rodriguez and Francisco Barcenas.*

*Reporter—Rodriguez was captured and sent to State Prison where he died. How did you and Barcenas come out?*

*Vasquez—We went to Santa Cruz County, where we were assisted by Gracia Rodriguez, brother of Narciso. (Gracia was killed near Watsonville about two years ago by Miguel Soto. Soto was tried and acquitted. Judge Collins of this city defended him,—Rep.) One day we three suddenly met the constable of Santa Cruz and two other officers on the outskirts of Santa Cruz, who called out for us to "stop and surrender!" We concluded to fight. Barcenas was shot dead; Gracia got away. I was shot through the body, the ball striking me on the right side below the nipple and ranging diagonally lodged in the back under the left shoulder. It has never been extracted. I got away after shooting the constable, but was laid up in the Cantua Canyon a long time with the wound.*

*Reporter—Before this and shortly after your release from prison you have been accused of abducting the wife of a Mexican resident of San Juan. Is this true?*

*Vasquez—No, I will tell you about that affair...At the house of Abelardo Salazar in San Juan in 1871, I first met Procopio. One night we three, Barcenas, Procopio and myself, were in the house. Barcenas seemed to like the wife of Salazar, and after we left he told me he was going to get her away. I told him all right, it was none of my business. A few days afterwards...I met Barcenas at the Salazar house, and he went in the house and got the wife into the stable, then came and told me he wanted me to get her away for him. I consented, the woman wanted to go and so I took her away. We first went to the saloon of Salazar's partner, one Gonzales, where Barcenas got the woman's clothes, by telling Gonzales some lie. Barcenas took the woman to Natividad. I had nothing to do with her.*

*Reporter—One of the indictments found against you, charges you with attempting to murder Abelardo Salazar. I would like to hear your side of the story, for no statement whatever regarding the matter has yet been published.*

*Vasquez—Certainly. My difficulty with him was caused by the abduction of his wife. Some enemies of mine in San Juan went to him and told him that I was the one who had taken his wife away. He threatened to kill me on sight, and one night while walking in San Juan with one of my* friends, we came upon Salazar. He stopped and said, "Vasquez, I want to speak to you."

I said, "all right," for I had done nothing. He asked me if I took his wife away. I laughed in his face and told him no; that I would bring Gonzales as a witness to that effect. Without saying a word—I was within two feet of him at the time—he drew a pistol and fired at me. The bullet struck me in the neck on the right side and came out below the shoulder. [Vasquez here exhibited to our reporter the scar on the neck made by the bullet] I was blinded by the powder, but ducked my head and fired at him several times, he returning the shots. I don't think I hit him. I got away and was near death for many days afterwards. Salazar got out a warrant for me, but I was not arrested. I was not guilty of any crime towards him, as you will perceive.

Reporter—Salazar has been your enemy ever since, has he not?

Vasquez—Yes. After the Soap Lake and McMahon robberies Salazar went to Tom McMahon and stated that for $300 he would effect my capture. McMahon gave him the money, but Salazar, instead of hunting me, left immediately for Mexico, and I believe he has never returned.

Reporter—How did you find out all these particulars?

Vasquez—Oh, I find out everything. I have friends all over the country who used to keep me posted.

Reporter—Did you ever try to get even on McMahon for his efforts to have you captured?

Vasquez—No, I could have killed him at any time if I had felt so inclined....

Reporter—What did you do after your fight with the officers in Santa Cruz County?

Vasquez—As soon as I was able I went to Mexico, where I remained three months.

Reporter—Did Procopio go with you? It has been so reported.

Vasquez—No, I went alone. I came back by steamer to San Francisco. Procopio was there then. I immediately left for the lower country, and a short time afterwards Procopio was arrested in the city by Sheriff Morse.

Reporter—What induced you to leave San Francisco so suddenly?

Vasquez—Well, I considered it a safe move. I knew the officers wanted me, and San Francisco was no place for me to stay in.

Reporter—After this you and Jose Castro robbed the San Benito stage, did you not?

*Vasquez—No. Jose Castro was an innocent man. He was caught and hanged by the Vigilantes for the robbery, but he had nothing to do with it whatever. He is dead now, and I speak the truth and do justice to him. I was the man who planned and executed the robberies. I had one assistant, a young man, but I cannot give you his name.*

*Reporter—Have you any idea how Castro came to be suspected?*

*Vasquez—Nothing more than this. He kept a saloon on the San Benito, a short distance from the place where the stage was stopped. His wife was Concepcion Espinosa, who is a distant relation of mine. I used to happen into the saloon once in a while—in fact I was there immediately preceding the robbery—and I suppose that the people suspected Castro for these reasons. But not only was he innocent of taking an active part, but he knew nothing whatever about the matter beforehand.*

*Reporter—I forgot to ask you about the murder of a Portuguese butcher at the Enriquita mine in 1864 or 1865. You have been charged with that murder.*

*Vasquez—I had nothing to do with it. I was unjustly accused and had to leave the country, and that is one of the many reasons that induced me to continue in the bad life I had commenced.*

*Reporter—Were you and Procopio ever engaged in a robbery together?*

*Vasquez—No. I was slightly acquainted with him, that's all.*

*Reporter—How is it with Juan Soto?*

*Vasquez—I never was with him on any raid. At the time he was killed, I was in San Juan.*

*Reporter—Leiva says you first met him [Leiva] January, 1873. Is that true?*

*Vasquez—No. I first became acquainted with him at his house near the New Idria mines in May, 1873. I was there from May until the latter part of August nearly all the time. I would go out and remain a few days occasionally and then come back again.*

*Reporter—Leiva says that the first time he went with you was when the raid on Firebaugh's Ferry was made. Is that statement correct?*

*Vasquez—No. Chavez, Leiva and myself left his house a short time before the Firebaugh affair, and on the San Joaquin a few miles this side of Kingston we robbed two men going along in a wagon.*

*A few days since one of the men we robbed came into the jail to see me. He instantly recognized me and asked for a watch I had taken from him. I* didn't have it with me and so he had to go away without it (laughing).

Reporter—Did you tell him that Leiva was here?

Vasquez—Yes, and he went into the other part of the jail and saw and recognized Leiva as one of the party who robbed him.

Reporter—How did you happen to go to Firebaugh's?

Vasquez—I heard that Henry Miller would be there on a certain day with several thousand dollars to pay his herders. Myself, Chavez, Leiva and De Bert made the raid. We didn't find Miller and so we laid hands on whatever we could get.

I took a watch from a man they called the Captain. His wife came to me and throwing her arms around me asked me to return the watch, that her husband had given it to her during their courtship and they couldn't bear to part with it. I gave it back and then she said "come with me." I followed her to a room and from behind the chimney she took out another watch and gave to me. The Captain said "You haven't got a bad heart, after all."

Reporter—Did you not put up a job to rob the pay car of the S.P.R.R. shortly afterwards?

Vasquez—No, I did not. Why, I wouldn't know how to do that.

Reporter—It is said that you intended to tear up the track below the 21-Mile House, throw the car off and go for the coin.

Vasquez—(anxiously)—Who told you that?

Reporter—Abdon Leiva.

Vasquez—He lies, that's all.

Reporter—You did rob the 21-Mile House?

Vasquez—Of course.

Reporter—You have stated that Leiva killed two of the men at Tres Pinos and that Romulo Gonzales killed the other one. Did you see Leiva fire the shots?

Vasquez—No, I did not see the firing.

Reporter—Will you give me your statement of that affair?

Vasquez—No. I am to be tried for that and I shall say nothing until I speak in court.

Reporter—(persuasively)—I don't want you to say anything that you have not already stated to others. You told J. M. Bassett, editor of the Los Angeles Herald, that Leiva and Gonzales were the murderers, and that you and Chavez did not arrive on the scene until after the shots had been fired. That statement has appeared in print.

Vasquez—I have never stated anything of the kind. I have told no one about the Tres Pinos raid.

Reporter—Of course you are innocent of murder.

Vasquez—Yes, I never committed a murder in my life.

Reporter—If you had, I don't suppose you would be likely, at this stage of the game, to commit yourself?

Vasquez—(with a cunning look )—No, I don't think I would.

Reporter—When did you first become intimate with Rosaria Leiva, the wife of Abdon?

Vasquez—During the four months preceding the Tres Pinos affair and while I was stopping at his house.

Reporter—Leiva states that the reason he left your gang at Rock Creek was because he discovered that you had had criminal intercourse with his wife. He says when he found you asleep and the truth was discovered, that he pulled his pistol and was about to shoot you, when Chavez, who had been lying in the bushes a few feet distant, jumped up and drawing his pistol, induced him (Leiva) to forego his murderous intentions; that you, on being awakened, refused to lift a hand against Leiva because you had dishonored him; that he left you then and there, after vowing to be your bitter enemy henceforth. Is this story true?

Vasquez—(laughing)—Not at all. No matter what I had to do with his wife, that's my business. At Rock Creek Leiva told me that he wanted to lay off with the horses for a few days to recuperate, and asked me to recommend him to some ranch. I went to the Yono Varde ranch and made arrangements for him to stay there. He went with his family. Two or three days afterward he came to see me and then he left and gave himself up to the officers. We had no words at all and his story is a fabrication.

(Our reporter felt like telling Vasquez that his story was very thin, but did not, for good and sufficient reasons.)

Reporter—You had a fight with Sheriff Adams' party in Rock Creek Canyon. What members of your gang were with you?

Vasquez—Chavez and myself, only.

Reporter—I would like to obtain your account of that affair.

Vasquez—We knew that the officers were close behind us and we pushed rapidly up the canyon. We halted in some underbrush around a

*San Jose at the time of the Vasquez trial and hanging. The courthouse is the large white domed building. Just to the left of the courthouse is the jail that housed Vasquez. Photograph by Loryea & MaCaulay. San Jose Historical Museum.*

*turn in the road and near a high point that commanded a view of the road below. I saw Adams coming ahead and the others behind; I heard him urge them to come on; for a moment I hesitated as to whether I should kill him or not; he was within easy range and I could have dropped him on the first shot. Then I thought that it would only make matters worse for me, and so I fired over his head several times after I had shouted to Chavez to get the horses ready. I meant to keep the officers back until Chavez had the horses on hand, when I intended to fly. As I left the point I heard Adams say: "Come on—we can get them!" If the men followed Adams they might have caught us.*

(Adams' men refused to follow, and the Sheriff, at the end of some moments delay, charged alone on the thicket where the robbers had been seen. He was confident when the firing ceased that Vasquez and Chavez left, and he was right, as the result proved.)

*Reporter—Were you ever married?*

*Vasquez—No.*

*Reporter—How many times have you been wounded?*

*Vasquez—Eleven times. I received eight wounds when I was captured. I was shot in the hand when I escaped from San Quentin; in the neck by Salazar at San Juan and in the breast by the Constable of Santa Cruz.*

The interview ended here. The bandit evinced no desire to conceal anything in reference to his robberies, but as far as murderous operations were concerned he claimed to have clean hands. He is cunning, audacious, vain and egotistical, and has none of Leiva's frankness and apparent honesty.

The trial began on January 6, 1875, in the Third District Court of Judge David Belden in San Jose. Despite a valiant defense by Vasquez' three attorneys, the bandit chieftain was convicted and sentenced to hang on March 19. Through it all, Vasquez remained stoic and in good humor. More, he signed various proclamations imploring children to obey the teaching of their parents and not follow his example. He also appealed to his followers not to seek vengeance on any of the officers who were merely doing their duty. When he viewed the casket he was to be buried in, he felt the satin lining and commented, "I can sleep here forever very well!"

Standing on the gallows, the outlaw turned his head to aid Sheriff Adams in adjusting the noose. He uttered one word—"Pronto!" Tiburcio Vasquez was history.

The grave of Vasquez in the old Santa Clara Mission Cemetery, Santa Clara, California. The monument, in a beautiful, tree-shaded setting, is much more than the desperado deserves. Author's collection.

## Chapter Seven / NOTES

Several good contemporary biographies of Vasquez have been done, notably Beers, George. *Vasquez, or the Hunted Bandits of the San Joaquin*. New York: Robert DeWitt Co., 1875; Sawyer, Eugene T. *Life and Career of Tiburcio Vasquez, the California Bandit and Murderer*. San Jose: 1875; Truman, Benjamin Cummings. *Life, Adventures and Capture of Tiburcio Vasquez; The Great California bandit and Murderer*. Los Angeles: *The Los Angeles Star*, 1874. Greenwood, Robert. *The California Outlaw*. Los Gatos: The Talisman Press, 1960, is a reprint of the Beers book, but with Greenwood's own excellently documented account of Vasquez' life, along with many illustrations.

The Hennessey quote is from the *San Francisco Examiner*, December 2, 1997. For information on Jose Jesus Lopez , see Latta, Frank F. *Saga of Rancho El Tejon*. Santa Cruz: Bear State Books, 1976, and the *Fresno Bee*, April 14, 1935.

Anastacio Garcia was one of the more colorful of the early Hispanic desperadoes. He accompanied Henry Cocks' posse that killed Claudio Feliz in September 1852. Since Cocks was married to a daughter of Francisco Garcia, Anastacio was possibly related to him. A good account of the 1854 killing of Constable William Hardmount in Monterey is in the *Fresno Weekly Expositor*, October 29, 1873. The *Monterey Sentinel*, October 6, 1855, announced Garcia's surrender on the Hardmount charge and his subsequent release for lack of evidence. For an account of Garcia's lynching at Monterey, see the *Santa Cruz Sentinel*, February 28, 1857.

The *Los Angeles Star*, July 25, 1857, reports Vasquez' arrest for horse theft. For his various San Quentin incarcerations, see *List of Convicts on Register of State Prison at San Quentin*, Sacramento, J. D. Young, Supt. State Printing, 1889. The *San Francisco Daily Alta California*, June 27, 1859, gives a long account of the San Quentin prison break, listing "T Basquez" as one of those who escaped. Vasquez was recaptured in Amador County as noted in the *California Police Gazette*, July 23, 1859.

The convict capture of the prison schooner *Bolinas* was initially reported in *The San Francisco Herald* of September 28, 1859. Follow-up articles were in the *Herald* and *Daily Alta California* of September 29 and the *Sacramento Daily Union* of September

30 and October 1, 1859. The fight with the three horse thieves was reported in the *Union* of October 15, 1859, while the Vasquez letter was originally published in the *Martinez Gazette*, then picked up by the *Union* on October 26. Details of the story can be found in *History of Contra Costa County*, W.A. Slocum & Co., 1882.

For a biography of Faustino Lorenzana, see Reader, Phil, *"Charole," The Life of Branciforte Bandido Faustino Lorenzana*. Santa Cruz: Cliffside Publishing (n.d.). Greenwood gives a good account of Vasquez and his cousin Lorenzana's complicity in the butcher's murder.

The gunfight with Abelardo Salazar is mentioned in most Vasquez biographies, although Vasquez himself gives a different version of the abduction. The name of the town of San Juan was changed to the present San Juan Bautista about 1904.

For one of the many accounts of the Soap Lake robbery, see the *San Francisco Bulletin*, August 19, 1871. A long account of the fight in which Barcenas was killed appeared in the *Santa Cruz Sentinel*, September 16, 1871, as noted. A brief item in this same issue announced the capture of Narciso Rodriguez.

For a biography of Clodoveo Chavez and an account of his terrible death, see Secrest, William B., "The Return of Chavez," *True West*, January–February, 1978. The Victor Gardenas interview was in *The Fresno Bee*, June 13, 1934. The robbery at Firebaugh's Ferry is detailed in the *Fresno Weekly Expositor*, March 5, 12, 1873. The erroneous Vasquez death notice was in the *Expositor*, April 23, 1873. An account of the 21-Mile House robbery is in the *Gilroy Advocate*, August 2, 1873.

An account of the Tres Pinos robbery and murders is in *The Salinas Index*, September 4, 1873. The best account of the incident is a long letter by Andrew Snyder, owner of the store that was robbed. Snyder says Chavez wanted to kill him, but Vasquez threatened to blow off the top of his head if he did. Copy of letter in author's collection. Another Snyder account is in the Huntington Library, San Marino, California. See also the newspaper accounts of the Teodoro Moreno trial, *San Francisco Bulletin*, November 25, 27, 28, 1873.

The Jones Store robbery was reported in the *Fresno Weekly Expositor*, November 19, 1874. John Bugg is mentioned in newspaper accounts of the raid and also in a reminiscence published in the *Fresno Morning Republican*, March 26, 1922. See also "Leaves of the Past," *The Ash Tree Echo*, April, 1970. The Kingston raid and its aftermath is reported in the *Expositor*, January 28, 1874, the *Visalia Weekly Delta*, January 1, 1874, and the *Kern County Weekly Courier*, January 3, 1874. Harry Morse's report on trailing the wounded Chavez through the Coast Range is in the *Governor's Reward Papers*, California State Archives, Sacramento.

The Coyote Holes stage holdup is described in the *Kern County Weekly Courier*, February 28, 1874.

The capture of Vasquez was headline news across the state, notably in the *Los Angeles Star*, March 16, 1874, and the *San Francisco Bulletin*, May 15, 1874. Vasquez' seduction of his half brother Francisco's daughter, Felicita, is related by Jose Lopez in Latta, Frank. *Saga of Rancho El Tejon*. Santa Cruz: Bear State Books, 1976. Lopez, whose cousin was married to Greek George Caralambo, claimed he turned Vasquez in when he learned that Felicita was pregnant. The most accurate account of the capture is by George Beers, a member of the posse and a correspondent of the *San Francisco Chronicle*. Beers and Frank Hartley both shot and wounded the bandit leader. Beers' account is published in full in the Greenwood book.

The Vasquez interview in the *Los Angeles Herald* was reprinted in the *San Francisco Bulletin*, May 15, 1874. The bandit's arrival and interview in San Francisco is detailed in the *Bulletin*, May 27, 1874. The Belshaw comments are from the same issue. Beers, who was present at the Vasquez trial and sentencing, gives a good account of the proceedings. For an interesting sidelight on the trial, see Judge Belden's scathing sentencing lecture to the outlaw in Berry, M. D., John J., ed., *Life of David Belden*. New York, Belden Bros., 1891. For Vasquez' appeal, see People vs. Vasquez 49 California Reports, 560, [January, 1875].

**$300 REWARD!**

For the apprehension of Richard Perkins who broke jail on the night of the 9th of January 1876, at Bakersfield Kern County, convicted of highway robbery.

He is about 5 feet 8 or 9 inches high, weighs about 170 pounds, heavy set, sandy complexion auburn hair, blue eyes, very lame, recently had his right leg broken between the knee and ankle a man of more than ordinary intelligence. The above reward will be given for his arrest and delivery to me at Bakersfield, Kern County, Cal.

Bakersfield, Jan. 10, 1876.          W. R. BOWER, Sh'eriff.

*When he escaped from the Bakersfield jail, Dick Fellows, alias Richard Perkins, was the most wanted outlaw in California. Wells Fargo detective Jim Hume compared him to Black Bart as one of the nerviest badmen he had ever known. Author's collection.*

*Two stagecoaches passing each other on a narrow desert road. Dick Fellows and other highwaymen looked for such spots to stop their quarry. Wells Fargo Bank History Room.*

# 7 "With a price on one's head"

## The Autobiography of Dick Fellows

George B. Lyttle, alias Dick Fellows, as he appeared after his 1882 capture near San Jose. From a contemporary police mug book. Author's collection.

**L**ike many outlaws, Dick Fellows sought to vindicate his theft by saying he only robbed large corporations and not average working people. This was seldom the case, but it was a justification often utilized in an age when giant corporations and banks controlled politics to the detriment of many struggling small farmers and merchants. Since he was trained as a lawyer, Dick should have known better.

"I began to rob stagecoaches," he once wrote, "taking only the treasure belonging to the express company, Wells, Fargo & Co."…as if that somehow palliated his crimes. Anyone reading Dick's own story will easily ascertain that he was not only a horse thief and stage robber, but one who robbed individuals as readily as he did a corporation.

Born George Brittain Lyttle in Clay County, Kentucky, in 1846, the outlaw known as Dick Fellows was one of the more successful stage robbers in California history. And that is too bad. His parents, David and Drucilla Lyttle, were highly respectable people who gave their son every opportunity in life. A prominent lawyer, legislator, judge and businessman, David Lyttle saw to it that his son had a good education and hoped he would follow in his footsteps. But it was not to be.

The Civil War was raging when George enlisted in the Confederate army in July 1863. Only seventeen at the time, the boy was serving with the 10th Regiment, Kentucky Infantry, when he was captured in November. After a brief stint in an Ohio prison camp, he was paroled home to Harlan County, Kentucky, in late December 1863.

Back home, young George read law in his father's office, but he had hardly got his feet wet in his new profession before it became clear he had a drinking problem. An embarrassment to himself and his family, the young man thought a change of scene would be beneficial and he accordingly left home in 1866. He drifted for a time, appearing in Southern California the following year. A few setbacks in the Golden State quickly triggered his drinking again. His own story was that "at length I became almost besotted, grew desperate and drifted into the worst company in California. The little money I brought with me from home was soon squandered and to gratify my appetite for drinks, I began to rob stagecoaches." No doubt some of his drinking cronies in the Los Angeles saloons had experience in the "road agent" business.

George Lyttle assumed the name Dick Fellows in order to protect his parents' name should he be caught. In November of 1869 the dangers of his new occupation became apparent when he read of a bandit gang stopping a stage running between Fort Yuma and San Diego as noted in the *Los Angeles Daily News:*

*Los Angeles in 1869, as Dick Fellows knew it. Los Angeles Public Library.*

Stage Robbers.—Passengers by the San Diego stage, last night, bring an account of a daring attempt at stage robbery. Some sixty miles from San Diego the stage was stopped by four highwaymen, with the customary stand and deliver. Instead of delivering their funds, the passengers opened fire upon the rascals, and a fight ensued in which, as usual where passengers have pluck to resist, the robbers were worsted.

One of the scoundrels was shot through the bowels and killed, and the others made off. One passenger was wounded in the leg, and one of the stage horses was killed. The robbers are supposed to be part of a gang which have been passing bogus gold dust and depredating in the vicinity of San Bernardino.

Still, after various stickups and forays into horse theft, Dick found his new lifestyle to be exhilarating and much easier than steady work. His targets were the coaches of the Coast Line Stage Company which provided shipping and passenger service between Los Angeles and San Francisco. He seems to have operated primarily between Los Angeles and Santa Barbara. Many years later he chronicled his early days as a highwayman while serving a sentence in the Folsom state prison. Since he was well educated it is probably the best of such personal outlaw memoirs, taking into consideration the long-winded prose style of the era. Despite limiting himself to his first few years of outlawry, it is a rousing tale of a promising life gone terribly awry.

*In the year 1869 I had been robbing stages and become a fugitive. My stamping ground was about the head of Casteca Creek [Castaic Creek]. Lower down the stream was a Spanish-American settlement in Los Angeles County. A man called Ed Clark was my "friend, counselor and guide," and one fall, observing that there were lots of acorns at our rendezvous, advised me to invest a couple of thousand dollars in hogs and quit stealing.*

*As it was hardly safe for me to leave our retreat, Clark, with the assistance of a young Spaniard from the settlement, made a tour through the surrounding country, collected a drove of 600 hogs, all as lean as a rail fence, and laid in a supply of food for the winter. This took our last dollar, and we relied on the sale of our stock for whatever else we might need.*

*One morning after I had been down to the Spanish-American settlement to hire a man to help us with our rapidly increasing band of hogs, I met Clark some two miles below our cabin at work building a brush fence.*

"How did you succeed?" he inquired, naturally, as I rode up to where he was.

"I did not see the fellow I wanted," I replied, "as he had gone away from home and was not expected back until about sunset. But I left word for him to come up in the morning."

"I had flattered myself that there were no prospectors or hunters about here," he said, abruptly changing the subject, "and that we should have no inquisitive intruders, but just a few minutes before you came in sight up the creek I heard some repeating rifle reports in the direction of the cabin, and they were guns of the heaviest calibre, in fact sounded like cannon."

The thought struck me that some hunter unaccustomed to seeing hogs in that section might

The Coast Line stages were a favorite target of Dick Fellows for years. Los Angeles Daily News, February 23, 1869.

have taken ours for wild hogs and was killing them. What most interested me was to know something about who the hunters were, and where they came from. Expressing as much to Clark, I dashed spurs to my horse and started rapidly in the direction of the cienega, where he had thought he had heard the rapid and heavy firing. Suddenly turning a point within 200 yards of the house at the cienega, the situation was explained. Clark had built a fire on the grass to cook his dinner, hurrying away as speedily as practicable after finishing his meal, and had left live coals in the ashes where the fire had been. Soon after he returned to his work, the wind blew the little live coals about in the grass and it took fire. The dense matted grass and tules at the cienega was all burned off and the ground black.

When we piled up the supplies under the sycamore trees some flasks of powder had been placed at the bottom of the stack. The burning grass had ignited these and produced the tremendous reports Clark had heard two miles away. But the worst of it was that the powder flasks, in exploding, had sown broadcast over the entire valley every potato and onion and the beans, like fine shot, had been scattered to all points of the compass.

The only thing left to eat in sight was a bursted sack of flour lying in the top of one of the largest sycamore trees. Only about half the flour had spilt, but it would have taken two good choppers half a day to cut the tree down.

By this time Clark was on the scene and as he approached the cabin, dismay pictured in his kind old face, I fished out of the shallow streamlet in front of the door a three gallon keg of aguardiente that had been blown heavenward with the other things in the pack. It had come down on the grass and rolled into the brook. Unscrewing the plug I tilted it up, turning toward my partner, and drank his health, passing the keg to him as he came up. He drank and expressed his feelings by remarking: "Well, this is hell!"

### How I Determined to "Rustle" a Winter Supply.

I told him I thought it a matter of little importance. The hogs were all right. The fire died out at the foot of the sandhills, only the bunch grass on the basin having been burned. There was sufficient flour left for him to live on until I could "rustle" another winter supply. Therefore, I determined to rob another stage or two within the next few days. I explained my desire fully to my partner, who, while he sincerely deprecated the necessity for the measure, heartily concurred in my object.

Leaving Clark alone at the hog ranch with the understanding that I would try to engage someone to come up and help him, I would obtain winter supplies at Los Angeles and have them forwarded for him on the old Fort Tejon trail within a few miles of camp. I started on my expedition that evening.

I traveled all night, going up the Santa Clara Valley and out by way of Lyon's Station which stood a little way from where the town of Newhall is situated now. I crossed the ridge at San Fernando Pass. By daybreak, having jogged along leisurely, I was at San Fernando.

At dawn I was at the San Fernando station, within a few miles of the place at which I wished to meet the Soledad stage, bound out from Los Angeles. It was due at San Fernando about 3 o'clock that afternoon. I had breakfast and had my horse fed at the station by sunup. Before travel begun on the road at that point, I went out past the old San Fernando Mission, on the road through the cactus desert, called the San Fernando plain. At a point where the road crossed a deep barranca, or wet-weather water-way, I halted, and reconnoitered the place. I found it admirably adapted to my purpose. It was about half a dozen miles from San Fernando and nearly midway between that place and Cahuenga, the first station out from Los Angeles on that road. The course of the barranca was tortuous, affording a means of keeping my horse out of sight of the road and yet within a short distance from it. The banks of the barranca were fringed with tall cactus plants, and about over the sandy plain stood dense patches of cactus, at one of which, where the road crossed the wash, I decided to stop the stage.

About 1 o'clock the stage came in sight probably three-fourths of a mile from where I awaited it. I took up a position behind the dense clump of prickly pears, and looked to all my equipment, especially to the saddle cinch, a performance that at once made my knowing horse restive.

Presently the cloud of fine dust preceding the stage on the wind, which set in our direction, began to envelope us, and springing to my seat in the saddle I shouted, "Hold on there, driver!"

"All right," he called through the cloud of dust, and stopped his team. At the same instant I saw a man dressed in partial uniform of a United States soldier step out of the stage on the opposite side from me and secrete himself quickly in the cactus, drawing as he did so a pistol. I sprang on my horse because out of the road a horse could not turn around or be maneuvered properly because of the dense cacti. Immediately placing myself on the same side of the road with my soldier antagonist, I knelt down to peep under the cactus to locate him, where the branches of the plant become fewer nearer the ground. My bold soldier had been a little before me in making this maneuver, and as I stooped down to peep, he took a shot at me.

Springing to my feet I called out, "Hurry up, Bill; you and John go around on one side and I'll take the other," as if the rest of my party had just appeared on the battlefield. Instantly he called out, "I will surrender—don't shoot, boys." I lost no time in getting around to where he was, but proceeded cautiously, pistol in hand, and disarmed him. When he shot at me, which was at the next instant after I had stopped the stage, the horses became unmanageable, or the driver, availing himself of the opportunity, sped on, sweeping my horse away with them on the road. As I had not asked the stage driver to throw off the box, he kept it aboard and by the time I had disarmed the belligerent passenger the whole fleeting outfit had passed the wash and was safe from all pursuit.

### The Disadvantage of Meddling in Other Peoples' Business.

I brought the man to the road and told him to "put up his hands." He had $350 which I took as he begged me to leave him enough money "to pay his way out of the country." At that moment I heard my horse neigh, indicating that he had discovered I was not along with the company he had fallen in with. Presently, he appeared tearing along the road towards us.

I said to the fellow, "Here comes my partner," referring to the horse, "and as soon as he gets here you can proceed on your way." I handed him $50 and accompanied it with the advice that hereafter he keep out of difficulties which did not concern him. I assured him truthfully that he was the first individual of whom I had ever demanded money, although my profession was that of a stage robber. My horse having arrived, he started on toward San Fernando. I mounted and proceeded toward Los Angeles, intending to "hold up" the stage between that city and Cahuenga when it would be due from up the Coast that evening.

At Cahuenga there was a general store. Finding that I could get the supplies Clark needed at that place, I invested the whole amount I had obtained that day in goods and in paying the freight on them out to Casteca Creek. I proceeded through Cahuenga Pass toward Los Angeles city. Near the foot of Cahuenga grade there were then some densely wooded ravines. There I turned off the highway, following along a ravine until well out of sight of the road. I then dismounted, tied my horse and returned on foot to a copse of stunted live oak, from which I could, unseen, observe all travelers on that road.

For purposes of defense the position I had gave me confidence. The danger lay in the team becoming startled and dashing over the short distance to the plain before I could get the box or possibly going headlong off the grade and killing or seriously injuring some one aboard. The messenger, if there should be one along, would be sure to fire on the clump of live oak that sheltered me. Then the horses would light out, whether the driver willed it or not.

I heard the vehicle coming. The horses approached me in a trot, the driver resting his foot lightly on the brake, and I saw no obstacle to his stopping the team readily, and called out in distinct tones to him, "Hold up, there, driver."

"All right," he replied, and pressing his foot on the brake brought the team to a standstill and waited for the next command. "Lookout for your team," I shouted abruptly, as I perceived a passenger within the stage attempt to draw his pistol and a lady on the seat with him trying to prevent him from shooting. He shook her off instantly and leveled his pistol at me. It was just at that moment that I shouted "Look out for your team," the driver tightening his grip on the reins instinctively as he saw me present my pistol. Immediately the report of the passenger's pistol echoed through the adjacent hills. The horses leaped forward, the driver doubtless letting them go willingly, and of course I did not shoot, although two pistol balls had spattered the bark of my live oak. I surely felt that I should like to take a shot at that nincompoop if he had been by himself. The stage went along all right down to the plain.

Springing on my horse I pushed forward after the coach. It was getting darker every moment, and two or three miles further on there was a turn in the road where it descended into an arroyo or deep water-way traversing the valley at right angles with the main road. It kept along the bed of the creek some distance, then ascended to the plain again. By keeping close behind the stage I could easily get ahead of it at this elbow in the road, and be prepared to try conclusions with that bellicose passenger again where the stage would have to ascend from the bed of the arroyo to the plain.

All went along splendidly, and I got to the desired spot ahead of the stage without having been seen in time to make disposition for emergencies. Leaving my horse out of view from the creek-bed, I placed my cloak and hat in a half-stooping posture at the point where the stage had to come up the bank of the arroyo. The apparel was arranged to look as much as possible like a knight of the road, being supported upon a stick, with another protruding stick for a gun. I then took up my position on top of the arroyo bank at a little distance from the dummy.

When the stage had arrived at the foot of the little acclivity, I called out loudly, "Be on the alert ahead there, boys!" and then commanded the driver in a confidential tone to halt.

The stage stopped instantly and lying flat, with my bare head exposed over the edge of the arroyo's brink, I continued. "Throw out Wells Fargo's treasure box!" Out went the box on the strong bottom of the arroyo.

"Be careful not to shoot until you get the signal, boys," I said, as I proceeded to remove my fellow craftsmen so that the horses attached to the vehicle could get by. Just then I perceived the figure of a man slip out of the stage and start on a run down the creek, back the way the stage had come.

The elusive treasure box, the target of Dick Fellows and hordes of California highwaymen for many years. California State Library.

I put on the "dummy" and called out to the stage driver, "Go ahead now, sir," and up the bank went the vehicle, and as it reached the plain and cleared out I heard the ripple of laughter, indicating that the passengers had begun to understand the situation and that one of their number was taking a wild-goose chase at a late hour over a very rough creek bottom.

When the stage had disappeared I heard him still lumbering along down the arroyo. In a short half hour I knew the stage would be in Los Angeles and the news of the stage robbery communicated to the county officers. There was little time to deliberate what It was best to do. The express box I soon opened by breaking off the padlock with a stone. It contained $485. Pocketing the amount divested of the packages, I stopped to reflect "half a minute" on the situation.

### The Disadvantages of Being a Man With a Price on One's Head.

To return directly to the stronghold would be to "give it away." The sheriff's posse, I believed, would be out on that road the following day probably to Camulos in the Santa Clara Valley. The best thing, it occurred to me, was to quietly drop around by way of the racetrack, to the San Gabriel River on the side of Los Angeles, directly opposite where I then was, lay quietly about the willow and cottonwood groves until the posses should have had time to search the country about my old rendezvous, and then slip back to the mountain fastness where Clark had been left and devote the rest of my life to agricultural industries.

It is an old and a true saying that man proposes, but God disposes. I stayed several days hidden about the river, and feeling that there was no further need of remaining there, I prepared to start one evening for the mountains. The distance was about fifty miles. I could leave about dark and by daybreak be at the Casteca Creek settlement. Having kept pretty close during the time I had been there, my horse and I had not fared first-rate.

I stopped at a station and ordered supper and grain for my faithful companion. It was just after dark. There were four persons about the little station, which stood near the highway, not far from where Los Nietos now stands. Of these four individuals, two were artesian well-borers who had come out that day from Los Angeles on business connected with their trade. The other two persons were the stationkeeper and his wife. It was some distance from the house to the stable, probably a hundred yards, and I had the grain fed to my horse in a little box opposite the door of the station just across the road.

The two well-borers recognized me, but never let on. It transpired that while I attended to arranging the feed box and adjusting the cinch so that my horse could have his supper in comfort, a plan was agreed upon between the well-borers and the stationkeeper to endeavor to capture me for the rewards offered. Presently supper was announced. I was invited in and asked to be seated at the table.

Three things I observed placed me on the alert. The lady had disappeared after preparing the meal, while the three men appeared to stand in positions with reference to the one seat and covered table, on which a lamp was burning. The stationkeeper, perceiving that I noticed the circumstance of the single seat, explained that they had all been to supper.

Drawing back the chair as if intending to sit down to supper, I hesitated, glancing at the stationkeeper's face over my left shoulder. As I did so the man on my right presented a pistol at my head, cocking the weapon and calling out, "Surrender, Dick Fellows, or I'll shoot you dead!"

But he made the mistake of springing too close to me and I knocked the muzzle of the pistol down, the ball entering my right foot at the instep. I held on to the pistol, having grasped the barrel, blew the light out, so that the others could not tell at whom to shoot, then grappled with my first assailant, throwing him with great force into a corner and wrestling the pistol from him. Drawing him to his feet, I shoved him ahead of me to the door and marched out with him to where my horse stood nonchalantly munching his barley.

I proceeded to carry out the plan to get my horse without exposing myself imprudently to the fire of the occupants of the house across the road. When I had mounted I said, "So long, old partner," to the man who had served me reluctantly as a stalking horse in effecting my withdrawal from rather "a ticklish situation," and proceeded on my journey.

### How at Last I Fell into the Hands of Mine Enemies.

From the station described to Los Angeles, a distance of about fifteen miles, I proceeded leisurely, not intending to enter the city proper. I planned to stop at the house of a former acquaintance, who, I thought I could trust and to whom I intended to apply for help in my dilemma. He lived four or five miles from the courthouse, in the suburbs of the city. Although the bullet in my foot pained me, I should not have stopped on account of pain alone, but I reflected that there were no surgeons in the Santa Clara Valley. If the ball were left in my foot it might result in the ultimate amputation of my limb, and indirectly in my being captured.

If I should be able to get the ball extracted and the wound dressed I had no doubt that I could take care of myself, trusting, of course, greatly to the services of my faithful horse.

I arrived at the house of my friend, explained the situation and requested him to start at once and get a doctor. Accordingly he went away and returned with a surgeon, whom he had been able to find only after great delay. It was getting well along toward daybreak. I explained to the surgeon that we had been having "a bit of a time" at a dance not far off and that from motives which would appear later on I desired him to keep his professional visit of that night to himself a day or two. He promised to do so, and began the operation.

By the time the operation had been finished it was sun up. I concluded then to not attempt to move until dark. I hopped out to where my horse was at a long haystack back of the lot, jumped on his back, without a saddle, and rode him to the river. Far back from the road I let him drink, brought him up again and tied him behind the haystack so that persons passing along the road should not catch a glimpse of him. He was a notable animal, being of a brownish color with four white feet and a white face. These were the only objections to be found with him for the purposes of a professional stage robber, but these drawbacks had been overcome in my estimation by his traveling qualities and his gentle disposition.

I had observed that while he could not be seen from the highway in front of the house, there was a point in the road a distance off from which he could be seen by travelers on the road coming toward the city. I thought the distance too great for persons who had his description even to recognize him. When I had tied him I hobbled to the house for breakfast. It seemed very pleasant in that cozy dining room and I remained longer than I had at first intended. I had breakfasted, but still sat by the fire chatting with my host and hostess thinking every minute of going back to where my horse was, when he whinnied in a manner indicating something unusual. Springing from my seat on one foot, I cautiously peeped through the door and saw my horse being led hurriedly along by a posse of four officers. They turned at that moment into some willows on the opposite side of the road from where the house was and some 200 yards from it.

"They have captured my horse," I said, turning to my host. "What animals have you got in the stable?"

"I have nothing there but the span of mules I drove to town last night," he answered.

I said then, "They have me surrounded; I shall have to surrender. There is a reward of several hundreds of dollars for my arrest and you might as well get it." They rejected the idea at first on the ground of what their friends would think of their superstitious treachery to a friend. I told them not to be apprehensive on that score; that it would be easy for me to set that matter right, and to decide at once and not be acting over-scrupulous to their own loss. "Say I am your prisoner," I said to the gentleman, "hitch your mules to the buggy and take me into the sheriff's office and say you caught me off my guard and arrested me at your home."

Soon the team had been harnessed and presently drew up at the door. The gentleman, with one of my captured pistols lying on the seat, assisted me to get in and we drove off. The other pistol, my original and reliable one, I kept buckled under my coat. I anticipated that if the gentlemen by whom I had been wounded at the station should be of the posse at hand they might be inclined to "have it out" with me before we reached the sheriff's office. When it should transpire that they were to be left out in the distribution of the rewards, of course I should have regretted exceedingly not to have been prepared.

The posse, however, on an explanation of the situation being given them by the proprietor of the house, congratulated him heartily on his success in having captured me. They fell in behind the buggy peaceably and the procession moved on into the town. I pleaded "guilty" to the charge of assault to murder, having been convicted on one charge of "highway robbery."

In none of the apparently desperate encounters in which I became entangled in my youthful adventures did any one get a bullet or stab by myself. I was out for *money, but not for blood. Of course, now that the secret is out my profession as a stage robber is gone, even if I were free. For what driver would throw out the box to a fellow whom he knew would harm no individual without a cause!*

*Before long I shall be a free man again, and the problem that confronts me is a hard one. I have tried hog-raising and stage-robbing, the instruction of moral philosophy and literature. The first two were failures, the third hardly profitable.*

*Whether the last is a success I leave the reader to judge.*

*Dick Fellows*

*Folsom State Prison, June 14, 1894*

There is little reason to doubt Dick's tale, even though he was remembering events of more than twenty years earlier. He was in prison for life at this time and perhaps telling his story might even aid him to obtain a parole. Too, he was hardly a hero the way he told it, except in his grand gesture in setting up his friends to receive the reward for his capture. And, even this is apparently accurate, although there is confusion as to where the coach was stopped and how the robber was wounded. The tale appeared in the *Los Angeles Daily News* of December 10, 1869:

Caught at Last.—The attempted robbery of one of the coaches of the Coast Line Stage Company in Santa Barbara, some time since, and the wounding of the would be robber is doubtless fresh in the minds of the readers of the News. Since the attempted robbery the road agent has been non est. At last he has turned up under the following circumstances. Wednesday night a man without hat or coat, and with a pair of dilapidated pants, came to the house of Mr. Antonio Mallehowitz, some five miles from this city on the L.A. & S.P.R.R. He told some pitiful tale, and sold or traded to Mr. W. a bay horse, with white feet and a white spot on one leg, receiving therefor a hat, pair of pants, an overcoat and the balance in cash. Upon noticing his wounds, Mr. M.'s suspicions became aroused, and a few questions served to satisfy him that the pretended traveler was the robber concerning whom he had heard. Upon attempting to detain him, Fellows drew his pistol, but a glance at the muzzle of a double barreled shot gun in close proximity to his head induced him to accept the situation. He was brought into this city yesterday, and placed in jail. This capture completes the list of those who have been known to have been engaged in stage robbing hereabouts, during the past few months.

The *Los Angeles Star* was much more austere when it announced Dick's arraignment the following day:

> Dick Fellows was examined before Justice Grey and held on two charges—one, highway robbery in stopping a man on the road near Cahuenga and robbing him of his pistol and money; and the other, an assault with intent to kill. His bail was placed at $2,000, and, in default, he was remanded to jail to await the action of the Grand Jury.

Dick was waiting for his trial when a man named Olmstead came over from Santa Barbara and accused him of horse theft. After proving title to the animal Dick was riding when captured, he went on his way satisfied the thief was already in a bad situation. The young highwayman was convicted and sentenced to San Quentin for eight years. He was received at the state prison on January 31, 1870. From his ostentatious beginning in the legal profession, Dick had now descended into a horse thief, stage robber and convict.

Dick became Number 4378 and began serving his term. Prison was a new world to him. Originally referred to as Corte Madera, then as Point San Quentin and finally just San Quentin, the prison was located across the bay some 12 miles north of San Francisco in Marin County. It was situated on 130 acres, but the walled-in prison itself only took up some six acres. The wall was about twenty feet in height, the lower portion of stone and the upper half of brick. Besides various outbuildings, within the walls were three two-story buildings housing cellblocks and a long, one-story structure where various factories were located. Guard posts were placed both on the walls and outside of them. Two cannon emplacements were mounted on hills to the north and south.

Lining up with several other prisoners, Dick had his description written down in the prison ledger and was given his striped uniform. He could keep his hat and coat. The prison rules and routine were read and he quickly learned there was only work enough for about half the 800 prisoners. He was pleased to learn that a library had recently been established, so he would at least be able to read.

Eight years must have seemed like a lifetime. Dick knew what he had to do, however, and if there was any way to shorten his term, he would do it. He kept his nose clean, secured work in the prison library, taught Sunday school and managed to obtain a pardon after serving only half his term. On April 4, 1874, he walked through the gate a free man again.

Dropping out of sight for a time, Dick soon drifted back into his old habits. In November of the following year he appeared in Bakersfield, then drifted up into Caliente in the hills east of town. After reconnoitering the area, he planned to rob a stage transporting some $240,000 from Caliente to Los Angeles. When the coach pulled out on December 4, 1875, Dick loped out of town on a horse that had other ideas. He had not gone far when his mount bolted and threw him violently to the ground. Regaining his senses some time later, Dick saw that his horse was gone and he walked back to town.

Far from being discouraged, Dick rented another animal and again took to the hills, planning to stop the coach on its return trip from Los Angeles. This time he was successful. On the night of December 5, he managed to stop the coach and ordered the driver to throw out the treasure box. Waving the stage on, Dick tried to get the box up on his horse, but the animal bolted and disappeared into the night.

Knowing the officers would quickly be on his trail, the highwayman hoisted the box on his shoulder and staggered off towards town. In the darkness he plunged off an embankment and fell some 12 feet onto a railroad track, breaking his leg. In great pain, he managed to get some $1,800 from the box, then with some makeshift crutches again began hobbling toward town. After stealing a horse, Dick was quickly tracked down just east of Bakersfield and arrested. "He gave himself up with no trouble," reported the *Kern County Weekly Courier.* "He did not appear to know that he was arrested for stealing the horse, but took it for granted that it was for robbing the stage."

When captured by Kern County Deputy Sheriff Ed Mahurin, Dick offered him all the express loot but fifty dollars if he would let him go. This, the officer refused to do, but he kept his foot in the door. Instead he offered to spend as much of the money as necessary to either let his captive escape or work for Dick's release if he went to prison. In great pain from his injury and not having much choice in the matter, Dick agreed with the officer's scheme. Mahurin turned over $1,294 to the local express agent, keeping the $500 balance. When Wells Fargo detective Jim Hume showed up, he angrily demanded an accounting from the deputy who insisted the money must have been lost. Mahurin retraced his steps to "look" for the money, but when he only "found" $200, Hume had him dismissed from the sheriff's office.

Using the name Richard Perkins, Dick plead guilty to stagecoach robbery in the Kern County Superior Court on January 9, 1876. He was sentenced to eight years in the state prison. That night, as fellow prisoners entertained themselves singing and dancing, Dick pulled up some floorboards in the

A contemporary newspaper sketch of Dick taking his tumble after the Caliente robbery. Author's collection.

makeshift jail and disappeared into the night. For nearly a week he wandered about, trying to keep out of sight and eat regularly. He was seen from time to time by ranchers and the *Courier* was alternately amused and frustrated by the fugitive's antics:

The latest from Perkins is that he came to Cox's on the Cotton Ranch on Thursday night and demanded a blanket and some food. Cox came over and gave the alarm, and everybody struck out after this broken-legged desperado. We expect to hear of him walking into the Sheriff's office and borrowing a pistol next. A wonderful fellow is Perkins, and he'll be just mean enough to go and get caught as soon as we have gone to press, so that we cannot give the glad tidings of his capture.

Dick was eating breakfast at a settler's cabin on the morning of the 14th when he was surprised and captured by the Santa Clara county sheriff. He was quickly whisked off to San Quentin where he was admitted on January 16 as Number 6834. Late the following month he wrote a letter to "his friend Hume," airing some concerns and gripes:

*San Quentin, Cal., February 26, 1876.*

*Mr. J.B. Hume—Dear Sir: I have heard that ex-deputy Sheriff Mahurin, of Kern County, has intimated that he intends to sue your company for the reward offered for my arrest, or rather his share of it, and I feel confident that he intends doing no such thing and has made such pretension, if he did make it, merely in hope of being permitted to remain in quiet possession of that he already has of your money,*

Bakersfield was still a rough frontier town when Dick Fellows had his experience there. Author's collection.

which amounts to about as much as his reward would have been had he been true to his office and friends. Without any spirit of revenge, I think it a shame that this doubly-dyed scoundrel, without even the redeeming feature of that little honesty said to exist among thieves, should not only go unwhipped by justice, but retain what doubtless seems to him so handsome a reward for his treachery, and that after being detected in it. He will also doubtless get his share of the $200, pretended to have been found on my trail, and which I know to have been money that I turned over to him.

I received precisely the same sentence in Kern that I did in Los Angeles (eight

James B. Hume, Wells Fargo's chief lawman, regarded Fellows as one of the most desperate outlaws he had to deal with. California State Library.

years). I believe I had the sympathy of many good men in Kern County until that affair of jailbreaking in which I only incurred a needless expense to others, and broke my leg over, and nearly perishing for days and days in these cold sloughs, without food or shelter, only to be recaptured at last by a band of unscrupulous nincompoops, who had the bad taste to divert from their legitimate calling as sheepherders to add to the distress of an unfortunate fellow-being, who was only endeavoring to flee the country. As they crowded around, each discussing his relative importance in effecting the capture, I could not help thinking (save the profane comparison) that unless shepherds had woefully degenerated since Oriental times, the infant Jesus himself would have met "Short Shrive" at their hands, if Herod had had the foresight to offer a suitable reward....

*I do not think your company ought to be very hard on me. I never have directed against them particularly any matured scheme for plunder…unless it was that I should try to live honestly…and if at any time compelled to trespass, to supply my immediate wants, I would aim at affluent corporations, and never molest poor persons or private individuals.…*

*Feeling that I already owe an apology for this trespass on your time, I close, with very high regard, your obedient servant.*

Richard Perkins.

Hume must have rolled on the floor over some of those comments.

The worst thing about prison was the boredom. Convicts got up about six-thirty, dressed, made up their bunks, then stood at the doors of their cells with their night bucket. As trusties unlocked the cells, the prisoners filed out to empty their buckets in the "Rose Bowl" or cistern, then washed up in cold water before marching to breakfast.

Some of the prisoners ate at their factory mess facilities, but most ate at the main mess hall, sitting at the five hundred numbered bench seats flanking the foot-wide tables. Waiters plied the aisles between tables, ladling out the

*A view of San Quentin and lined-up convicts when Dick Fellows was there in 1871. The "Stones," the first cellblock built in 1854, is shown at right. It was demolished in 1959. California State Library.*

stew and beans that made up their meal. A slab of bread was dropped next to the steaming tin of coffee. The banging of a guard's mallet signalled for the eating to begin. Fifteen minutes later, the mallet again signalled—this time that the meal was over. Standing up, the prisoners were then marched to their jobs or left to pass time as best they could in the open yard. Another meal was served just before noon, with evening supper being signalled at about three-thirty. After that, they were marched to their cells for the night. It was the same monotonous routine, day after day.

Still being quite lame, Dick wasn't immediately assigned any work. He had plenty of time on his hands and wrote to the *Kern County Weekly Gazette*, describing a fire that had destroyed most of the prison factory building in May of 1876.

*The conflagration, under the circumstances, was a sight worth while to see. On the one hand the fierce menacing flames, and on the other, a scarcely less formidable array of bristling cannon and Henry rifles....For a wonder the whole affair was unattended with loss of life or serious injury to anyone. One man, who had been employed in the attic where the fire originated and whose retreat down the elevator was cut off, escaped through a dormer window on to the roof and ran diagonally across it, in the most excited manner, to the corner of the building and made several motions as though he would precipitate himself to the pavement, some fifty feet below; and strange to say many in the excited crowd below shouted to him to do so—"jump off"—while apparently they had ample time to procure a ladder for him. They must have apprehended an explosion, though that could hardly have been attended with worse consequences. He finally escaped by dropping from the roof to a half open iron door and thence to the landing of a flight of stairs running up on the outside of the building. Some commodious wooden structures in way of kitchen dining rooms, etc. are but just completed, and it is understood I believe that the cabinet makers will commence operations again soon....As for my part, I am door keeper in the dining room or, as the "boys" express it, "watching the grub pile." There however, the parallel between myself and the dog in the manger ceases.*

He signed his letter, "Lame Dick," probably his prison nickname. The fire no doubt meant little more to the convicts than a break in the monotony.

It was an older, but no wiser, Dick Fellows who was released early for good behavior on May 16, 1881. He worked briefly for a newspaper, then tried his hand as a Spanish language instructor, but with indifferent success. It was all the excuse he needed to go back on the road and on July 19, 1881, he held up the San Luis Obispo stage. The loot, however, was minimal and in

August he stopped two more coaches. Cheered by these successes, Dick held up another coach on December 27 and stopped the San Luis Obispo stage again on January 2, 1882. But the pitcher had gone to the well once too often.

In San Francisco, Jim Hume of Wells Fargo sent operative Charles Aull to look into the rash of robberies. In two days Aull had identified Fellows as the robber and put out circulars in the Santa Clara Valley hoping someone would spot him. And someone did. He was recognized by a rancher and Dick was soon on his way to San Jose with a constable named Burke. Dick chatted amiably with the officer who quickly let down his guard with the noted "lone highwayman." In San Jose, the two went into a saloon for a drink. As they left the place, Dick suddenly sprinted off down the street and quickly disappeared up an alley. While Aull and posses of lawmen scoured the countryside and distributed new flyers, San Jose's police chief, Dan Haskell, received a telegram. The fugitive had been seen in the Los Gatos area. Taking Constable Juan Edson along, the two lawmen quickly had the outlaw back in custody.

On Sunday, February 5, 1882, some 500 locals visited Dick in the San Jose jail. As the gawkers filed past his cell, the outlaw chatted with a *San Jose Mercury* reporter while disposing of lunch:

The San Quentin fire of 1876. Marin County Historical Society.

"Well, I wonder if this is the kind of a table they furnish prisoners?"

"And yet," suggested the reporter, "that's a better table than you have been accustomed to lately."

"You're right there," said Fellows, as he laughed good naturedly. "I haven't dined in first class style for some time."

"I dare say that's a better dinner than you have tasted for several days," said the reporter as Fellows slashed off a piece of steak and commenced operations in earnest.

"Well, to tell the truth," he replied, "I haven't been living very luxuriantly. Dr. Gunckel's apples were very good as a desert, and his English porter isn't bad, but I failed to cultivate much of an appetite for his bran mash. Still, it isn't bad for a diet," and he took another morsel of steak with evident relish. "You're on the Mercury, ain't you?" he continued after a pause.

"Yes."

"I got hold of a copy today, containing a spirited account of my escape. I worked on the Santa Cruz Echo for awhile, for Stevens. He's gone to San Diego, I hear; he couldn't make a go in Santa Cruz. He's an energetic sort of fellow, but hasn't any judgement. He got all the whiskey dealers down on him by his persistent temperance hullabullo. I tell you what, a newspaper man has to have a consideration for all classes."

Dick very nearly escaped again in San Jose. The officers were continually amazed at the desperate chances he was willing to take. California State Library.

"Quite true," coincided the reporter, "and that's why I am here this evening. The public just at present are all interested in Dick Fellows, and would like to know how you have passed the time since your escape from Constable Burke. I have heard several persons say they were sorry you had been caught."

"Well, why shouldn't they? No one can make any complaints against me except the express company. I've had rather a rough time of it, though. The night I escaped I hid in a sort of machine shop. I stayed there until the next night, when I went into

Gunckel's barn. The cellar was handy, and I lived very well until I was unceremoniously routed out.

"That night I traveled toward Los Gatos and hid the next day in a straw stack out in a field. While in Gunckel's barn I got a hatchet, with which I cut the chain connecting the handcuffs on my wrists. Friday night I broke into the kitchen of a farm house and got something to eat. I also took a case knife out of which I made a saw, and finally succeeded yesterday forenoon in cutting the handcuffs in two and getting rid of them."

Wells Fargo Detective Charles Aull. Author's collection.

"About noon I stopped at a house and read an account of my escape in the Weekly Mercury. I then struck up the road toward Guadalupe, and entering a canyon came to a cabin. A woman was there who told me her husband, who was working the mine, would soon be back for supper and that if I would wait until he came I could have something eat. I had been there but a short time when the dog began to bark. I supposed her husband was coming, and therefore was not uneasy. In a few minutes I learned my mistake, for two officers entered and I was a prisoner. There was no use resisting; they had the drop on me. I have felt all the time that I could escape only by a miracle. Every man, woman and child in the county was on the lookout for me. I passed a team and wagon yesterday, and its occupants doubtless thought I was Fellows and at once sent word to headquarters. I had no show at all."

Dick then went on to verify that he had indeed engaged in six of the seven recent stage holdups of which he stood accused. When the San Luis Obispo robbery of July 19, 1881, was mentioned, however, Dick interrupted.

"I don't have the honor of doing that last named job. I own up to the rest."

Standing trial in Santa Barbara, Fellows chose to defend himself. His defense was that Wells Fargo was engaged in an illegal business and as such it was no crime to steal from them. It was perhaps just as well Dick hadn't gone into law. In any case, the judge sentenced him to life in the new state prison at Folsom in the foothills east of Sacramento.

The following morning Dick surprised and subdued his guard who was bringing him breakfast. Sprinting from jail, the outlaw mounted a horse he found staked out in a nearby lot. He was promptly thrown to the ground, however, and seized by pursuing lawmen. Before leaving for Folsom state prison, Dick penned the following letter to the local newspaper:

*Jail, Santa Barbara, Cal. April 3rd, 1882. 10:30 p.m.*

*Editor, Press. Dear Sir: I have just noticed your article on this date in reference to my recent attempt to escape, and also your editorial in regard to my past career entitled, "It Don't Pay," and after thanking you for your kindly notice, I have to say that both are in the main correct. I most heartily concur in what you have to say in the last named article, and would only add that the same may be said of any unlawful calling, no matter what the provocation. My unfortunate experience has thrown me into the society of thousands of law breakers from every clime and all walks of life, and in every instance the result is the same. It is the same sad story; "It don't Pay" in any sense. I learn that the boat will leave in a few minutes, and I bid you and the people of Santa Barbara Good Bye.*

*Dick Fellows.*

On April 6, 1882, Dick entered prison as number 470. Initiated by an act of the legislature in 1858, land was acquired for the branch prison at Folsom in 1868, but it wasn't until October 17, 1878 that actual work on the site was begun. A quarry on the property furnished granite for administration buildings, cell blocks, and various other structures that were erected on 483 acres overlooking the American River near the town of Folsom. An early visitor described the prison as being "finely situated for the most important requisite in an institution where several hundred desperate and hardened criminals are to be kept. At the slightest attempt to revolt, the Gatlings and small arms of five commanding guard houses could be turned upon the yard below, and immediate destruction would follow any insurrection."

*A prison mug shot of Dick taken some time during the late 1880s. California State Archives.*

Despite its depressing granite walls, the guard towers, relentless discipline, and the drudgery of the quarry, convicts tended beautiful gardens on the slopes and terraces of the new prison. When he arrived, Dick probably looked around and again decided to keep his nose clean with an eye to somehow gaining his freedom. But it was to be a long and weary vigil.

# Application for Executive Clemency.

To His Excellency J. N. GILLETT, Governor of California:

SIR: I hereby make application for _Pardon_

from the _State Prison_ at _Folsom, California_

and respectfully represent as follows:

Name _Richard Fellows_ ; Prison No. _470_ ; Age _68_ ;

Nationality _American_ ; County where convicted _Santa Barbara_;

Crime _Robbery_ ; Date of sentence _April 4th 1882_;

Term of sentence _Life_ ; Sentence expires _____;

Name of Judge _David P. Hatch_ ; of Prosecuting Attorney _— Kincaid, dec'd —_

Name of Attorney who defended. (Whether retained by defendant or appointed by the Court.) _Preliminary examination Victor H. Metcalf — no other_, was retained by defendant. please see appended statement.

If case appealed to Supreme Court, give its number or other designation

Where were you born? _Kentucky, Harlan County_, Where have you lived? _Kentucky, Ohio, Virginia, Tennessee, California, lived in latter State upward of forty years._

Were you ever before convicted of any crime? _Yes_ ; If so, state when, where, and what for _Los Angeles 1870 Robbery and assault to murder, Marin 1876 Robbery._

What was your former trade or occupation? _Attorney at Law, in Kansas city._

By whom have you been employed? _Last employed in California by Bascom A. Stevens, Editor Santa Cruz Echo as solicitor and local reporter, during year 1881._

Have you ever been addicted to the use of liquor, morphine, or opium? _the former in youth_

Are your parents living? _No_ ; If so, state name, age, and place of residence

Are you married? _No_ : If so, give name and place of residence of your husband or wife

Have you any children or other relatives dependent upon you for support? _yes_

If so, state name, age, and place of residence _Children & deceased brother and sister, Barbourville, Knox County, Kentucky_

Were you living with and supporting your family at the time of your conviction? _No_

If not, state reasons _At time of my conviction on this charge Father was living and provided for all his children_

Have you ever made previous application for executive clemency? _In an informal way_

Give any reasons you may have why you should be granted executive clemency. (Facts to sustain these grounds may be shown by affidavit and appended hereto.) _Disproportionate sentence and quarters of century good record in this prison, advanced age and others dependent upon me for aid. Judge Hatch appeared before the Hon. Board of State Prison Directors here and asked them to recommend clemency in the case which they have done twice, as has also the Supreme Court of California, on investigation of the case_ (Signature of prisoner) _Richard ___

_appended statements and letters, herewith, submitted under oath, as true and bona fide_

Subscribed and sworn to before me, this ___ day of ___

*Dick Fellows' pardon application showing that he practiced as an attorney in Kentucky and worked as a salesman and local reporter on the Santa Cruz Echo newspaper. California State Archives.*

His affable nature and education quickly gained the "retired" outlaw easy jobs and by 1885 he was the prison's Instructor of Moral Philosophy. He was also the chaplain's assistant and tutored inmates in both the English and Spanish language. In time he also recognized that if there was any good news about incarceration, it was being deprived of the demon rum. "I have been so long without drinking liquor," he wrote to a friend in 1893, "that I have confidence in myself of being able to avoid it, otherwise I should not care to live either in prison or out. I enjoy myself better here than I ever did at liberty after I became addicted to drink...."

Hoping perhaps there would be some mutual influence for good between them, Warden Charles Aull, the former Wells Fargo detective who had helped capture Dick in 1882, put the murderous train robber, Christopher Evans, in Dick's cell. The two men got along well since both liked to talk, read and write. Dick had seen more than he wanted of prison life, however, and by the mid-1890s he was actively working for some means to be free again. He talked to the warden at every opportunity and began corresponding with an attorney in Los Angeles concerning a commutation of sentence or a pardon. His cause was greatly furthered when both detective Jim Hume and his boss Wells Fargo President John J. Valentine agreed that Dick had been punished enough and would probably make a good citizen.

After the turn of the century he reestablished contact with his family in Kentucky and they too began working for his release. Finally, the great day arrived. On March 8, 1908, he received his pardon and walked through the prison gates a free man. And then disappeared.

Train robber Chris Evans, left, and Dick in their Folsom cell as depicted in a contemporary newspaper sketch. Author's collection.

*Another prison mug shot of Dick taken in his last years at Folsom. California State Archives.*

There are stories of his going to Mexico, teaching school in Tennessee and Louisiana and simply returning home to Kentucky, but no one knows for sure what happened to him. No records or death certificate have yet surfaced and like another noted stage robber, Black Bart, Dick Fellows vanished as though he never really existed.

## Chapter Eight / NOTES

The "robbing corporations" quote is from a letter, Dick Fellows to Rev. Thomas D. Garvin, January 10, 1893. Folsom Prison, Governor's Pardon Files, California State Archives, Sacramento, California. Bill Miner and Black Bart, both stage robbers of Fellows' era, made similar statements. See Boessenecker, John *Badge and Buckshot.* Norman, Oklahoma and London, University of Oklahoma Press, 1988.

Biographical information on George B. Lyttle, alias Dick Fellows and Richard Perkins, is from family letters in the Governor's Pardon Files, California State Archives, and U.S. Census Reports: 1850, Harlan County, Kentucky. His brief stint in the army is recorded in Confederate Service Records, National Archives, Washington DC., courtesy Lee Edwards. See also Edwards, Lee. "The Disappearance of Dick Fellows." *Historic Kern,* Quarterly Bulletin of the Kern County Historical Society, Vol. 44, No. 1, March, 1994.

Dick's drinking problem and move to California is chronicled in the previously cited Garvin letter. The disastrous San Diego stage robbery is reported in the *Los Angeles Daily News*, November 12, 1869. Information on the Coast Line Stage Company is from Outland, Charles F. *Stagecoaching on El Camino Real.* Glendale, CA The Arthur H. Clark Company, 1973.

Dick's autobiographical article on his Los Angeles stage robbing days is from the *San Francisco Examiner*, June 24, 1894. "Casteca Creek" refers to Castaic Creek, located roughly some 40 miles north of Los Angeles in the Coast Range of mountains. Castaic is a well-known landmark on I-5 between Bakersfield and San Fernando.

Little is known of Ed Clark, Fellows' companion on Castaic Creek. Although Dick refers to him as "old," Clark was about 38 years of age at this time and a widower. His wife, Amanda Tennessee McLean, had been drowned in February, 1862, during a flood at Fiddletown in Amador County. It was a double tragedy for Clark, since his wife had been pregnant at the time. Clark stayed with his wife's family for a time, and when they moved south to what is now Ventura County, Ed went with them and eventually met Fellows. Clark died on July 26, 1901, at the Tuolumne County Hospital in Sonora and is buried there in the local cemetery. He was a great uncle by marriage to Carlo M. De Ferrari, the noted Tuolumne County historian. Letter, De Ferrari to the author, August 9, 1997.

Dick's route from Castaic Creek to San Fernando by way of the Santa Clara Valley was probably less travelled than the more direct Fort Tejon trail, with less chance he would be seen. Dick's robbery site was obviously in the area now known as the San Fernando Valley, a desert at that time.

The horse described by Fellows as a "notable animal" was undoubtedly stolen. The outlaw's capture is verified by the newspaper notice in the *Los Angeles Daily News*, December 10, 1869. The notice of Fellows' arraignment appeared in the *Los Angeles Star*, December 11, 1869. The Olmstead reference is from the *News*, December 24, while the *Star* reported his sentence on January 22, 1870.

Fellows' arrival at San Quentin and his prison number was obtained from "Register and Descriptive List of Convicts under Sentence of Imprisonment in the State Prison of California," California State Archives, Sacramento. History and data on San Quentin State Prison is from Lamott, Kenneth. *Chronicles of San Quentin*. New York: David McKay Company, Inc., 1961. See also the Annual Report of State Prison Director for the Year 1859, Charles T. Botts, State Printer, Sacramento and various other reports in state legislative journals of the period.

The robbery attempt near Caliente was detailed by James B. Hume in the *Sacramento Record-Union*, January 1, 1885. The successful second attempt and its aftermath was reported in the *Kern County Weekly Courier*, December 11, 1875. The Mahurin incident is described by Hume in the *Record-Union* as cited above, and also in Dillon, Richard, *Wells, Fargo Detective*, New York, Coward-McCann, Inc., 1969.

Fellows' jail escape was recorded in the *Kern County Weekly Courier*, January 15, 1876, the "Cox's Ranch" sighting being in the same issue. Details of his capture are given in the *Courier*, January 22, 1876. Dick's first letter from San Quentin was published in the above cited *Record-Union* article, while his second letter was printed in the *Kern County Weekly Gazette*, April 1, 1876.

The five coastal stage holdups are all recounted in the above cited *Record-Union* article and the *San Francisco Daily Morning Call*, January 28, 1882. Fellows' capture and escape in San Jose is reported in the *San Jose Mercury*, January 28, 29, 1882. His recapture is noted in the *Mercury* of February 3, 4, 1882. The interview is in the *Mercury*, February 5, 1882. Dick's conviction, escape attempt and farewell letter at Santa Barbara are in the *Santa Barbara Press*, as reported in the *Mercury*, April 22, 1882, and the *Sacramento Record-Union*, January 1, 1885, as previously cited. See also the *San Francisco Daily Morning Call*, January 23, February 5, 7, and April 6, 1882.

Information on the history of Folsom prison is from Ford, Tirey L. *California State Prisons, their History, Development and Management*, San Francisco, The Star Press, 1910. See also (no author given), *As Prescribed by Law, A Treatise on Folsom Prison*, Represa, CA: The Represa Press, 1940.

Fellows' 1893 letter is the previously cited note to Rev. Garvin. The sharing of a cell with the noted train robber Chris Evans is reported in the *San Francisco Examiner* article in which his memoir appeared. The Los Angeles attorneys who helped secure Dick's pardon were Judge and Mrs. Ida Hatch. Letters from Mrs. Sally B. Hatton, of Barboursville, Kentucky, his sister, and George B. Turner, among others, are in the Governor's Pardon Files, California State Archives. Other data is from research by Lee Edwards of Bakersfield, California.

The Evans home near Visalia was something less than pretentious. There was always hope for a better life, however, until Chris got tired of waiting. A contemporary newspaper sketch. Author's collection.

Chris Evans worked as a laborer, a miner, in warehouses and on the large combines and wheat harvesters on the plains of the San Joaquin. Author's collection.

# 8 "A bullet sped past my left eyebrow"

*Chris Evans' Account of
the Fight at Young's Cabin.*

Chris Evans' mug shot as he entered Folsom state prison in early 1894. The career of this "remarkable man," as Jim Hume called him, was ended.
*California State Archives*

Just why Hollywood has yet to discover the story of Christopher Evans and John Sontag is difficult to understand. It is one of the true, classic tales of the Old West. All the elements of epic drama are there—the greedy railroad barons robbing the farmers of the San Joaquin with their high freight rates; familial love and devotion; farmers accused of train robbery and beset by bounty hunters after blood money; gunfights and ambushes and finally the showdown shootout between a posse and the two outlaws.

Year after year Hollywood churns out films based on far lesser material. Perhaps the story of Evans and Sontag is just too much of a cliche, even for Hollywood. After some one hundred years of "Western" novels and films, the material is perhaps too familiar. At first glance it appears to have all been done before.

Oddly enough, a version of the saga was filmed in 1914 by one of the participants, following his release from prison. But that is getting ahead of our story.

A rough log cabin near Ottawa, Canada, was the birthplace of Christopher Evans in 1847. Like so many others, his Catholic parents had probably emigrated from Ireland during the great potato famine. Chris claimed to have left home at an early age, crossing the border and enlisting in the U.S. Army during the Civil War. Since no records of service have ever surfaced, he may have joined a Minnesota unit that chased Indians, rather than Confederates. Later there were stories that he served with Custer's cavalry. If so, his service would have been brief since Chris himself once stated he had lived in Tulare County since 1869.

In California Evans labored at lumbering, mining, farming and teamstering. In November 1874 he married fifteen-year-old Molly Byrd whose family owned a ranch 25 miles northeast of Visalia in the southern San Joaquin Valley. In 1876 Chris operated a steamboat on Owens Lake in Inyo County, but moved back to Visalia after a brief sojourn in Washington state. He bought some land on the edge of town and here built his home and outbuildings for a farm. Although he lacked much formal education, Evans read prodigiously and grew to love quoting the classics and great poetry.

Chris Evans as a young man in 1878. This drawing is from a photograph in a locket carried by his wife. Author's collection.

Although their first born had died in infancy, Chris and Molly's daughter Eva grew up to be very close to her father. Young Elmer also died at an early age, but daughters Ynez and Winifred added to the joy of the young couple. The family saw hard times and Chris did whatever work he could find. From 1878 to 1882 he worked in a mine in San Luis Obispo County. Later he would pilot gang-plows, work harvesters, and do warehouse work for the Bank of California. On occasion he even worked for the Southern Pacific railroad, supervising Chinese track crews.

At this time the Southern Pacific was thoroughly despised in the vast San Joaquin Valley because of excessive freight rates and the bloody 1880 Mussel Slough shootout. Five settlers died in that fight, slain by a U.S. marshal's party in a dispute over railroad land titles. Two of the marshal's party had been shot and killed, also.

Evans had all he could do to take care of his growing family. By 1887 there were five children in the household, with Chris away much of the time harvesting wheat or operating gang scrapers carving out irrigation ditches for the many farmers of the area. The same year he met an unemployed railroad brakeman named John Sontag.

Born John Contant on May 27, 1860, in Minnesota, Sontag's father died while he was just a boy. When his mother remarried a man named Sontag, John took his stepfather's name. His brother George, three years younger, kept the original family surname. John moved west when his devout Catholic family insisted that he become a priest. In California he went to work on the Southern Pacific, but in 1887 he was seriously injured in the Fresno railroad yards, an incident reported in the *Fresno Weekly Expositor*:

> John Sontag, the brakeman on the railroad who was so severely injured while coupling cars the other night, is resting quite

comfortable. Dr. Rowell expresses his opinion that only one rib has been broken, and backbone severely wrenched. Good nursing and Father Time will pull him through.

Sontag spent time in the Sacramento railroad hospital, but claimed to have been dismissed while he was still ill and had refused easy work by his old employers. When Evans met Sontag at Tulare, the two men "hit it off" immediately. The crippled railroad man was invited to live with his new friend and work the farm when Evans was away. The association would have memorable consequences.

During the summer of 1890 Evans and Sontag mortgaged some of the Evans' property to lease a livery stable in Modesto. Chris had always loved horses and looked forward to operating a business that would keep him home instead of constantly working for others at distant sites. The stable, a

Modesto was a growing town along the Southern Pacific Railroad when Evans and Sontag opened their livery stable. It was a dream that turned into a nightmare. McHenry Museum.

large, two-story structure measuring 100 by 120 feet, was owned by Thomas Wallace. The lease included all of Wallace's stock, buggies, harness and feed, although Evans also furnished some animals of his own. The new firm was only in business some four months when disaster struck.

Shortly after 2 o'clock on the morning of January 7, 1891, William Hall, the night stableman, saw the glow of a fire. He rushed out to see the whole stable roof in flames and began yelling at the top of his lungs. Evans rushed from his nearby home, but there was little they, or the arriving firemen, could do. A sixteen-year-old neighbor boy who slept upstairs was burned to death.

First press notices stated that eleven horses had died in the blaze, but several days later it was reported that twenty-two animals had been buried in an adjoining corral. Wallace began rebuilding immediately, the insurance picking up most of the cost. Although the *Modesto Evening News* reported that the lessees would remain in possession of the business, when the rebuilt stable opened in early March, Evans was back at his old farm in Visalia.

Modesto Evening News, *January 3, 1891.*

Meanwhile the Southern Pacific troubles had escalated. Although train robbery had blossomed in the Midwest during the 1870s, the crime was slow to gain a foothold in California. Late on the night of August 30, 1881, however, a passenger train chugged up the grade in the Sierra Nevada Mountains between Reno and Sacramento. At a prominence known as Cape Horn Mills, the engine plowed to a jarring halt as it struck an area where a track had been pried up. A gang of bandits, led by Ed Steinegal and George Shinn, were all rookies in the game and at the last moment panicked and fled the scene. Both Steinegal and Shinn were tried and convicted of the crime.

A different approach was tried in November 1883. While the northbound Southern Pacific train was stopped at Modesto, some six or seven "roughs" boarded a coach and began robbing the passengers. One of the bandits was thrown from the car as the irate passengers took potshots at his accomplices, who promptly fled. The gang was later rounded up by a Lathrop constable.

A more organized attempt took place on February 22, 1889, when train No. 17 headed south after leaving Pixley in Tulare County. Two masked robbers were on the tender and, after stopping the train, they dynamited the express car and reportedly obtained some $5,000. Ben Wright was at the Pixley depot that night and later recalled the exciting event:

> The train came and left Pixley each day between the hours of 7 and 7:30 o'clock each evening. It was the only train that went south each day. The train would stop in Pixley, and the train crew and people would go to the hotel for dinner....As I looked down the tracks, I saw the engineer and two men going toward the front

of the train. The two men were carrying shotguns and went almost to the engine before climbing aboard. It was not unusual to see men armed, and almost every man carried a shotgun because many times a person could get a shot at a jack rabbit, coyote or other game....

Sometime later we heard the whistle of the train and saw the red lights approaching as the train backed into Pixley.

Wright's account was verified in the *Tulare Daily Evening Register* the next day:

Just as the train was pulling out of Pixley two men wearing long masks reaching below the waist climbed upon the engine and covered the engineer, Pete Bolger, and the fireman, C. G. Elker, with

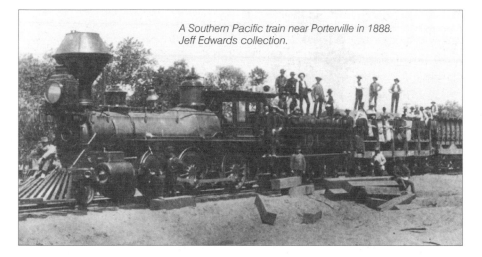

A Southern Pacific train near Porterville in 1888.
Jeff Edwards collection.

revolvers. They were also armed with shotguns which were strapped to them and hung at their sides...the train was started on its way, the rest of the crew and the passengers little dreaming what was transpiring on the engine.

When a little more than two miles from Pixley, one of the masked men gave the order to stop the train....When the train came to a stop one of the men threw a bomb under the express car which exploded and shivered the glass in the windows but did not break or derail the car....

Deputy Constable Ed Bentley was on the train and getting off went toward the engine to see what the trouble was about. This act probably cost him his life, for while he was stooping to look under the train, a shot came from the other side and he staggered back exclaiming, "I'm shot! I'm shot!"

The two bandits then brought up the engineer and fireman and threatened to shoot them if the express messenger didn't open the car door. When the door was opened, one of the outlaws gathered what loot could be carried, and the two then backed off into the night with their shotguns leveled on the trainmen.

*Officer wearing hat, coat and mask found at the Evans farm. Contemporary newspaper sketch. Author's collection.*

Bentley had been mortally wounded by the robbers. Another passenger, one Charles Gaber, was also found crumpled along the tracks. He too had been killed by the outlaws while trying to see what was happening. The bandit's tracks—a carefully prepared false trail—led off towards the Sierra Nevada. The dollar amount of the robbery was never made public.

Another train holdup took place near Goshen, a few miles northwest of Visalia, in January of 1890. Again it was a pair of masked men and this time a tramp was killed. The bandits got away with a reported $20,000. On February 6, 1891, a train was held up south of Pixley, at Alila. In an exchange

of gunfire between the two bandits and the express messenger, the train's fireman was killed. This time the bandits fled towards the Coast Range, instead of the Sierra. The Dalton brothers were strongly suspected of this holdup, but they couldn't be found.

A holdup near Ceres in September 1891 was unsuccessful. In the hunt for the robbers and the resulting hard riding by posses, only Grat Dalton had been rounded up. Convicted of the Alila robbery, Grat escaped the Visalia jail and fled to Oklahoma where he was killed with brother Bob and two others during the foolhardy 1892 attempt to rob two banks at Coffeyville, Kansas. Badly wounded during the aborted raid, Emmett admitted that his brothers had done the Alila job.

*Convicted of the Alila robbery, Grat Dalton escaped jail at Visalia and fled to Oklahoma. Author's collection.*

After the Evans stable disaster in Modesto, John

Sontag made a trip home to Minnesota. He told his younger brother, George, how he and Chris Evans had held up the trains at Pixley, Goshen, and Ceres. Curious as to their own abilities in a holdup venture, the brothers robbed a train outside Chicago in November of 1891. John had no sooner left to return to the coast, than Chris Evans appeared in Mankato using the alias, Charles Naughton. Evans and George now held up a train at Kasota Junction in Minnesota, but received no loot for their trouble.

George Contant, with a prison record due to an embezzlement conviction in Nebraska, was quickly suspected of these two robberies. When Evans and Contant returned to California, Pinkerton and express agency detectives watched every move they made. In a letter to his friend William Pinkerton, San Francisco Police Detective Isaiah W. Lees described the surveillance of the train robbers:

George Contant was as handsome as his brother John and both had a proclivity for easy money. Troy Tuggle collection.

> San Francisco, August 19, 1892
>
> W.A. Pinkerton, Esq.
>
> Dear Sir. Yours of the 10th inst., referring to the Mankato, Minn. train robbers and their connection with the Southern Pacific train robbery at Collis, at hand. I note all you say about our old friend Warner of the American Express Co. and our office being engaged in tracing the Mankato robbers, and the services rendered the S.P.Co. and W.F. & Co. by Mr. Hartshorn of the American Express Co. assisted by your office, in following them to this coast, and finally locating them at Fresno, and proving beyond a doubt they were John Sontag, alias Con[t]ant and Chris. Evans of Visalia, who had been at Mankato as Naughton. Evans and John Sontag are undoubtedly as desperate a pair as have turned up for many years anywhere, and I fully agree with you that the Collis robbers should have been detected right in the act, with the information that was given to the S.P. and W.F. & Co. people, prior to the robbery.
>
> I.W. Lees, Capt. of Detectives.

The "Collis robbers" were the three bandits who stopped another Southern Pacific train at Collis, near Fresno, on August 3, 1892. The suspects were the Contant/Sontag brothers and Chris Evans whose haul was a reported $50,000. They made careful plans to cover their tracks and establish alibis, but George was quickly picked up in Visalia and interrogated. When railroad detective Will Smith and Deputy Sheriff George Witty arrived at the Evans farm to talk to Chris and John Sontag, there was a sudden burst of gunfire as the two bandits chased the wounded lawmen from the scene.

Hastily fleeing to the nearby hills, the two fugitives returned to the farm that night. While placing supplies in their buggy, a lurking posseman opened fire and killed their horse. Both Evans and Sontag returned the fire, killing Deputy Sheriff Oscar Beaver before again disappearing into the mountains.

Evans and Sontag would always deny that they had robbed any trains, but their denials would have made much more sense if they had surrendered peaceably at this time. Mrs. Evans' only explanation was that her husband had "gone crazy." Sontag, too, had behaved inexplicably. At the time he was engaged to young Eva Evans and he was trading a chance for a happy marriage for the life of a fugitive. Even if there hadn't been evidence that the men were indeed train robbers, their actions at

The wrecked Southern Pacific express car at Collis as sketched by a newspaper artist of the time. Author's collection.

the Evans home certainly cinched matters to most people. Innocent suspects just don't shoot officers and flee to the mountains!

Drunk and telling conflicting stories when first taken into custody, George Contant was tried and convicted for the Collis robbery in October, 1892. He was shipped off to Folsom state prison to begin serving a life term.

There was little doubt that the train robbers had been identified at last and a ten thousand dollar reward was quickly posted for the two fugitives. Besides the local lawmen, bounty hunters and detectives began arriving in

Visalia. "Today on the 11 o'clock motor there arrived ten shotgun messengers, or trailers, from Texas and Arizona," noted the *Visalia Daily Times* of August 11. "These men are employed by the Southern Pacific Company." Among the arrivals was Vic Wilson, a deputy U.S. Marshal from Tucson, Arizona, and Frank Burke, a deputy sheriff from Yuma who brought along two Yuma Indian trailers, Pelon and Cameno. The party attached themselves to a posse consisting of S.P. detective Will Smith, one of the officers at the Evans' home fiasco, Constable Warren Hill of Sanger, Andy McGinnis, and Al Witty. The group was quickly in the mountains and on the trail.

John Sontag had told everyone who would listen of his grievance against the railroad. It wasn't hard to suspect him of being a train robber. Author's collection.

The two fugitives had vanished into the wilderness of the Sierra Nevada. For over a month there were rumors of sightings and speculation, but that was all. Then on September 10, Vic Wilson's posse found a trail leading them to a recent campsite at Sampson Flat in eastern Fresno County.

Vernon C. Wilson was a tough officer from Arizona, but he had no chance in the ambush at Jim Young's cabin. Author's collection.

For several more days they followed the trail to various sites, then decided to stop by Jim Young's mountain cabin to leave a message for a posse member.

Young had a small plot of land in a clearing where he raised crops, including corn and watermelons. The cabin was a one room affair of logs and shakes, with a loft. The main trail ran in front of the place, with a fence and gate opening onto the foot path leading to the cabin. Deputy Frank Burke remembered exactly what happened:

Monday we remained at Sands Baker's place and this morning we started for Sampson's Flat to watch the trails for the outlaws. We started to go to Young's house to get some potatoes and to leave a note for John Broder, who was expected back the next day. Wilson, McGinnis,

Pelon, one of the Yuma Indian trackers who stood their ground at Young's cabin. Author's collection.

myself and Witty had dismounted and started down the hill to the house on the south side. Wilson and McGinnis led off and I was about 20 yards behind, with Witty behind me. I started off to a watermelon patch ... suddenly, when the men were about 5 steps from the house, we saw the two men run out and shoot.

Unfortunately, Evans and Sontag were in the house. There was no back door from which to make an exit and their only choice was to surrender or fight. They decided to fight. Jim Young wasn't home, but they sent a visiting Englishman out to the pump to get him out of the way. The two fugitives then watched the approaching lawmen from a chink in a log. Chris Evans told the story from there:

*The tall man advanced, and by his side to our astonishment came Andrew McGinnis. The balance at that moment were outside the gate.*

*We waited until the first two men came within fifteen or twenty feet of the door, then we thrust our shotguns through the window panes and blazed away, one barrel each.*

Young's cabin as it appeared around the turn of the century. In this reenactment of the ambush, men posing as Evans and Sontag have just shot down Wilson and McGinnis who lay before them. Annie Mitchell collection.

Both men reeled and fell, and as I swung open the door swiftly and came out through the smoke toward them, McGinnis cried out to Sontag:

"For God's sake, don't John!'

We dashed by the two fallen men and opened fire on the balance of them. Witty fell and bellowed like a calf. Burke tumbled over the fence to the right of the gate, and I sent a Winchester bullet after him to increase his speed. He flew down the gulch and we saw him no more.

Sprinter [Will] Smith, with a wild cry, wheeled his horse, clapped spurs to its flanks, dropped his head against the horse's neck and flew back up the trail, scattering his gun, his belt, his coat, and for all I know everything that he had along the road. One Indian bawled for him to stop, but that only increased his terror.

### How the Indians Behaved.

Sanger Constable Warren Hill was also in the Young's cabin fight. Author's collection.

The Indians meanwhile had taken to the rock pile at the left of the gate and were fighting in true Indian fashion. I did not mind them so much, because I had fought Sioux and Cheyennes and I knew their tricks. These fellows simply thrust their rifles above the rocks and blazed away without taking any aim, so they failed entirely to hit us. Pretty soon I made it so hot for them that they thought distance would lend enchantment to the view and dashed away down the road.

Warren Hill started to run away with his horse, but a Winchester bullet dropped the animal and Hill took to Burke's horse.

All this occurred in the twinkling of an eye, and it was with a jump that I discovered we were attacked from the rear. John Sontag suddenly dropped his right arm and cried out that it was broken, while a bullet sped past my left eyebrow, leaving the scar. Whirling about we saw that McGinnis had revived and had turned over on his back to fill me with lead from his Winchester rifle. I was compelled to put another bullet into him to stop him.

The coast now being clear I examined Sontag's arm. No bones were broken, and taking off the coat we found that it was only a flesh wound, and not a very bad one at that. We bandaged it with a handkerchief and walked slowly away through the corn field.

I left my shotgun in Young's house for the reason that Sontag's injured arm did not permit us to pack away all four of our guns.

The next two weeks we retired to a hospital life, and while the posses of detectives and blood money hunters were chasing each other up and down steep *trails we were in a comparatively comfortable state.*

*However, to be serious, we never killed anyone except in self-defense. We are entirely guiltless of the train robbery and are thoroughly conscious of our innocence. As to the killing we have done, it seems to me it has been a pretty good riddance for the country of the so called 'bad man.' Take Oscar Beaver. He killed 'Sheepman Cripe' near Lemoore in cold blood, and another time he shot a fellow in the Laurel Palace Saloon in San Francisco. As for Andy McGinnis, he shot a young Negro lad who was sleeping in a box car at Modesto and was concerned in the whitecap business there. I never kept track of Vic Wilson's graveyard, but everybody always knew that he was terribly dangerous.*

Andy McGinnis had experience as an officer but was after bounty money when he was killed at Young's cabin. A newspaper sketch from a photograph. Author's collection.

*So far as the question of train robbery is concerned, we are entirely innocent, while, as I said before, the killings we have committed have been purely in self defense. We have plenty of provisions now, a first-rate fortress, and we are ready to defy any of the posses that may come our way.*

Southern Pacific railroad detective Will Smith was relentless in his pursuit of the outlaws, but made a poor showing at Young's cabin. John Boessenecker collection.

Evans' interview was granted to *San Francisco Examiner* reporter Henry "Petey" Bigelow who was able to gain access to the outlaws through mutual friends. It was a great scoop at the time, but certain contingents of the press sneered that it was a fake. In a later letter to the *Examiner*, Evans sought to validate the interview and gave details of the meeting as well as some additional particulars of the Young's cabin affair:

*He took down our statement in long hand writing and, with the exception of stating that we both shot from the window in Young's cabin, it was perfectly correct. When Mainwaring went out of the house with the bucket the door was wide open and was left that way. We sat down on the floor under the window and watched our enemies approach*

through a chink between the logs. When about fifteen feet from the door I said, 'Now!' and rising up drove my shotgun through the windowpane, and killed Wilson. Mr. Sontag at the same moment fired from the doorway and shot McGinnis, who said as he fell: 'Oh, my God, John!' We sprang past them, and I fired at Witty as he ran. He bawled, and Mr. Sontag said 'You hit that fellow in the side.' While shooting at the Indians I felt a bullet strike me from behind, back of the eye, which knocked my head sideways. I was in the act of making Pelon a good Apache, but McGinnis' bullet struck me as I was pressing the trigger and spoiled my shot. I whirled around, throwing in a cartridge as I did, and saw McGinnis trying to shoot me again. I shot him in the left temple; the gun dropped from his hands; he quivered one instant, and Andy McGinnis climbed the Golden Stairs.

Taken a few days after the September 13, 1892, ambush, this photograph by Visalia photographer E. M. Davidson shows Young's cabin just as it looked at the time of the tragedy. Author's collection.

Right or wrong, Evans and Sontag felt they had little choice but to fight at Young's cabin. They had no doubt convinced themselves that the lawmen would take no chances with them after what had happened to Smith, Witty and Oscar Beaver at the Evans home. As a result, Vic Wilson was found with more than 100 shot in his body—most in the bowels. McGinnis had been struck by 36 shot and a Winchester bullet had torn through the left side of his jaw.

At the time there were rumors of others being in the house who had fired on the posse from the upstairs loft. Some of the possemen stated as much, trying to increase the outlaws' firepower to help explain their own poor showing. Actually, the author interviewed one Sam B. Williams of Fresno many years later. Sam claimed to have been in the cabin at the time and told me all about the fight. He did not participate, however. He was just a lately arrived Tennessee farm boy who had been invited to spend a few days at the cabin by Jim Young, whom he had met at the Fresno railroad station.

Evans was quite exhilarated by the Young's cabin scrap. In a safe hideout he later wrote a poem about the event which was found by a deputy sheriff. It showed, perhaps better than anything else, his arrogance and newly acquired callousness toward human life. The poem itself hardly compared to Tennyson—or even Black Bart:

*Although tattered and showing the ravages of time, this old poster displays the reason the mountains above Fresno and Visalia were crowded with bounty hunters. Courtesy Paul Calkins and Juanita Browne.*

## THE GAME OF EUCHRE

*Of Sontag and Evans I'll sing you tonight,*
*the sentiment here I think is all right.*
*They played a lone hand, the joker they hold,*
*in the glorious state that is noted for gold.*
*A posse on Know to the mountains did go,*
*and to Sontag and Evans they made a great show.*
*But the two held the joker, the joker they played,*
*and two of the posse were on the ground laid.*
*One of the posse (you know who I mean),*
*made the longest footrace that ever was seen.*
*You could play cards on the tail of his coat,*
*as his feet hit the ground for he jumped*
*like a goat.*
*At the house you have heard, where the*
*shooting occurred,*
*A large melon patch grew, and lay sparkling in dew.*
*This man of the posse, whom you all know,*
*When the patch his eye for a melon did go*
*But a change in the programme suddenly come,*
*the man dropped the melon and started to run.*
*Some say he is running on still, and will never*
*stop running till he gets to the mill...*

There was more to this epic ballad, but unfortunately, it doesn't get any better.

Friends and family kept the two outlaws supplied in the mountains, but their record of robbery and murder was now so outrageous that they could seldom rest from the pressure of the lawmen.

When local lawmen seemed unable to make any progress in the case, U.S. Marshal George Gard came up from Los Angeles. He had been summoned by Wells Fargo detective John Thacker. Gard and Thacker assembled a special posse of just three men: Hiram Rapelje, a Fresno County deputy sheriff, Tom Burns, a private detective working for the Harry Morse

Agency of San Francisco, and Fred Jackson, a Nevada lawman and friend of Thacker's son, who happened to be visiting several nieces in Fresno at the time.

It was a top secret operation and the three men were smuggled out of town in a wagon at night. Gard later joined them in the field. They rested days and at night watched the trails the outlaws were known to frequent. They made dry camps and ate jerky and other uncooked food without making campfires. And it paid off.

On June 11, 1893, the posse rested at an old shack alongside a trail Evans and Sontag sometimes used while visiting Visalia. It was near an old landmark called Stone Corral. Late in the day the posse spotted the two outlaws walking toward the shack. It was the exact reverse of the Young's cabin situation. As soon as they were sure of the strangers' identity, the lawmen opened fire, badly wounding Sontag. The two groups exchanged gunfire until it was too dark to see. Evans' own account of the fight is as dramatic as it is exciting:

*The first intimation I had of danger was a bullet. John and I was walking leisurely down the trail and were just sitting down upon the old manure heap near the cabin. Suddenly there was a report and a bullet flew past Sontag's head. Then we knew we were in for it. It was the worst fight I ever was in; worse, in fact, than a big battle with the Sioux Indians I was in once upon a time.*

*The manure heap was small and only two feet high. It served as a death trap because of its flimsy protection. We flung ourselves behind it, however, kneeling on*

Deputy U.S. Marshal Fred Jackson.
Author's collection.

*the ground, and proceeded to pump lead into the cabin. It was about half an hour before sundown. The door of the cabin was aslant and we could not see exactly where our adversaries were placed at first, but presently after the first four shots, we could tell that they were not inside, but round the corner of the house. I directed my fire toward that point and presently was hit in the middle of the right eyebrow, the bullet plowing a hole across the bridge of the nose. This splashed blood across my eyes and blinded me so badly that I could not see the sights on the rifle.*

*They must have fired 200 shots into that dung heap during the battle. We had plenty of ammunition, but the whizzing bullets came ripping through the straw and caught me in the forearm, shattering it badly. Next, my other arm went by the board and I was left helpless. John Sontag, however, kept up the return fire bravely. He is always exceedingly cool when under fire, and he never lost his nerve a minute, although repeatedly hit. He did not give up heart though til just before dark, then a bullet striking him in the forehead knocked him backward like a tenpin. He cried:*

*"My God, Chris, I'm done for this time."*

*It's a wonder that the wound in the chest which he had received ten minutes before had not floored him, for the blood was flowing through his shirt fearfully and his face was a dreadful sight. He begged me to blow his brains out, but I had not the heart to do it.*

*I waited until the stars came out, and then knowing that John's case was hopeless I helped to cover him with straw and resolved to make a break for high land. You see they did not fire from behind the cabin all the time, but would flank us firing at long distance.*

No desk officer, U.S. Marshal George Gard had much experience as a Los Angeles sheriff and police officer. Author's collection.

*Why, at one time they fired at 200 or 300 yards range. Well, when I made up my mind to leave, I slid on my belly, Indian fashion, through the grass. It was then that a man running along the fence took a quick shot at me and plowed my back with a bullet. I rose to my feet with a jump and dashed up the slope over a low hill. The man did not follow me....*

Fred Jackson had been badly wounded in the leg during the fight. After Evans left the area, Hi Rapelje obtained a wagon from a nearby farm and rushed his wounded partner to a doctor in Visalia. In town, Rapelje advised Deputy Sheriff George Witty to round up a posse and return with him to where Gard and Burns maintained a surveillance over the wounded Sontag in the field. Not knowing how badly the outlaw was hit, the lawmen decided to wait until morning before approaching him.

Witty, Sam Stingley, and Constable William English rode back to the battle scene with Rapelje. A photographer named E. M. Davidson and reporter Jo P. Carroll also tagged along. At the scene, Marshal Gard accepted a drink from Rapelje's whiskey flask, then pointed to where the wounded outlaw lay. Strung out across the field, the crowd of men cautiously approached Sontag who was barely visible under the pile of straw. Deputy Witty took the fallen bandit's pistol from his hand and announced that he was arresting him. After Davidson had taken several photographs, Sontag was placed in a wagon and brought to town. As he lay in the Visalia jail, Sontag told his own story of the fight:

*We were on our way to Visalia. We were not in Visalia last Thursday. Chris regretted the Pine Ridge (Young's cabin) affair; he never wanted to kill anybody, except blood-money detectives. Oh, no; you will never get him. He was as cool as any man. At Pine Ridge McGinnis fired three shots after he was shot. He shot Chris and one of the Indians hit me. I did not see Burke. Burke fired two shots. The Indians did all the shooting.*

*We were going to town for clothes. We haven't had a cent of money for a month. We did not intend to hold up a train. We intended to leave here some time, but had no clothes nor money.*

*When Chris fired at the officer I thought his gun had gone off accidentally. After I had been shot I asked Chris to shoot me, but he wouldn't do it. I begged him to kill me. "Shoot me through the head before you go," I said, but he still refused to do it. After a little while Chris said, "Are you getting any better," and I told him*

*Only four men in this famous photo of the wounded Sontag took part in the battle near Stone Corral. Hi Rapelje is second from left, while Marshal Gard is third from right with a handkerchief on his head. Tom Burns is to Gard's right. The others are local ranchers and a reporter. Fred Jackson was in Visalia under a physician's care. Author's collection.*

John Sontag, the wounded outlaw. Wells Fargo Bank History Room.

no; then he asked me if I could move, and I said no. We had two shotguns, two rifles, and two six shooters. Chris carried away a Winchester rifle.

*Chris was always sorry he shot Witty; thought he was Will Smith.... We would have shot Hume, Thacker or Smith though. We never had it in for the county officers; they were only doing their duty in hunting us—but we were after the blood-money detectives.*

*We could not have been convicted of train robbery, as we had no hand in it. The Southern Pacific did me a hard turn when I was hurt while in their employ... and when Detective Smith started to arrest me I was determined I would not be taken by any Southern Pacific man. That's the reason I made the resistance to my arrest.*

*No, I have no word to leave, and have no kick coming. I am only sorry I did not make a better job in killing myself.*

The badly wounded Evans was picked up some eight miles away at a relative's house the day after the Stone Corral fight. Sontag was already in custody when Evans was brought in and assigned a suite in the Tulare County jail. As soon as possible, Molly Evans and daughter Eva arrived at the jail and pushed through the crowds of people. As Eva later recalled, it was an emotional meeting:

*As I stood beside him, John took my hand in his and I laid my other hand on his forehead where the bullet had grazed it. His beard had been removed and his face was framed in a bandage that covered the hole in either cheek where his bullet had gone in and out. The agony that held him until the end, already gripped him. As he lifted his eyes to mine it was all I could do to keep from crying out. There was more there than a broken body. I saw a broken heart.*

Chris Evans was badly shot up and lost an eye and arm as a result of his wounds. But he survived. Sontag's worst wound was from a bullet that shattered his shoulder, then ripped through his upper body just missing the spine. In a few days tetanus set in, resulting in lockjaw, and a tooth had to be broken out so he could drink through a straw. When Eva saw him for the last time, she recalled that his "beautiful eyes were dull with suffering; he was dying of peritonitis. He took my hand... then closed his eyes. I waited for him to speak or to open his eyes. When he did neither, I leaned over and kissed the closed eyes."

Eva Evans. A contemporary newspaper sketch from a photograph. Author's collection.

In a Visalia saloon Witty was heard to remark that only the men who did the shooting should get the rewards. But ten thousand dollars was a lot of money and later he modified his statement to say that if he did get any reward, he would give it to the widows of Oscar Beaver, Vic Wilson, and Andy McGinnis.

When the rewards were finally paid, Tulare County Sheriff Eugene Kay accepted $5,000 for his undersheriff's arrest of Evans at a relative's home. Undersheriff Hall had raced, and beaten, a Fresno posse to the scene. Rapelje and Hall nearly came to blows, but the Tulare officer was allowed to retain his prisoner. The other $5,000 was divided as follows: Gard received $1,500, Jackson $1,500 and $1,000 each to Burns and Rapelje.

Chris Evans, wounded and in the Visalia jail. He lost an eye and lower arm and hand. Tulare County Historical Society.

"Those retrievers from Visalia have no right to any of it," growled Marshal Gard. "The case is like that of one man shooting a quail and another man getting to it first when it falls and asserting that it belongs to him."

Gard wasn't the only one grumbling, however. George Witty, despite his previous assertions, began to feel that he had arrested Sontag and should have the reward. In early October 1895 Witty brought suit against the Southern Pacific Railroad and Wells, Fargo Express Company in the United States Court at Los Angeles. Tom Burns, Harry Morse's detective, was particularly vitriolic about Witty's claim and accused Sam Stingley of perjuring himself in Witty's behalf. Friends had interfered during several confrontations between Burns and the Witty crowd.

On the night of October 9, a party of officers and their witnesses were returning on the Los Angeles train to Visalia after a day in court. Several had been liberally garnished in the local saloons before leaving. When Witty stepped onto the platform for some air, he was followed by Burns. There was another argument, a scuffle and several shots. As they grappled, the two men fell from the moving train. Shot in the arm and hand, Witty's wounds were not serious, but both men were injured in the fall. Neither pressed charges.

On December 11, 1896, the court ruled that Witty had no claim to the reward and he must pay the court costs. Oddly enough, both men died in 1901, Burns in a personal fight in Arizona, and Witty by his own hand in San Francisco.

Sontag died of his wounds on July 3, 1893, and was buried in Fresno the next day. As if all this wasn't enough drama for the Evans and Sontag saga, Molly Evans and daughter Eva began performing in a San Francisco stage drama depicting the outlaws' story, ostensibly to obtain funds for Chris's defense.

On June 27, 1893, George Contant led a bloody escape attempt at Folsom. Three convicts were killed and several others, including George, were badly wounded. After fourteen years, George's prison sentence was finally commuted in 1908. His book, *A Pardoned Lifer*, came out the following year and in 1914 he formed a film company. His movie of Evans and Sontag was well received and was quite popular for a time.

Chris Evans and George Contant did their time in these cold and bleak granite cells at Folsom state prison. This shows two tiers of cells with their doors standing open. Note huge padlocks used to secure them. Author's collection.

*Fresno in the 1890s was no longer a frontier town. Chris Evans' trial, in the distant courthouse, was a reminder that the "Wild West" wasn't completely dead yet. Fresno City and County Historical Society.*

After a dramatic escape from the Fresno County jail, Evans was recaptured and sentenced to Folsom state prison for life. He was a model prisoner and for a time shared a cell with Dick Fellows, the notorious stage robber. The two seemed to have gotten along well, both men being well read and of a literary bent. Dick wrote letters and sent an article to a local newspaper on his early adventures in Southern California. Evans was of a more thoughtful mien. In 1900 he published a book, *Eurasia*, which described an idyllic socialist state where women had equal status in government by law. Needless to say, it never made the best-seller lists, but it was an interesting insight into Evans' character.

Pardoned in 1911, Evans was banished from the state. He spent his few remaining years in Oregon with the family that he loved, but had nearly destroyed. His outlaw past dimmed in time. When he died on February 9, 1917, the *Portland Journal* gave him a sentimental and sympathetic obituary:

> A shower of lilies rested on the casket. There were other flowers, a large bed of carnations, and lilacs and roses, but in the dim light of the room, the lilies shone more beautifully than all the rest… In the gray case of wood, unmindful of sighs and of tears, was sleeping one who had known the storms and snows of life. But the peace of the ages had come to Chris Evans.…

This morning the bride of bright days and drear, sat silently as the Rev. Father E. P. Murphy read the prayers of the church, and spoke of the love that passeth all understanding. "God reads the heart, it is not for man to read it," declared the pastor.

The final chapter was written. Chris Evans never took anyone into his confidence as to just why he had turned outlaw. His killings, he insisted, were self defense. He was never convicted of, nor ever publicly admitted to, being a train robber. Why this devoted father and husband would put his family at risk and become a hunted outlaw is one of the more curious questions of California history. An exasperated Molly Evans simply said her husband had "gone crazy!" But it wasn't that simple, either. Perhaps even Chris Evans didn't know just what had driven him into a life of crime.

In any case, the pastor was right. No man ever read the heart of Chris Evans.

As an old man Chris Evans must have often wondered himself why he had brought such grief on himself and his family. *Tulare County Historical Society.*

# Chapter Eight / NOTES

Information on Chris Evans' family is from the Canadian Census Report: Canada West, 1851, 1861, Carelton County, Nepean Township, Ontario, Public Archives of Canada, Ottawa; my thanks to Lee Edwards for his help. See also Kinkela, Evelyn Evans, McCullough. *An Outlaw and His Family.* unpublished ms. in the Huntington Library, San Marino, California; Smith, Wallace. *Prodigal Sons.* Boston: The Christopher Publishing House, 1951. Dr. Smith, with the encouragement of Mrs. McCullough, utilized her manuscript in writing his own biography of Evans and Sontag. When his book was published, the writer was taking a college course from Smith and we sometimes discussed Western matters while walking from class. Smith told me that Eva had tried to sue him for using her manuscript in his own work, even though she had written and urged him to do so. The suit went nowhere, of course.

No army record for Chris Evans has ever been located, leading some historians to believe he merely joined a Minnesota volunteer unit that chased Indians during the Civil War. Too, he would never allow his family to seek a veteran's pension. Lee Edwards to the author, July 3, 1997. and the Kinkela manuscript.

For the Southern Pacific influence in the San Joaquin Valley, and the Mussel Slough troubles, see Brown, James L. *The Mussel Slough Tragedy.* n.p., 1958. Information on the Sontag brothers is from Warner, Opie L. *A Pardoned Lifer, Life of George Sontag.* San Bernardino, CA: The Index Print, 1909. John Sontag's railroad accident was reported in the *Fresno Weekly Expositor*, August 31, 1887.

The Modesto stable fire is detailed in Smith's *Prodigal Sons* and in the *Modesto Evening News* January 7, 8, 10, 14, 1891.

A good account of the Cape Horn Mills train incident is in Boessenecker, John. *Badge and Buckshot.* Norman: University of Oklahoma Press, 1988. The attempted robbery at Modesto was reported in the *San Francisco Chronicle*, November 13, 1883. There is much material on the Pixley train robbery in the *Pixley Enterprise*,

November 26, December 3, 1980. The Wright interview was conducted in 1954 and was utilized in the *Enterprise* of November 26.

The *Tulare Daily Evening Register* quote was published on February 23, 1889. Other details are from this same issue and the *Fresno Bee*, April 24, 1966. For a general picture of the Valley train robberies see, Glasscock, C.B. *Bandits and the Southern Pacific.* New York: Grosset and Dunlap, 1929. For an encyclopedic approach, consult Patterson, Richard. *The Train Robbery Era.* Boulder: Pruett Publishing Company, 1991. Also helpful was O'Connell, Daniel, "Sontag and Evans." *Police Officers Journal*, August–September, 1936.

The Alila robbery is laid at the Daltons' door by no less than Littleton Dalton, another brother. See Latta, Frank F. *Dalton Gang Days.* Santa Cruz: Bear State Books, 1976. Too, Emmett Dalton made a sworn statement after the Coffeeville raid that the Dalton brothers were responsible for the Alila, California, train holdup as reported in the *Visalia Weekly Delta*, October 13, 1892. In later years and in his books, however, Emmett always denied he and his brothers committed the robbery.

For Evans' and the Sontag brothers' Midwest train robberies and subsequent shadowing by detectives, see the *Visalia Weekly Delta*, January 29, 1893, and Warner's *A Pardoned Lifer.* The I. W. Lees letter to William Pinkerton is from the Pinkerton Archives, Los Angeles, California, courtesy John Boessenecker.

The fight at the Evans home is reported at length in the *Fresno Morning Republican*, August 6, 1892, The *San Francisco Examiner*, August 7, 1892, and of course the Visalia press. Beaver's death is reported in the same papers. See also, Huddleston, Charles, "A California Story," *Valley Voice*, June, July, August, 1992. Huddleston is a great nephew of Beaver and tells the story from a family viewpoint.

For the fight at Young's cabin, see the *Visalia Daily Times*, September 13, 16, 22, the *Visalia Weekly Delta*, September 15 and the *Fresno Morning Republican*, September 15, 1892. The Burke quote, appeared in *The Republican*, noted above. See also the *San Francisco Examiner*, September 15, 1892. Henry Bigelow's interview, containing Evans' account of the Young's cabin fight, appeared in the *San Francisco Examiner*, October 7, 1892. Evans' letter validating the Bigelow interview was originally published in the *Examiner* and reprinted in the *Fresno Morning Republican*, June 14, 1893. The wounds of Wilson and McGinnis were detailed in *The Republican*, September 16, 1892. Sam Williams' story was the basis for Secrest, William B. "He Saw the Posse Die." *Frontier Times*, July, 1966.

Chris Evans' "Game of Euchre" poem was published in the *Fresno Morning Republican*, March 3, 1894. It was found at one of Evans' hideouts and was originally published in the *Reedley Exponent*.

Gard told how his posse came to be formed in the *Visalia Weekly Delta*, June 15, 1893. For detailed accounts of the Stone Corral fight, see the *Delta* of June 15, and the *Fresno Weekly Republican* of June 16, 1893. The San Francisco newspapers provided good coverage of the fight from their valley correspondents, including illustrations made from photographs taken at the scene—something the valley newspapers were not yet equipped to do.

Evans' recounting of the Stone Corral fight is from the *Fresno Weekly Republican*, June 16, 1893. Sontag's story is from the *Visalia Weekly Delta*, June 15, 1893. Eva's comments are from her manuscript, *An Outlaw and His Family*. Articles on the rewards were in the *Republican*, April 14, 1894, and the *Delta*, May 3, 1894. The rewards squabble, Los Angeles court hearing and the Burns-Witty shooting are in the *Republican*, October 9, 11, 1895; *Delta*, October 10, 17, 1895, and transcripts of the Circuit Court of the United States, Ninth Circuit, Southern District, October–December, 1895. National Archives, courtesy John Boessenecker. For Tom Burns' death, see the *San Francisco Chronicle*, June 20, 1901. Witty's self-destruction is detailed in the *Republican*, August 17, 1901.

John Sontag's death is reported in the *Fresno Morning Republican*, July 4, 1893. Evans and Dick Fellows are noted as sharing a Folsom cell in the *San Francisco Examiner*, June 24, 1894. For a curious look at Evans' ideas about how society should be, see Evans, Chris. *Eurasia*. San Francisco: The James H. Barry Company, 1900. Chris Evans died in Oregon on February 9, 1917. Four sons served as pall bearers. See Smith, *Prodigal Sons* and Eva McCullough's previously cited manuscript. The quoted obituary is from the *Portland Journal* of February 12, 1917. See also the *Portland Morning Oregonian*, February 10, 1917.

A coach full of tourists stops to enjoy the view in Yosemite sometime around the turn of the century. Author's collection.

During the last half of the nineteenth century the astonishing beauty of California's Yosemite Valley was the subject of paintings, photographs and visitors from around the world. Those traveling to the valley were subjected to days of wearying and dusty stagecoach rides over rugged mountain trails. An ever-present danger was a holdup. While bandits and road agents described their crimes in previous chapters, what of the victims? What of those people standing alongside a stagecoach afraid that any moment they might be shot down by a nervous or startled bandit? Here are tales of the first and last stage robberies on the Yosemite road and the reactions of some of the participants.

# 9 "Throw out the express box!"

## Holdups on the old Yosemite Road

Walter Farnsworth was driving the stage when it was stopped and robbed in 1905 and a passenger was allowed to photograph the robbery. Author's collection.

The first tourist parties to California's magnificent Yosemite Valley began arriving in 1855 on foot and mule back over crude mountain trails. It was a rough trip, but the scenery was so breathtaking that even women were sidesaddling their way into the valley at this early day.

Over the years businessmen and merchants in the foothill towns and along the trails realized what a bonanza a growing tourist trade could be. Grading began on three competing tollroads into the famous valley and on June 17, 1874, a procession of stagecoaches and freight wagons began the journey on the new Coulterville Road onto the floor of Yosemite Valley. By late July of the following year, both the Big Oak Flat Road and the Mariposa Road also had been completed into the valley. Tourism has been growing steadily ever since.

But there were others who saw a different type of opportunity in the newly established roads. Loafers and criminals watched the passengers dismount from the trains and stagecoaches at the stations along the way. Most of the travelers had money. Sometimes there was an express box. It wasn't long before the holdup virus had spread to the Yosemite roads.

And, while the Fates have not left us with first-person accounts from the various road agents involved, other more unwilling participants were delighted to speak up.

On the morning of August 13, 1883, a stage driven by Ernest Stevens was on its way from Wawona to Yosemite. It was close to 11 o'clock, near Grouse Creek, when three masked men stepped onto the road and commanded the driver to stop. Stevens reined up and the bandits quickly ordered him to unhitch his horses. After he had done so, the outlaws began firing their pistols and hazing the animals off down the road. Ignoring two women riders, the bandits took nearly $2,000 from four male passengers, then disappeared into the surrounding brush and tree-shrouded, mountain wilderness. The road agents were never captured.

The next coach to be stopped was pulled over by Milton Harvey Lee and his brother-in-law, John Herbert. Lee was a bad apple and had served two prison terms, but he was no Black Bart. On May 7, 1884, they stopped the Yosemite coach about 23 miles from Madera as it came down out of the hills. Their loot was about $60 and three watches. On

*Milton Harvey Lee, a pioneer in holding up the Yosemite coach. Author's collection.*

June 7 both bandits were picked up in San Jose and brought to Fresno for trial. They were easily convicted and sentenced to twenty years each in San Quentin.

A year later on May 22, 1885, two stages were on their way from Madera

*Stage robber John Herbert, Milton Harvey Lee's brother-in-law. Author's collection.*

to Yosemite. It was five o'clock in the evening near Fish Camp, when two masked men stepped out in front of Phil Toby's coach with leveled shotguns.

"Phil, stop and throw down the express box."

"The box is not in my stage," replied Toby, "and if you don't believe it you can get in and see."

One of the bandits checked out the coach and found Toby to be correct. Both outlaws wore masks with black applied to their hands and any exposed parts of their faces. Each had a pistol, with one carrying a rifle and the other a shotgun. Their clothes were worn inside out and one of the robbers was taller than the other. There were a dozen people in the coach, and the outlaws ordered the six male passengers to get out and line up along the road. Four women and two children remained in the coach. In their haste the outlaws overlooked some $4,000 in diamonds worn by the women. As the bandits began collecting money and valuables from the passengers, another coach, driven by Jake Foster, pulled up behind them. Foster was quickly told to get his hands up and keep his passengers quiet.

Taking money, cuff links, railroad tickets, watches and rings, the bandits were later described as being very "bunglesome and clumsy" in their collecting of the loot. Finishing their work, the two gunmen prodded the male passengers back into the coach. One of the robbers then said, "Drive on, Phil," punctuating his command with three pistol shots. The horses of the waiting coach were startled at the shots, but the two bandits quieted them and repeated the preceding performance with Foster's passengers.

The second coach only had two passengers, but this time they also obtained an express box. Finished with their task, the two robbers told Foster to move on, then broke open the box. There was little of value in it, however, and the two men lost no time in disappearing into the forest.

The two stage holdups were remarkable for a number of reasons, as we shall see. Local newspaper accounts had little to say about the passengers, other than to give their names and repeat whatever they had to say about the bandits and their lost possessions. By a particularly curious quirk of fate, one of the passengers did take the time to write up the incident. His name was W. Chance and his article was first published in the *London Times*. Later it was picked up and printed in the *San Francisco Daily Morning Call*, August 30, 1885. It is a hilarious diatribe by an outraged Englishman warning his fellow countrymen to stay away from America's "Wild West":

*I hope that the following account of an adventure which befell my wife and myself while traveling in California, and of which I have seen no mention made in the papers, may serve as a warning to those of my fellow-countrymen who intend visiting the "Far West."*

*We had arrived at San Francisco from Japan, and were on our way to visit the celebrated Yosemite Valley. Leaving the railway at Madera on the morning of the 23d of May last, we were conveyed the remaining 100 miles by stage (a* char a banc

*drawn by six horses) the road journey occupying two days. Our party consisted of twelve persons— six men, four ladies and two children—all Americans except ourselves. Late in the afternoon of the first day at a spot called Fresno Flats, some twenty miles from*

Type of light stage used on the Yosemite road at the time of the robbery. Author's collection.

A posed photograph of a stage robbery showing how Prescott and Myers did their work. *It is undated, but probably around the turn of the century. This print was obtained many years ago from a man who thought the photo might be an actual holdup taking place, but the stilted poses seem to say otherwise. Author's collection.*

*Clark's Hotel, our resting place for the night, the stage was stopped by two masked men, armed with guns and revolvers. One with his gun covered the driver while the other levelled his at the passengers.*

*We were all completely taken by surprise. They threatened to shoot upon the slightest move on the part of any of us. "If any man moves I'll shoot him, or woman either," were the exact words used. We were none of us armed, nor, indeed, with ladies present, would resistance in either case have been justifiable. We were then ordered to alight, ranged in line, and made to hold up our hands under a threat to shoot if we disobeyed. One of the robbers, revolver in hand, went down the line and relieved us of our watches and chains and money, while the other, standing a short distance behind, kept his gun levelled at us, as he had been doing all along, ready to shoot if we made any show of resistance.*

*The robber actually had the cowardice to hold his revolver to the face of each lady as he searched her. Our stage carried the box of the Wells Fargo Express Company containing money and valuables. The highwaymen asked for and were given this, and for its sake, doubtless, the stage was attacked, the unfortunate travellers suffering themselves in consequence. As long as the Wells, Fargo Company are allowed to send the treasure entrusted to them in an ordinary stage the attacks will continue.*

*But travelers can be warned what to expect. My advice to them is to leave behind valuable watches, not to take with them more money than they actually require for the visit to the valley. The tourist must not expect to hear anything of these robberies at any of the ticket offices or hotels in San Francisco or elsewhere. In fact, the possibility of their occurrence is certain to be denied. I may add that we found American tourists from the East quite as ignorant as ourselves of these occurrences and equally indignant at their possibility.*

Mr. Chance's tale is verified by an article in the *Mariposa Gazette* dated May 30, 1885. The passengers of Foster's coach are listed as "W. H. Waite and wife, of Providence, R.I., Mr. Chance and wife, of Raymond's Excursion Party, Mr. Harris, of Los Angeles and Mr. Duncan with a party of four." This makes ten passengers in all, but if Mr. Chance's figure of twelve is correct, the two children were apparently not enumerated. He was incorrect, however, in stating that the Wells, Fargo box was in his coach, when actually it was in the second stage driven by Jacob Foster.

Here is a wonderful chain of circumstances. A stage is robbed in the California foothills. One of the passengers is an Englishman who returns home and writes an angry letter that is published in the *London Times*. In some way the letter is picked up and published in the *San Francisco Daily Morning Call* a few months later. It seems it was a small world after all, even then!

Late that night first news of the holdup was telegraphed from Madera to Fresno County Sheriff O. James Meade and the authorities at Merced. A message was also sent to Mariposa where Sheriff John Mullery and his Undersheriff, William J. Howard, were promptly in the saddle. Mullery and Howard reached Wawona at 7 A.M. the next morning. They immediately sought out the robbery site and spent the day scouring the area for clues. Sheriff Meade and Merced County Deputy Sheriff Hi Rapelje arrived at 5:30 that evening. Working with John Washburn, one of the stageline owners, and others, the officers covered much territory in a short time. Local rancher "Indian Tom" Beasore helped track the outlaws also, as the lawmen questioned local residents and located vital bits of information.

Mariposa Sheriff Mullery, Beasore and others of the investigating officers located tracks leading to the home of rancher Charley Myers. At 3 o'clock in the afternoon they met up with Deputy Sheriff Howard and later ran into Sheriff Meade and Rapelje and exchanged information.

Howard was a legendary character in Mariposa County. He had been one of Harry Love's California Rangers during the hunt for Joaquin Murrieta in 1853 and engaged in various shooting scrapes when he wasn't serving as a lawyer, peace officer or district attorney. He was usually referred to as "Captain," but the source of his title is obscure.

William J. Howard was a prominent ranc. stable owner and deputy sheriff when he worked on the Prescott and Myers case. Author's collection.

The lawmen decided to pick up Charley Myers at his house, ten or fifteen miles from Fresno Flats. Surrounding the house, the lawmen found only his brother-in-law, Willie Prescott, sleeping peacefully in bed. Prescott was the other suspected stage robber and told the officers Myers had gone to visit his wife and child who were staying nearby with a friend named Bass. It was decided that Sheriff Meade and Rapelje should go and arrest Myers, while Howard stayed with Prescott.

Arriving at the Bass home, the officers called Charley Myers to the door and Sheriff Meade announced that he was under arrest. Myers was furious and angrily stated he would whip anyone who called him a stage robber. The burly Rapelje stepped closer and asked where he had been on the day of the robbery. Myers replied that he had been hog hunting with his brother-in-law, Willie Prescott.

Tom Beasore helped track the outlaws. From an old newspaper print. Author's collection.

The two suspects were taken before Justice Johnson at Fresno Flats on June 2 and charged with the double robbery. Both men steadily maintained they had been out hog hunting in the mountains on the day of the robbery. The *Fresno Weekly Expositor* reported:

Myers and Prescott, charged with the Yosemite stage robbery, were bound over to appear before Superior Court for trial. Their bonds were fixed at $2,000 each. Sheriff Meade will bring them to Fresno tonight. It is said that the officers have a strong case against the men....It will be quite a feather in the official caps of those officers named if they have succeeded in getting off with the right persons, as well as numerous dollars in their pockets.

The amount of bail given the two suspects was reported in the *Mariposa Gazette* as $10,000. Both men declined paying such a large amount and they were ushered into a cell to await their examination on June 11, 1885. Meanwhile, as if the Englishman, Mr. Chance's, letter had been read by the whole country, tourism had indeed taken a drop in the Yosemite country. The *Weekly Expositor* reported:

> The travel to the Yo Semite has fallen off greatly since the robbery of the coaches a few weeks ago. This is to be regretted for different reasons, among others the people are depriving themselves of a great pleasure because of a groundless fear. With the precautions that are taken travelers to the valley are as safe as they would be on any highway in the world.

Mr. Chance would have chuckled over his afternoon tea and crumpets if he could have read this. Still, Californians took stage robberies in stride. Writing to the *Expositor* on June 4, a Madera correspondent mused that while men were generally on the warpath about transgressions of this nature, some women viewed such matters from a more detached and giddy perspective:

*Merced County Deputy Sheriff Hiram Rapelje worked closely with other lawmen of the area to track down the stage robbers. Author's collection.*

> But while the stern males are on the alert, prepared for hideous war, the feminines take it differently. As a sample, one inquires, with the sweetest smiles and eagerness, "Do you think they will rob us?" "Oh, no, madam," says Captain Badger, with a responsive and most bland smile and courtly manner, "there is no danger at all. You needn't be the least alarmed, madam." "Oh," says she, "I do wish they would!" and her face fairly beamed with enthusiasm at the idea of a romantic encounter with the real, live robbers in the dark forests of the mountain glens.

Just how much reward money was at stake isn't known, but Henry Washburn, one of the brothers who owned the stage line, had offered $250 for the arrest and conviction of the 1883 stage robbers. Wells, Fargo also had a standing reward of $300 for those who molested its treasure boxes. Other rewards may have been offered, but in any case it was good money for those times. When the case of Prescott and Myers came up on the morning of September 9, 1885, Howard, Rapelje, Meade and some of the other officers were there as both witnesses and to protect the expenditure of their own money in the investigation. They couldn't have been happy to be informed that Pat Reddy and Walter D. Grady were defense counsel on the case.

Famous criminal lawyer Patrick Reddy became quite wealthy acquiring mining claims as payment for legal work. *Eastern California Museum.*

Pat Reddy was the most celebrated criminal lawyer on the West Coast. A self-made man, Reddy came to California in 1861 where he mined and gambled for a living. He was handy with a pistol, also, and in Virginia City in 1864 he was badly wounded in a shooting incident and lost his arm. Seeing little future for a one-armed miner or gambler, Pat took up the law and became one of the most prosperous mining litigators on the coast. At the time of the Prescott and Myers case he was also a state senator for Mono, Inyo, Kern, Tulare and Fresno counties.

Grady was also well known and had defended Lee and Herbert, the two stage robbers of the previous year. George Goucher, of Mariposa, was the prosecutor. A jury was selected on September 3, the trial beginning the following day.

Stage driver Phil Toby was the lead witness and testified as to details of the robbery. A stage passenger was called next, then William Howard was called to take the stand and remained there for several days.

Howard told of finding a spot near the robbery site where two men had laid down on a blanket. Nearby, at the side of the road, the Wells Fargo box was found broken open. Howard and others found boot tracks at the spot, then followed them from the site past a neighboring ranch to Myers' corral. Both Howard and several other witnesses testified that one boot had a worn spot that made it easy to identify. Tom Beasore corroborated this, saying he had measured the length of the boot track with a stick, notching the stick to indicate the width.

When the prosecution called witness after witness to testify as to the tracks and their validity, Reddy objected. He insisted the track evidence should be thrown out since it had not been proved by any of the witnesses that the tracks belonged to the robbers. The court disagreed and allowed the evidence for what it was worth.

When Deputy Howard identified a can of blacking as being found at Myers' place, defense lawyer Reddy objected, saying such material could be found in any paint shop in the country. "Mr. Reddy," noted a newspaper account, "continued his oratory on the point of his objection, when he was asked by Mr. Goucher of the opposing counsel if he were through with his speech?"

"You don't call that a speech, do you?" replied Reddy. " If you call that a speech, you will be astonished when you hear one."

Various witnesses testified that the two robbers were armed with a shotgun and rifle and it was shown that Prescott and Myers had taken a shotgun and Winchester along on their hog hunt.

When Deputy Hi Rapelje testified concerning a sack of clothes discovered under a bale of hay in the Myers barn, Reddy questioned him closely. The sack contained two undershirts, two overshirts and a pair of overalls. One of the shirts had been identified as belonging to Charley Myers by several locals who had seen him wearing it. The undershirts were shown to have black markings around the neck and cuffs—the prosecution implying this was made by the blacking applied to the robbers' hands and faces. After a severe grilling, Reddy asked Rapelje if the black marks could have been the result of the "perspiration of a hard working man?"

"No," replied the question-weary deputy, "I never worked hard enough to know."

The Fresno County Courthouse as it looked at the time of the Prescott and Myers trials. Author's collection.

Rapelje was becoming weary of waiting to be called and recalled to testify, not to mention the badgering of the defense attorneys. While hanging around the Fresno County sheriff's office on September 1, his friend, Deputy Sheriff Johnny White, asked if he would like to go along while he served a warrant on a Bakersfield horse thief. Rapelje jumped at the chance.

The fugitive, Gervasio Romero, was finally located at some sheep shearing pens west of town. Approaching the pen where Romero was shearing a sheep, White called out to him and quickly read the warrant. Romero picked up his vest and began backing away. As the two officers moved toward him, the fugitive pulled his pistol and fired at White, barely missing him. He then fired at Rapelje, the bullet barely missing his left ear. By now both lawmen had their pistols out and shot for Romero's legs. When he didn't go down, they fired again at his body and he dropped dead.

The coroner's report verified that Romero had two bullets in his legs and one in the chest. He had bragged the night before that he would never be taken alive.

Back in Judge Campbell's courtroom, Pat Reddy knew his craft well. He objected constantly and questioned every bit of evidence. He made one witness admit lying to Howard. When he asked John Washburn, one of the stage company owners, if he was prejudiced, Washburn replied that he thought the defendants were guilty, but he was not prejudiced.

Although the defense steadily maintained the defendants had been in the mountains hog hunting at the time of the robbery, they couldn't prove it. When asked to retrace their journey, neither Prescott or Myers could recall just where they had been, nor locate the spot where they had spent the night. Witnesses testified that both men knew the mountains well.

Reddy kept up the attack, determined to wear down the court and jury. The *Weekly Expositor* reported:

John Washburn helped investigate the Prescott and Myers holdup. Author's collection.

Hon. P. Reddy occupied nearly the entire day Saturday [the 19th] in his argument for the defense in the stage robbing case. The argument was not only eloquent, but it was able and ingenious. The jury being worn out, Mr. Goucher, for the prosecution, did not make his address until today, when he made a most convincing and able argument. The instructions were given, and the case submitted to the jury this afternoon.

After a trial lasting twenty-two days, the jury brought in a verdict of "guilty" and the two prisoners were sentenced to a prison term of twenty years. Of course Pat Reddy immediately appealed and with good cause. Sheriff Meade, who had expended his own funds in the investigation and now had a stake in the rewards, had taken the jury out for drinks on two different occasions. Ruling that the defense hadn't had the same opportunity, the California Supreme Court set aside the decision and ordered a new trial.

The second trial began in early January, 1887. A few new witnesses were scraped up, but it was pretty much a replay of the first trial. The courtroom was no longer packed as before. On January 25, Judge Campbell retired the jury, but they soon announced they could not agree on a verdict. A new date was set and when the third trial began, the *Fresno Morning Republican* correctly summed up the situation on December 1, 1887:

*Reel B. Terry was a skilled district attorney, but Pat Reddy had too many factors in his favor during a third trial. Author's collection.*

The facts in this case are well known to all our readers, it having been reported upon the occasion of both their first and second trials. The prosecution, as is nearly always the case, has been the side to suffer by the delays and reversals of judgment, etc., but a strong effort will be made to place the same evidence before the present jury.

A new district attorney faced Reddy this time. Reel B. Terry was the Texas-born nephew of the famous Judge David S. Terry of duelling fame. A good lawyer who backed up his rhetoric with a pistol, Reel Terry was prepared for the endless objections and stalling of Pat Reddy. But it made little difference. On December 24, the jury announced that they were hopelessly deadlocked. There were seven votes for acquittal and five for conviction. "District Attorney Terry and Senator Goucher," noted the *Republican*, " made as strong a case as could have been made from the evidence at their command and it was generally thought that a conviction would result." Terry moved to discharge the prisoners which was done. No rewards were paid.

Both Prescott and Myers were generally believed to have been guilty of stage robbery and they left the area soon after their acquittal. Prescott changed his name to Hatch, married and was living quietly in Fresno when he was charged with wife beating in May of 1899. He was easily convicted this time and spent a year in the county jail.

Charley Myers and his wife Hattie moved to Portland, Oregon. When his wife divorced him, Myers married Kitty Wittle in 1899. After his father's death, Charley and his new wife moved back to Fresno Flats on the Yosemite road. His wife, Kitty, became upset when outsiders would ask where she was from and she would say "Fresno Flats." "Oh that's where Charley Myers robbed the stage," they would respond.

Tradition has it that when these comments were made once too often, Kitty Myers began petitioning Sacramento to change the name of the town to Oakhurst. The old timers wouldn't sign the appeals, but enough newcomers signed to make the difference. Fresno Flats was officially changed to Oakhurst, but the new name wasn't commonly used until after 1925. And all because of a suspected stage robber who hadn't even been convicted.

Troop I, 15th U.S. Cavalry in the Mariposa Grove in 1901. Fresno County Library Collection.

When the federal government granted the Yosemite Valley and Mariposa Big Trees area to California in 1864, it was the beginning of an era. On October 1, 1890, Yosemite National Park was created and elements of the Fourth Cavalry and various administrative officers began arriving the following April. Entering the park in the spring and withdrawing in the fall, the army mapped and explored the area, maintained trails, and kept out poachers, sheep and cattle. In the winter, several rangers would try to maintain the status quo until spring. The presence of the troops seemed to inhibit road agents for a time. But it was too good a field to ignore and by 1900 the "gentlemen of the road" were again becoming active.

On June 2, 1900, a telegram was received in Madera announcing that five stagecoaches had been held up by a lone highwayman two miles west of Grub Gulch. Actually, only three stages had been stopped, along with two wagons hauling freight and wood. A. H. Foster, driver of the first coach stopped, was carrying some quarrymen to the Big Trees. One of the other

coaches was filled with tourists on their way to Yosemite, while the other was transporting a load of Chinese workers. The bandit was a small man wearing a mask and wielding a shotgun. He stopped all of the wagons one at a time as they pulled up behind each other in the road.

The passengers were told to get out and line up, then the usual collections were made. Only cash was taken, no jewelry. A. H. Foster, the driver of the first coach, was handed a small, hand-printed card on which was written, "The Black Kid."

Two soldiers, riding in advance of a troop of cavalry on its way to Yosemite, rode into the gathering and before they knew what was happening were confronted by the bandit. He told them to drop their cartridge belts and weapons, dismount and join the others standing under some trees along the road.

*Reminiscent of the Black Kid's great escapade, this photo has been authoritatively identified as a "spoof of the Veith experience." Apparently it was taken on the old Yosemite road. The driver was identified as Bright Gillespie, one of the coach drivers stopped by the Black Kid. This print was in the collection of former Fresno County Sheriff Robert D. Chittenden. Special Collections, Henry Madden Library, California State University, Fresno.*

By this time the affair was taking on all the aspects of a picnic. When Foster asked the highwayman if he was going to wait for all the stages, the answer was yes. There was some beer on board his coach and Foster suggested they might as well have a drink while they waited.

"I was going to ask him to join us," recalled Foster later, "but I thought he might suppose I was getting too familiar on short acquaintance."

The two wagons hauling freight and wood now pulled up and the drivers were robbed. The fifth, and last, vehicle was the stage full of Chinese workers. Despite the language difference, the robber's shotgun soon had the Asians contributing to his "cause." Nearly $250 in contributions had now been made, but the picnic was about to end.

The bandit looked around at the crowd of people and vehicles and knew that he was pushing his luck. Foster was told to load up and proceed, the two soldiers being ordered to get in the coach also. Two of the passengers were then ordered to get on the trooper's horses and move on. Neither was accustomed to horseback riding and the animals ran off down the road.

Dr. A. J. Pedlar who went after the Black Kid while unarmed and had a close call. Author's collection.

Dr. A. J. Pedlar, a Fresno physician, was with the cavalry troop that now was fast approaching the scene of the robberies. The good doctor later recalled his experience that day:

*A sergeant and a private were an hour ahead of the column, to secure beef supply at Grub Gulch. They were behind the first stage. Only non-coms were permitted to carry ammunition as we were not aware we were passing through the 'enemy's country.' No pistols were loaded and carbines were carried in the boots....*

*Two passengers excitedly galloping down the grade brought word of the robbery to the cavalry. The column was strung out for a quarter of a mile to avoid dust....The major, his son and I, pushed forward and at 75 yards sighted a freight wagon stopped in the road. Unconscious of the fact that the bandit, near a front wheel, had us covered by his gun and called on us to halt, we galloped up to the wagon to learn from the teamster that we had frightened the robber, who had just taken to the brush. Ordered to hurry up the troop, I hurried back 150 yards and the troop came up at a gallop.*

*The major had gone to the right in the direction taken by the robber. On my return with the troop and while ammunition was being hastily located (only a few*

The stage station at Ahwahnee on the road to Yosemite.
Mariposa County Historical Society.

had any) I rode past the wagon and at about 50 yards from it, started to enter the brush. I had no weapon of any kind. As I faced to the right, I came face to face with the 'Black Kid.' He was 60 yards off coming my way through dense brush. Between us, most of the ground was quite open. We met by chance, saw each other at the same instant. He covered me instantly, and his appearance as well as his promptness I shall never forget. Bareheaded, his face blackened, a narrow uncolored ring around his eyes, his cloth mask gone, he would have made a good Kodak picture. He claimed the right to make the first 'snap-shot' and I did not tarry to argue the matter. Wheeling my horse, I hurriedly reported to the major the whereabouts of the game....

Doctor Pedlar and the cavalrymen searched the brush for nearly an hour, but could not locate the elusive highwayman. Leaving behind a lieutenant and six troopers to continue the search, the cavalry moved on to Ahwahnee. The *Fresno Morning Republican* of June 9, 1900, reported:

Newspaper sketch of one of the photographs found in the captured Black Kid's satchel. Author's collection.

In his flight the bandit left a satchel containing bandages and salve, some salt, and strangely enough, there were two pictures in the satchel. The bandages and salve were evidently intended as a precautionary measure in case he should be wounded and the salt to make game more palatable in the event he should have to kill what he should eat for some days. But the pictures cannot be so easily accounted for. It may be, and it seems highly probable, that he placed the photographs in the satchel to deceive the officers.

Neither civilian posses or the soldiers ever caught The Black Kid. It was said the bandit fit the general description of a man who held up several stages consecutively on the Big Oak Flat road two weeks previously.

$\mathbf{A}$ nton Veith was having a good time. He had just returned from a visit to Yosemite and was spending a few days with his brother, a local fruit rancher. Veith was Austrian consul at Milwaukee, Wisconsin, and was on a tour of the West for his agricultural newspaper, the *Milwaukee Herald,* which he edited. His brother had invited a group of friends to meet Anton and join them in a gala dinner celebration at the Sequoia Hotel in Fresno.

The *Fresno Morning Republican* had given a good account of Anton Veith's adventure on the way to Yosemite. His coach had been stopped by a highwayman and robbed on August 15, 1900, and everyone at the party wanted to hear all about it. The incident was even more remarkable since Veith had taken a photograph of the robbery in progress. With a smile, Mr. Veith took a sip of wine and puffed on his cigar as he began his tale:

*Do you know on the way up we were discussing what we would do in case of a holdup. I had never been in any robbery adventure of that kind and had often wondered what would happen. At one of the two stations, two blacksmiths got aboard and I asked them what they would do in case of an attempted robbery. Supposing, I said, that you had with you the earnings of a lifetime, would you give it up if a robber would stop us here? One said that he might make another fortune, but had only one life and thought he would give up quickly. I said that a bullet didn't always hit, and I would take the chance the other way, if my fortune was at stake.*

*But I didn't lose any fortune. I see by some of the papers that I am supposed to have lost great sums, but as a matter of fact I lost but forty dollars. Another forty that I had in an inside pocket the man didn't find.*

*And I must say that he was a thorough gentleman. I can't imagine a man being more considerate of the people he was robbing. In some ways he was very clever, in others very careless. There was a half dozen times that I might have shot him if I had had a pistol, and he didn't try to find out whether the men had any or not. There was not a gun in the crowd.*

Anton Veith, the man who took the stage robbery photo. Author's collection.

*After dinner I was dozing in the back seat of the stage, when suddenly I heard some one call out, "Get down." I looked to the left of the stage, and there was the fellow* standing with gun slung over shoulder, and pistol pointed at us. Why he should have had the end of the gun bound up with a glove, I do not know, unless he did not want the bore of the gun known. The men in the party got down. Then he asked the driver

The remarkable photograph of a stage holdup taken by Anton Veith. It is perhaps the only authentic photograph of its kind. The author copied this print from an original in the Veith family album. Author's collection.

if he had a gun and the driver said "No or he would have used it before." The women were permitted to keep their seats, nor did the driver get down, as was reported. He stood us men along in a row, I next to the German guide, Maelzen. I asked the guide in German whether if I jumped the man he would help me, but he shook his head. The robber demanded to know what we were talking about, but I said nothing. After searching the men, he started toward the stage, and I looked around at him, whereupon he asked what I was looking for.

"Because I want to see you," I said. He then went on to search the women. He caught one of the ladies trying to hide some money in a camera and took it, but got little else. One had slipped her money under the driver's seat. By the time he got to the Austrian lady on the back seat, he seemed to get angry at not getting anything and started to search her and I said "That lady hasn't any money." Then he stopped. He certainly was a gentleman.

Then again see how foolish he was when he let me get those snap shots of him. I went to the stage to get the camera, and he didn't know but what I had a revolver there. You can see by the picture how he posed for it. I was glad I managed to get the stage and those fellows in it, standing out there where he had lined them up.

After we had all gotten back in the stage, he seemed to think things over and was disappointed at not getting more coin. He said "Now, is that all the money you have?" and we said it was. In searching me he had taken everything out of my pockets, and some of the trash he had thrown away. I had told him that my watch was an heirloom and would be worth little to him and he gave it back. I now told him that he had taken from my pocket this little rosary. I told him that it was a cherished pocket piece that I had carried for many years. He searched through all his pockets but couldn't find it. Then he said, "Well, I'll leave it on the road somewhere and someone will find it for you" and sure enough, the sheriff afterward found it and returned it to me. How was that for being a gentleman?

Two Madera County lawmen such as those who hunted the various Yosemite stage robbers. Author's collection.

Then he called out to the driver to move on and the man started the horses. I was again on the back seat and as we drove off I could see him back on the road waving his hand at us and I waved back. He was certainly all right.

It was my first experience in a holdup and it was certainly worth the $40. I don't know of any other case in which a photograph has been taken of a criminal at the time of the commission of the crime. The whole affair—our talking over the possibility of the robbery, then the surprise of its really happening and being taken by such a courteous robber makes it a memory worth having.

Probably there were those who questioned Veith's boasts about wanting to tackle the bandit, but they didn't know the man. Many years later the driver of the coach that day, Walter Farnsworth, corroborated Veith's story.

"That newspaperman wanted to tackle the gunman," Farnsworth recalled in 1954. "We stopped him though, he might have been shot. I was up in the box holding the horses."

Thirty years ago when I interviewed George Veith, Anton's Nephew, at his home, he showed the author many mementos of his uncle, including his photo album with the original holdup photo and his Austrian army uniforms. With his military background there is not much doubt that he would indeed have tackled the highwayman if the opportunity had presented itself.

Despite a protracted hunt for the robber, he was not apprehended. There were other robberies, notably in July of the following year when, once again, five coaches were stopped and robbed. Other holdup incidents took place during the summer of 1906 and 1907. In 1911 the last robberies of horse-drawn Yosemite coaches took place when four stages were stopped.

When motor coaches took over the stage lines, robberies still occasionally took place. On July 24, 1920, a lone bandit stopped five coaches and collected some $300. His mask revealed his eyes and nose and later he was identified and prosecuted. He was reported as being around fifty years of age by several of his victims. Perhaps he was one of the earlier robbers dating back to the turn of the century—maybe even "The Black Kid." His identity is not known, lost to the mists of time as are the coaches that rumbled down the grades into the great Yosemite Valley so long ago.

*The End*

## Chapter Nine / NOTES

For background on Chapter Nine I have relied on Russell, Carl P. *100 Years in Yosemite, The Story of a Great National Park.* Yosemite National Park: Yosemite Natural History Association, 1968, and Sargent, Shirley. *Wawona's Yesterdays.* Yosemite National Park: Yosemite Natural History Association, 1961. Also helpful were Johnston, Hank. *Yosemite's Yesterdays.* Yosemite National Park: Flying Spur Press, 1989, and Millar, June E. "History of Fish Camp, Mariposa, County" typescript in California History and Genealogy Room, Fresno County Public Library, Fresno, California.

The August 13, 1883, robbery is detailed in the *Mariposa Gazette*, August 18, 25, 1883. The Lee and Herbert robbery is recounted in Secrest, William B. *Dangerous Trails, Five Desperadoes of the Old West Coast.* Stillwater, OK: Barbed Wire Press, 1995.

The robbery of May 22, 1885, was announced in the *Fresno Weekly Expositor,* May 27, 1885. A much longer article appeared in the *Mariposa Gazette*, May 30, 1885. The arrest of Charles Myers and William Prescott was announced in a long article in the *Gazette*, June 6, 1885. The article gave many details of the investigation as did the many trial stories appearing in the press in the following years.

John Washburn, who helped investigate the robbery, was one of the more prominent citizens of the area. He and his brothers, Edward and Henry, owned the Wawona Hotel, which John operated, as well as one of the toll roads leading to Yosemite, a stage line and various other enterprises. The brothers were naturally interested in a quick capture of the robbers to minimize any bad publicity attached to their thriving tourist business. See Sargent's *Wawona's Yesterdays* and Marguerite-Dexter and Staff. *Mariposa Gazette 1854–1979,* Commemorating 125 Years of Continuous Publication. Mariposa, California, 1979.

The comments of the Madera correspondent appeared in the *Fresno Weekly Expositor* of June 10, 1885. The letter of Mr. Chance, the irate Englishman, appeared first in the *London Times* and then in the San Francisco *Daily Morning Call,* August 30, 1885.

Information on William J. Howard is from Cosley-Batt, Jill L. *The Last of the California Rangers*. New York and London: Funk & Wagnalls Company, 1928 and the author's files.

Hiram L. Rapelje had been appointed a Merced County deputy sheriff by Merced County Sheriff J. L. Crittenden in late 1884. He had a long career as a lawman in Fresno County and in 1893 was a member of the posse that captured Chris Evans and John Sontag, the train robbers. Rapelje's participation in the shooting of Gervasio Romero is detailed in the *Fresno Weekly Expositor*, September 9, 1885. A typescript biography of Rapelje has been done by the author.

A son of John Beasore and an Indian mother, Tom Beasore had been born in the Fresno Flats area in 1860. At the time of the stage robbery he was a local rancher and part-time deputy sheriff and considered a good tracker. Sweet, Nathan. "The Beasore-Taylor Story." typescript in June English Collection, Special Collections, Henry Madden Library, California State University, Fresno, California. See also *As We Were Told*, Coarsegold, CA: Coarse Gold Historical Society, 1990.

For biographical information on Patrick Reddy, see Palazzo, Robert. "The Fighting Reddy Brothers of the Eastern Sierra." *The Album, Times and Tales of Inyo-Mono*, 1996; Shuck, Oscar T. *History of the Bench and Bar of California*. Los Angeles: The Commercial Printing House, 1901. Indications of Walter D. Grady's boisterous career can be found in English, June. "W.D. Grady    Anti-Divisionist." typescript in collection of author. See also *San Francisco Examiner*, January 21, 1897, for account of Grady biting a chunk from a waiter's ear.

The article noting the drop in tourists to Yosemite due to the holdup was in the *Expositor*, June 17, 1885. Notice of the Fresno arraignment of Prescott and Myers is in the same issue. Comments by the giddy woman who wanted to be robbed were from the *Fresno Weekly Expositor*, June 10, 1885.

There is extensive trial coverage in the *Fresno Weekly Expositor*, September 9, 16, 23, 1885. The story of the sheriff taking the jury out for drinks is from the *Fresno Bee*, October 11, 1942, quoting from the state supreme court decision; *People v. C.W. Myers et al.*, 70 California Reports, 582 (Aug. 1886). The defendant's conviction is noted in the *Expositor*, September 30, 1885. The second trial is given much less notice in the local press, but some coverage is in the *Expositor*, January 12, 26, 1887. The third trial is reported in the *Expositor*, December 1, 7, 8, 9, 12, 13, 14, 16, 20, 24, 25, 1887.

Aurelius "Reel" B. Terry was a nephew of the noted, ex-California Supreme Court justice David S. Terry. Young Terry had lived with his uncle for a time in Stockton while studying law. Judge Terry had been living in Fresno since June, 1887, where he practised law and held various properties. A fiery Southerner with a history of violence, Judge Terry was shot and killed by the bodyguard of another judge whom he had assaulted at Lathrop, California, in 1889. Material on Reel Terry can be found in Clough, Charles and Secrest, Jr., William B. *Fresno County—The Pioneer Years, From the Beginnings to 1900*. Fresno: Panorama West Books, 1984. See also Buchanan, A. Russell. *David S. Terry of California, Dueling Judge*. San Marino, CA: The Huntington Library, 1956. Material on both men is in the files of the author.

William Prescott's wife beating and jail term is reported in the *Fresno Morning Republican*, May 19, 1899. Charles Myers' later life, divorce, remarriage and renaming of Fresno Flats to Oakhurst, is related in Mason, Ruth and Bill. "An Overview of the History of Fresno Flats and the Surrounding Area, 1850–1986," typescript in Fresno County Library, California History and Genealogy Room, Fresno, California.

The sojourn of the U.S. Army as custodians of Yosemite National Park is related in the previously cited *100 Years in Yosemite*. The "Black Kid" holdup and the Veith robbery were originally researched for my booklet, *The Great Yosemite Hold-Ups*. Fresno, CA: Saga West Publishing Company, 1968. A principal source was the *Fresno Morning Republican* of June 3, 9, 12, 1900.

The Veith robbery was reported in the *Republican* of August 16, 18, 19, 1905. The Anton Veith interview was in the *Republican* of August 20, 1905. George Veith, nephew of Anton Veith, was interviewed by the author in the early 1960s, although the notes have since been lost. It was a most interesting evening and he generously allowed me to take the family album to a photographer to make copies of the famous holdup photo and others.

Walter Farnsworth, the Veith stage driver, was interviewed in the *Fresno Bee*, August 29, 1954. Norman Bishop, curator of the Yosemite Museum in 1966, was most helpful, as was the Yosemite Natural History Association. Resources and staff of the Fresno County Library were much appreciated, as always.

# Bibliography

The following is a select bibliography of the primary sources consulted during the research and writing of this book. For additional sources, see the Notes section for each chapter, which provides full documentation of minor sources, as well as those listed below.

## BOOKS

*As Prescribed by Law, A Treatise on Folsom Prison*. (no author given). Represa, CA: The Represa, Press, 1940.

Bancroft, Hubert H. *California Pastoral, 1769–1848*. San Francisco: The History Company, Publishers, 1888.

————, Hubert H. *History of California, 1846–1848*. San Francisco: The History Company, Publishers, 1886.

————, Hubert H. *History of California, 1848–1859*. San Francisco: The History Company, Publishers, 1888.

————, Hubert H. *Popular Tribunals*. Vol. I. San Francisco: The History Company, Publishers, 1887.

Beckwourth, James P. *The Life and Adventures of James P. Beckwourth, written from his own dictation by T.D. Bonner*. New York: Harper, 1856.

Beers, George. *Vasquez, or the Hunted Bandits of the San Joaquin*. New York: Robert DeWitt Co., 1875.

Berry, John J., ed.. *Life of David Belden*. New York and Toronto, Canada: Belden Bros.,1891.

Boessenecker, John. *Badge and Buckshot*. Norman: University of Oklahoma, 1988.

Brown, James L. *The Mussel Slough Tragedy*. n.p., 1958.

Clark, Francis D. *The First Regiment of New York Volunteers*. New York: George S, Evans & Company, Printers, 1882.

Ellison, William H., and Francis Price, eds. *The Life and Adventures in California of Don Augustín Janssens 1834–1856*. San Marino, California: The Huntington Library, 1953.

Engelhardt, Zephyrin, Father. *Mission Nuestra Señora de la Soledad, Mission San Miguel Archangel*. Santa Barbara: Mission Santa Barbara, 1929.

Flinn, Charles J. *Life and Career of Charles Mortimer, etc.* Sacramento: William H. Mills & Co., 1873.

Ford, Tirey L. *California State Prisons, their History, Development and Management.* San Francisco: The Star Press, 1910.

Garner, William Robert. *Letters from California, 1846–1847.* Berkeley: University of California Press, 1970.

Gay, Theressa. *James Marshall.* Georgetown, CA: The Talisman Press, 1967.

Glasscock, C.B. *Bandits and the Southern Pacific.* New York: Grosset and Dunlap, 1929.

Greenwood, Robert. *The California Outlaw.* Los Gatos, CA: The Talisman Press, 1960.

Ham, Randall E. *A Buckeye in the Land of Gold, The Letters and Journal of William Dennison Bickham.* Spokane, Washington: The Arthur H. Clark Company, 1996.

Harlow, Alvin F. *Old Waybills.* New York, London: D. Appleton-Century Company, 1934.

Harlow, Neal. *California Conquered, War and Peace in the Pacific, 1846–1850.* Berkeley: University of California Press, 1982.

Hawgood, John A. *First and Last Consul.* Palo Alto: Pacific Books, 1970.

Hawkings, David T. *Bound for Australia.* Phillimore, England: Chichester, 1987.

———. *Criminal Ancestors.* Wolfeboro Falls, NH: Alan Sutton Publishing Ltd., 1992.

Holliday, J. S. *The World Rushed In.* New York: Simon & Schuster, 1981.

Huddleston, Charles. *A California Story.* Visalia: Visalia Instant Press, 1980.

Hughes, Robert. *The Fatal Shore.* New York: Alfred A. Knopf, 1987.

Kantor, J. R. K., ed.. *Grimshaw's Narrative.* Sacramento Book Collector's Club, 1964.

Lamott, Kenneth. *Chronicles of San Quentin.* New York: David McKay Company, Inc. 1961.

Latta, Frank F. *Dalton Gang Days.* Santa Cruz: Bear State Books, 1976.

———. *Saga of Rancho El Tejon.* Santa Cruz: Bear State Books, 1976.

Monaghan, Jay. *Australians and the Gold Rush, California and Down Under, 1849–1854.* Berkeley: University of California Press, 1966.

Mooney, James L., ed. *Dictionary of American Fighting Ships.* Vol. III, Washington: Naval Historical Center, Department of the Navy, 1981.

Mullen, Kevin J. *Let Justice Be Done.* Reno: University of Nevada Press, 1989.

[ Munroe-Fraser, J.P.]. *History of Contra Costa County, California.* San Francisco: W. A. Slocum & Co., 1882.

Ohles, Wallace V. *The Lands of Mission San Miguel.* Fresno: Word Dancer Press, 1997.

Older, Fremont. *My Own Story*. New York: The Macmillan Company, 1926.

Oneill, Owen H., ed. *History of Santa Barbara County*. Santa Barbara: H. M. Meier, 1939.

Outland, Charles F. *Stagecoaching on El Camino Real*. Glendale: The Arthur H. Clark Company, 1973.

Patterson, Richard. *The Train Robbery Era*. Boulder, CO: Pruett Publishing Company, 1991.

Reader, Phil. *"Charole," The Life of Branciforte Bandito Faustino Lorenzana*. Santa Cruz: Cliffside Publishing, n. d.

*Report of Jas. B. Hume and Jno. Thacker, Special Officers, Wells, Fargo & Co's Express, Covering a Period of Fourteen Years, giving losses by Train Robbers, Stage Robbers and Burglaries, etc.* San Francisco: H.S. Crocker & Co., 1885.

Sawyer, Eugene T. *Life and Career of Tiburcio Vasquez, the California Bandit and Murderer*. San Jose: 1875.

Secrest, William B. *Lawmen & Desperadoes*. Spokane, WA: The Arthur H. Clark Company, 1994.

Smith, Wallace. *Garden of the Sun*. Los Angeles: Lymanhouse, 1939.

————. *Prodigal Sons*. Boston: The Christopher Publishing House, 1951.

Stewart, George R. *Committee of Vigilance: Revolution in San Francisco, 1851*. Boston: Houghton Mifflin, 1964.

Truman, Benjamin Cummings. *Life, Adventures and Capture of Tiburcio Vasquez; the Great California Bandit and Murderer*. Los Angeles: The Los Angeles Star, 1874.

Warner, Opie L. *A Pardoned Lifer, Life of George Sontag*. San Bernardino: The Index Print, 1909.

Wells, Evelyn. *Fremont Older*. New York: D. Appleton Century Company, 1936.

Williams, Mary Floyd, ed. *Papers of the San Francisco Committee of Vigilance of 1851*. Berkeley: University of California Press, 1919.

————. *History of the San Francisco Committee of Vigilance of 1851*. Berkeley: University of California Press, 1921.

Wilson, Elinor. *Jim Beckwourth*. Norman, OK: University of Oklahoma Press, 1972.


PERIODICALS & JOURNALS

Edwards, Lee. "The Disappearance of Dick Fellows." *Historic Kern*. Quarterly Bulletin of the Kern County Historical Society. March, 1994.

Leonard, Ralph J. "The San Miguel Mission Murders." *La Vista*. San Luis Obispo County Historical Society. June, 1980.

O'Connell, Daniel. "Sontag and Evans." *Police Officers Journal*. August–September, 1936.

Ramey, Earl. "The Beginnings of Marysville." Part III. *California Historical Society*

*Quarterly.* March, 1936.

Ricards, Sherman L. and George M. Blackburn. "The Sydney Ducks: A Demographic Analysis." *Pacific Historical Review.* February, 1973.

"Roster of Fremont's California Battalion, Mexican War, 1846," *The Madera County Historian,* Madera County Historical Society Quarterly. September, 1961

Secrest, William B. "He Saw the Posse Die." *Frontier Times.* July, 1966.

————. "The Return of Chavez." *True West.* January/February, 1978.

Sherman, General William T. "Old Times in California." *North American Review.* March, 1889.

Wheat, Carl I., ed. "California's Bantam Cock, The Journals of Charles E. DeLong, 1854–1863." *California Historical Society Quarterly.* March, 1930.


UNPUBLISHED MATERIALS

Byram, Edward. San Francisco Police Record Books and Journals, 1876–1908. Collection of John Boessenecker.

Coleman, William T. Statement. The Bancroft Library, University of California, Berkeley, California.

Daggett Scrapbooks, Vol. 3. California Section, California State Library, Sacramento.

De la Guerra Collection, Folder 821, 1848 - 50. Santa Barbara Mission Archives, Santa Barbara, California.

Kinkela, Evelyn Evans, McCullough. "An Outlaw and His Family." Unpublished ms. in The Huntington Library, San Marino, California.

Letter: Lee Edwards, Bakersfield, California, to the author, July 3, 1997.

Letter: Carlo M. De Ferrari, Sonora, California, to the author, August 9, 1997.

Letter: Sharon Hosler, Napa State Hospital, Napa, California, to the author, January 16, 1987.

Letter: M. Thomas, Archives 1, Reference Branch, Textual Reference Division, National Archives, Washington DC, to the author, February 7, 1998.

Moore, Benjamin F. "Early Days in California." Manuscript in Wells Fargo Bank History Dept., San Francisco, California.

"Memoirs of Doña Catarina Avila de Rios, the Widow of Sergt. Petronilo Rios." Manuscript No. D-35. The Bancroft Library, University of California, Berkeley, California.

Snyder, Andrew. "True Story of the Vasquez Murders at Tres Pinos." Collection of Edna Zyl Modie.

## GOVERNMENT DOCUMENTS

California State Assembly. "Report of Committee Relative to the Condition and/Management of the State Prison." In: Assembly Journal appendix, Document Number 26, 1855 session. Sacramento: B.R. Redding, State Printer, 1856.

California State Legislature. "Annual Report of State Prison Director for the Year 1859." In: Legislative Journals appendix, 1860 session. State Printer, Sacramento, California.

California State Legislature. "Report of the Directors of the California State Prison." July 1, 1871. In: Legislative Journal appendix, 1872 session. Sacramento: State Printing Office, 1872.

California State Legislature. "Report on the State Prison by the Joint Committee of the Senate and Assembly." 1872. In: Legislative Journal appendix, 1872 session. Sacramento: State Printing Office, 1872.

California Death Certificate Index, 1905 -. California Section, California State Library, Sacramento, California.

California Supreme Court Reports. People v. Vasquez, 49 Cal. 560 (Jan. 1875).
———. People v. Myers et al., 70 Cal. 582 (Aug. 1886).

Canadian Census Report: Canada West, 1851, 1861. Carelton County, Nepean Township, Ontario, Public Archives of Canada, Ottawa.

Confederate Service Records. National Archives, Washington DC.

Governor's Pardon Files. California State Archives, Sacramento, California.

Governor's Reward Papers. California State Archives, Sacramento, California.

"List of Convicts on Register of State Prison at San Quentin." Marin County, California, Sacramento, J.D. Young, Supt. State Printing, 1889.

Police mug books. Sacramento City Archives, Sacramento, California.

"Register and Descriptive List of Convicts under Sentence of Imprisonment in the State Prison of California." San Quentin, California State Archives, Sacramento, California.

United States Army. Records of the 10th Military Department. Letters Received, 1846–1851.

United States Census Reports: 1850, Harlan County, Kentucky.

United States Circuit Court, Ninth Judicial Circuit, Southern District. George W. Witty vs. The Southern Pacific Co., et al, February, 1896.

## NEWSPAPERS

California Chronicle (San Francisco)
California Police Gazette (San Francisco)
California Star (San Francisco)
Daily Alta California (San Francisco)
Fresno Bee
Fresno Morning Republican
Fresno Weekly Expositor
Fresno Weekly Republican
Gilroy Advocate
Grass Valley Union
Indianapolis News (Indiana)
Kern County Weekly Courtier (Bakersfield)
Kern County Weekly Gazette (Bakersfield)
Los Angeles Daily News
Los Angeles Herald
Los Angeles Star
Los Angeles Times
Mariposa Gazette
Martinez Gazette
Marysville Herald
Milwaukee Herald
Modesto Evening News
Monterey Californian
Monterey Sentinel
Morning Oregonian (Portland, Oregon)
Napa Register
Nevada Democrat (Nevada County, California)
Nevada City Daily Transcript
New York Herald
New York Sun
Pixley Enterprise

Placer Herald (Auburn)
Portland Journal (Oregon)
Reedley Exponent
Sacramento Bee
Sacramento Daily Union
Sacramento Democratic State Journal
Sacramento Record-Union,
Sacramento Times
Sacramento Transcript
Sacramento Daily Union
Salinas Index
San Andreas Independent
San Francisco Argonaut
San Francisco Bulletin
San Francisco Californian
San Francisco Chronicle
San Francisco Daily Morning Call
San Francisco Evening Picayune
San Francisco Examiner
San Francisco Herald and Mirror
San Francisco Herald
San Francisco Star and Californian
San Joaquin Republican (Stockton)
San Jose Daily Patriot
San Jose Mercury
Santa Barbara Press
Santa Cruz Sentinel
Sonora Union Democrat
St. Louis Republican (Missouri)
Stockton Argus
Tulare Daily Evening Register
Union City Times (Indiana)
Visalia Daily Times
Visalia Weekly Delta
Yreka Weekly Union

# Index

B orn in Fresno, California, in March of 1930, William B. Secrest grew up in the great San Joaquin Valley. After high school he joined the Marine Corps where he served in a guard detachment and in a rifle company in the early years of the Korean War. Returning to college, he obtained a BA in education, but for many years he served as an art director for a Fresno advertising firm.

Secrest has been interested in history since his youth and early began comparing Western films to what really happened in the West. A hobby at first, this avocation quickly developed into correspondence with noted writers and more serious research. Not satisfied in a collaboration with friend and Western writer Ray Thorp, Secrest began researching and writing his own articles in the early 1960s.

Although at first he wrote on many general Western subjects, some years ago Secrest realized how his home state has consistently been neglected in the Western genre and concentrated almost exclusively on early California subjects. He has produced hundreds of articles for such publications as Westways, Montana, True West, and the American West, while publishing seven monographs on early California themes. His book I Buried Hickok (Early West Publishing Co.) appeared in 1980, followed by Lawmen & Desperadoes (The Arthur H. Clark Co.) in 1994 and Dangerous Trails (Barbed Wire Press) in 1995. A biography of noted San Francisco police detective Isaiah Lees has been accepted for publication. A current project is a biography of harry Love, the leader of the rangers who tracked down Joaquin Murrieta.